MASTERING WITCHCRAFT
A Practical Guide for Witches, Warlocks & Covens

The witches' wheel

MASTERING WITCHCRAFT

A Practical Guide for Witches, Warlocks & Covens

by Paul Huson

With illustrations by the author

A PERIGEE BOOK

For William Bast

A Perigee Book
Published by The Berkley Publishing Group
A division of Penguin Putnam Inc.
375 Hudson Street
New York, New York 10014.

All rights reserved. This book or parts
thereof, may not be reproduced in any
form without permission.

Copyright © 1970 by Paul Huson

Published by arrangement with
G. P. Putnam's Sons
Berkley Windhover edition: May 1977
First Perigee edition: 1980

The Penguin Putnam Inc. World Wide Web site address is
http://www.penguinputnam.com

Library of Congress Catalog Card Number: 79-111530

ISBN 0-399-50442-7

Printed in the United States of America

31 30 29 28 27 26 25 24

Foreword

In the circle of firelight which we are pleased to call an enlightened scientific civilization, we usually feel secure in the knowledge that most of our worst childhood terrors and nightmares were merely fantasy. But if and when the firelight happens to dim, at those times when the unknown presses hard upon us, in the presence of death or insanity or insurmountable calamity, we again know instinctively that science is ultimately irrelevant, and we once again experience the old childhood terrors.

We are still powerless in the face of overmastering fate. Science still completely fails to come to grips with that outer darkness beyond the flickering ring of light.

However, down the ages it has seemed to some intrepid souls that only with weapons forged from the darkness itself, and by the aid of those others before them who have made it their business to know the ways in and out of the unseen world, can any man maybe hope to bend to his will an indifferent fate, whose roots appear to reach back into the outer regions of that night.

Among those who understand the darkness which is no darkness to them anymore are those that tread the way of witchcraft. They of their own accord have walked beyond the ring of firelight and learned the paths in the wilderness beyond.

Now that Aquarius is upon us, the gates have swung back revealing as never before the secret workings of those who practice the Black Arts. No more are we constrained by common law to hide our doings; the stake and the noose are things of the past, and we may once more choose our own gods, bright or dark. The day of the pale Galilean is passing, and the restrictions imposed by his devotees are losing their thrall upon the public mind, leaving people free once more to return to the old teachings of joy and love and knowledge of arts once forbidden.

Our Lady Habondia and her horned consort hold court once more. Should you wish to tread the dark path of witchcraft, the way is open to you now.

Whether you believe the Christian bugaboos and fear to lose your soul in return for the powers or, like us, consider the gamble well spent, is up to you.

Should you decide the former, then read no further. The aim of this book is solely to teach you the first steps to becoming a witch or a warlock.

But remember, the choice was yours. We take no responsibility for the results you may achieve, good or bad. Witchcraft is witchcraft. The seeds of success or destruction lie within you and you alone. Night is jealous of her secrets and guards them in many ways; but those who succeed in wooing her may reap many rewards.

On the other hand, those who timidly shun the darkness win temporary respite only, until such a time as the darkness itself reaches out and takes them when they are least forearmed.

Contents

	FOREWORD	5
	INTRODUCTION	9
1	FIRST STEPS	19
2	PRELIMINARY PREPARATIONS	37
3	DIVINATION	62
4	SPELLS FOR LOVERS	95
5	COUNTERMAGIC AND PROTECTION	136
6	VENGEANCE AND ATTACK	172
7	THE COVEN AND HOW TO FORM ONE	207
	APPENDIX 1. THE PLANETARY HOURS	244
	APPENDIX 2. GLOSSARY OF WITCH WORDS AND TERMS	247
	BIBLIOGRAPHY	253

Introduction

BEFORE taking any practical steps upon the road to becoming a full-fledged witch, it would be advisable for you to be acquainted with at least the essence of witch history. By this I do not mean such things as the overfamiliar accounts of Gilles de Rais' necrophilic exploits and massacres or Mother Shipton's quaint prophecies, but rather a general survey of those events in witchcraft which stand out as signposts of the black craft's history.

Witch history is steeped in legend, hidden in antiquity. There are few written sources, and those that exist are generally obscure, of an oblique nature, casting light upon rather than informing directly. For instance, Italian witch lore presents us with the following creation story:

In the beginning the Great Darkness, Diana, divided herself into two equal and opposite forces, night and day. The night was ruled over by Diana herself as the moon, the day by her alter ego and brother, Lucifer, the sun. Diana, inasmuch as the moon is ever pursuing the sun across the sky, became enamoured of her brother the sun and seduced him in the shape of his pet cat. The offspring from this union was a daughter, Aradia or Herodias, the archetypal "avatar" or patroness of all witches.

In this legend of Diana with its gnostic overtones, there are reflections of the Cabalistic tradition of Naamah, the seductress of the Fallen Angel Azael. Naamah is synonymous with Babylonian Lilith, and Azael is none other than Babylonian Shamash, the Sun God in his underworld aspect as Lord of Riches and Artificer of Metals. In fact he is the alter ego of Tubal

Cain himself, Naamah's own brother. Azael, or Azazel, is in fact one of the modern witch's gods.

Which brings me to the crux of the matter. According to ancient magical legend, Azael was originally one of those beings of primordial fire, first created dwellers in the high heaven, referred to by the Christian church as messengers, or angels, by the Greeks as *daemons*. Azael and his followers, according to old lore, in defiance of their masters, elected to descend upon the earth countless eons ago, for the purpose of educating and civilizing primitive man as he then existed. Whether it was part of their original plan or merely a side issue, these angelic beings, "Sons of God" or "Watchers of the Heavens," as they were entitled, elected to mate with humankind. The Book of Genesis briefly records the legend thus:

> And it came to pass, when men began to multiply on the face of the earth, and daughters were born unto them, that the Sons of God saw the daughters of men that they were fair, and they took wives of all which they chose . . .

However, the ancient Book of Noah written several hundred years before the birth of Christ is more explicit:

> . . . And the angels, the children of heaven, saw and lusted after them [the daughters of men] and said one to another: "Come let us choose wives from among the children of men and beget us children" . . . And all the others together took unto themselves wives, and each chose for himself one, and they began to go in unto them and defile themselves with them, and they taught them charms and enchantments, and the cutting of roots, and made them acquainted with plants . . .
>
> And Azâzêl [Azael] taught men to make swords, and knives, and shields, and breastplates, and made known to them the Metals [of the earth] and the art of working them . . .
>
> Semjâzâ taught enchantments, and root cuttings, Armârôs the resolving of enchantments, Barâqîjêl astrology, Kôkabêl the constellations, Ezêqêêl the knowledge of the clouds [weather lore], Araqiêl the signs of the earth [husbandry], Shamsiêl the signs of the sun, Sariêl the course of the moon . . .*

---

* "Book of Noah" from Charles Canon, *Book of Enoch*, London, Society for Promoting Christian Knowledge, 1962. Reprinted from Oxford University Press edition, 1912.

According to that collection of ancient Cabalistic lore, the Zohar, Great Azael and his cohorts had had to assume tangible bodies in order to descend upon the earth. Because of their revolt against higher authority and the ties with this world which they had subsequently formed, they were unable to divest themselves of these material forms and reascend into the heavenly spaces again. It is from these exiled beings that all true magical knowledge and power is said to be derived. Laban, reputedly one of the greatest adepts in magical art of pre-flood times, visited the mountaintop wherein they dwelt, to learn his wisdom. This idea has lingered on and finally became a fundamental part of legends of magical initiation all over the world, from Chaldea to Tibet. The offspring of the Sons of Heaven, however, proved to be a mixed blessing for the world. Like their progenitors, they were gigantic in stature—"great giants whose height was three thousand ells." Some of these Nephelim, as the descendants of the house of Azael were known, were, like Nimrod, men of renown and great in wisdom. Others, however, turned in the opposite direction and increasingly devoted themselves to the pursuit of hideous delights and necromantic pastimes besides which Gilles de Rais' antics are said to pall into insignificance.

> . . . And they [the Giants] began to sin against birds, and beasts, and reptiles, and fish, and to devour one another's flesh, and drink the blood. Then the earth laid accusation against the lawless ones . . .*

Legend has it that the Watchers, in despair at the evil that had been unleashed upon the world by their hand, took counsel among themselves and wielded their power to cast down the lands wherein the Nephelim dwelt, overwhelming the entire population in one day and night by volcanic upheaval and subsequent flood, of such a planetary magnitude that to this day, throughout many parts of the world, there yet remains evidence of this appalling cataclysm in the form of layers of silt and debris beneath a certain level of geological strata, as well as the recurring legends of the flood and Atlantis current throughout the Western hemisphere.

The early Christian writer of the tale of Beowulf recounts

* *Book of Enoch, ibid.*

how, written in runes upon the hilt of an enchanted sword said to have been made by the Nephelim themselves, King Hrothgar of the Danes reads:

> . . . The story of ancient wars
> Between good and evil, the opening of the waters,
> The Flood sweeping the Giants away, how they suffered,
> And died, that race who hated the Ruler
> Of us all, and received judgment from his hands,
> Surging waves that found them wherever they fled . . .*

We again find traces of this lore in the Norse legend of the giants' revolt, and similarly in Greek mythology concerning the gods' dealings with the rebellious Titans. It is a persistent theme. The Zohar intimates, however, that though most of the giants yielded up their lives in the flood, many of their spirits partaking as they did of the angelic nature of their fathers, proved indestructible, and lived on, invisible yet powerful even in their disembodied state. On occasion, these shades are said to gain access to the world of men by reincarnating in human shape, and are referred to as intruders, ancient alien souls transmigrating from the past. Otherwise, collectively in their immaterial shape, they constitute the so-called demonic hierarchy with which the modern witch has dealings on occasion. It is the Watchers, the Mighty Ones of the Heavenly Places, the parents of giant and human alike as seen in symbolic and archetypal form as the parents of humanity, whether as masters of wisdom and love or simply as benevolent powers of fertility and hunting, that constitute the witch's true deities.

Diana and Lucifer of the above-mentioned witch legend are but figurative forms of these Mighty Ones. Although the legend is overlaid with later gnostic overtones such as the latinized names "Diana" and "Lucifer," these are not inappropriate, and indeed they preserve many of the seeds of truth. "Gnostic" itself in its etymological derivation means much the same as "witch": "One who knows," "one who concerns himself or herself with the hidden wisdom." It is the tattered remnants of the wisdom of the Watchers, or gods, which constitutes the lore of the witch.

The wisdom was said to have been borne away from the Lost

---

* *Beowulf*, translated by Burton Raffel (Mentor Books U.S.A. 1963).

Lands prior to the cataclysm by certain survivors, who knew the minds of the Watchers, and fled the oncoming doom. The knowledge is said to have been preserved until such a time as bit by bit in devious manners it could be secretly reintroduced to humanity once more.

Babylonian legends of Uta-Napishtim and the Biblical Noah or his Greek parallel, Deucalion, all contain echoes of this belief. Witch lore, morever, tells of settlers from the Lost Lands coming in their wanderings to the land which is now Britain and Northern Europe, or Middle Earth as it was called in Old English, and mingling with the neolithic cultures then in existence. It was the people produced by this intermingling that the iron-bearing Celts discovered on their sweep westward across Northern Europe and into Britain around 500 B.C.

The indigenous Britons, or Prytani as they then were called, were a strange people, who buried their dead in great burial mounds, or barrows, used bronze as their only metal, and relied for weapons chiefly upon slender arrows with delicate elder-leaf-shaped flint tips. Their religion, which was connected in some way with the moon and stars, was conducted amidst stone circles, surrounded by a bank and ditch (the original witch circle, in fact). The Prytani appear to have kept very much to themselves, isolating themselves within raths, or large circular encampments, the only contact between the two races being made by the Celtic shamans, or Druids, a word probably signifying wise ones, or wizards. Much or all of the Druidic lore would appear to have been drawn from contact with the Prytani. Indeed many druids were probably born of Prytanic fathers to Celtic mothers. The legendary Merlin was maybe one such as this, born of "mortal" mother and fathered by a "devil" or "elf." In fact elves were but the Teutonic names bestowed upon the remaining Prytani five centuries later by the Germanic invaders of Britain.

Arthurian legend has it that King Arthur's half-sister Morgan la Fay (like Merlin) was also of elven descent, accounting for her magical prowess. Nimué, the Lady of the Lake, and Vivian, Merlin's enchantress, were of course completely elven in their ancestry. To this day there remain certain Scottish families which claim elven descent, for by the time of the Roman invasion of Britain within the first century A.D., the Prytani had almost all retreated to the northernmost tip of the country, and were occupying the lands north of what is now Perth and Argyll in Scotland.

This may also account for the old witch belief of the north as being the holy direction. The northern abodes of the rulers of the Picts, as the Prytani were known by the Romans, were often mysterious vitrified forts, towers whose outer stones had been fused together by great fires, making them practically impregnable to all attack. This is probably the origin of the witch's Glass Castle, which you will encounter later on. We know for a fact that glass castles such as these existed at Craig Phadrick at Inverness, Dun Fionn, Achterawe, and Dundbhairdghal.

By the eleventh century A.D., subsequent to successive invasions of Britain, as it was now called, by Teutonic Angles, Saxons, Jutes, Danes, and lastly Normans, Prytanic lore had been completely overlaid by a conglomeration of Celtic, Roman, Saxon, and finally Christian beliefs, gnostic and otherwise. The Prytani themselves, now referred to by either their Saxon epithet, Elvenfolk, or simply as People of the Heath or heathens, were rapidly dwindling into legend. The elven king and queen in their enchanted hill which opened up on the ancient holy festivals of Halloween and Beltane were fast passing out of public memory, recalled only by the wise, or as they were known in the old English tongue, the Wicce and Wicca, Wizards and Witches. The legend of the Elvenfolk's ancestry still survived, however, in heavily Christianized form. They were the remaining offspring of the fallen angels. Neither devils, like Satan and his cohorts, nor angels, but somewhere between the two. Neither good nor bad, merely indifferent.

It is at this point that organized Christianity began to take a hand, and bore down heavily on all those suspected of either having consorted with or actually being elves or "faery folk."

The heresy trials of the Waldenses, Albigenses, and Knights Templar had spanned the twelfth, thirteenth, and fourteenth centuries, as Mother Church consolidated herself and waged war against the forces of dissolution and darkness manifesting as rival doctrinal factions within her bosom. It was not till the fifteenth century that the actual cult of witchcraft became established as an entity in the mind of the Church's "instrument of justice," the Inquisition. This cult was in fact based upon traditional witch beliefs, but strung together in a way reminiscent of the accounts of the religious rites that the Church had chosen to believe were celebrated by the recently defunct heresies of the past two centuries.

Joan of Arc was burned as a witch and consorter with the faeries in 1431, and in 1484 Pope Innocent VIII formally declared war on all "witches" in a Papal Bull. This was closely followed by the Inquisitors Kramer and Sprenger producing their infamous handbook on witch finding, the *Malleus Maleficarum,* or Witches Hammer, in 1486, a book incidentally used by Protestant and Catholic witch hunters alike.

The sixteenth century saw a great revitalization of interest in the past in the form of the Renaissance. Scholars began to study the antiquities of the classical world, and with them many of the old magical practices, always, however, relating it to a Christian framework, for safety's sake if nothing else. In Italy, Pico della Mirandola, Ficino and Giordano Bruno began experimenting with the old art of the employment of magical archetypal images, while in northern Europe Abbot Trithemius and his pupils Paracelsus, Cornelius Agrippa, and Wierus turned their attentions circumspectly to the Black Arts. In England, Dr. John Dee, preoccupied with the Lost Lands of Logres and the Star Temple at Glastonbury, began his Scrying Experiments using a "great chrystalline globe," or seeing stone. It was during the course of these experiments that certain parts of the pre-flood language are said to have been rediscovered, a so-called Enochian tongue, the original language of the Nephelim.

By the seventeenth century, the persecution of witches, by Protestants now as well as Catholics, seems to have fairly well decimated most of the centers of witch lore, save those preserved under heavy disguise of Cabalistic or alchemical learning. Even these by now had also become suspect, and apparently owing to this, secret brotherhoods such as the Rosicrucians and Freemasons were organized, for the very purpose of keeping the flame of the old wisdom burning.

By the eighteenth century Masonic and Hermetic lodges had become widespread and the power of the Church had been considerably reduced, indeed was waning fast, never to recover its old position of strength. Within the lodges, many old witch secrets were being rediscovered. Swedenborg reintroduced the concept of that principle which is known as clairvoyance, or ESP, and Mesmer began his researches on what he called animal magnetism, but that witches nowadays refer to simply as witch power. The powers of the deep mind were being rediscovered.

The nineteenth century, with its bias toward materialist science, saw a greater concentration on aspects of magical power under one name or another. In 1801 the English magus Francis Barratt had gathered together a school of twelve students of arcane lore with himself as leader, a traditional coven, in fact. It is probably to this magical society that the great French occultist Eliphas Levi, alias Abbé Constant, and Lord Bulwer Lytton had belonged, both of whom widely publicized the marvels of the newly rediscovered witch power, under the name of the Astral Light in Levi's case, Vril in Lytton's. Baron Reichenbach was also trying to put this same mysterious energy, which such mediums as D. D. Home, Eusapia Palladino, and the Fox sisters were flaunting before the public, on a firmer scientific footing in his experiments with what he designated "odylic force" or "od." The task was taken up in earnest by the English Society for Psychical Research when it was formed in 1882.

However, it was not until the end of the nineteenth century and the beginning of the twentieth that the occult world lost its somewhat strained "scientific" outlook of the previous hundred years, and turned its attention once more, after all the centuries, to the old gods.

In 1851 Helena Petrovna Blavatsky had met the aforementioned Rosicrucian magus Bulwer Lytton, and impressed by the encounter, had organized the Theosophical Society in 1875, the object of which was to establish a nucleus of the Universal Brotherhood of Humanity. The purpose of this nucleus was to study the supreme source of all the world religions, the central "Wisdom Religion" as vouchsafed to various peoples of the earth in such a manner as best suited to time and geographical circumstance, and which was said to have been in existence from time immemorial; the old wisdom of the Watchers, in fact. In Madame Blavatsky's society it was the Oriental branch of this Wisdom, comprising the teachings of Vedanta and Esoteric Buddhism, which was the main inspiration.

Closely paralleling this movement, however, the Hermetic Order of the Golden Dawn was formed in England a few years later, similar in ideal but pursuing a Western, Rosicrucian path bound up with a system of ceremonial magic comprising invocation of ancient Egyptian gods, Cabalistic formulae, and Dr. John Dee's sixteenth-century Enochian research. This erudite institution attracted many fertile minds including the poet W. B. Yeats, Arthur Machen, and Algernon Blackwood, all on the fringe or involved with the "celtic twilight," and all greatly preoccupied with the rediscovery of the old gods, as will be readily discerned if one acquaints oneself with their writings. A later, Christianized development of the original Order of the Golden Dawn was the "Stella Matutina." This offshoot attracted such minds as A. E. Waite, Evelyn Underhill, and Charles Williams to its ranks.

However, in magical circles, it is chiefly the names of Aleister Crowley and Dion Fortune that are best remembered as members of these mysterious schools, both, like Yeats before them, deeply involved with the reconstitution of the old mysteries, and the return to the elder gods. The researches of Freud, but especially Jung, had provided part of a link with the past via the image-magic of Trithemius and Bruno. The rest of the link was supplied by the magical dictum publicly propounded by Dion Fortune herself, that in essence all gods are one god, and all goddesses but one goddess; that the varying pantheons and hierarchies are but racial and regional permutations of the same ancient archetypes.

In 1951 the last English witchcraft act was repealed, removing the final official stigma upon the study and practice of the craft, in that country at least.

Three years later, an anthropologist, Gerald Gardner, published a work, *Witchcraft Today*, admitting, for the first time in history, to the existence of a definite witch cult similar to the one suspected by Margaret Murray in the twenties, a tenuous but widely spread body of magical practitioners who did not cloak their occult operations under scientific, Christian, or Cabalistic guise, but preferred simply to practice their arts in the old manner that they had inherited from the past, under the banner of the old gods. Most of the witch processes that remain to us now are simple and unsophisticated in comparison with the starry wisdom of the lost lore of the Watchers, fragments of which are daily in the process of being rediscovered through "legitimate" scientific research.

In fact our present-day witch magic is decadent. A patchwork quilt of historical odds and ends, religious flotsam and jetsam, but containing in the midst of that welter of confusing symbolism enough of the old secrets to make the processes work if properly pursued. The methods nowadays may seem to some childish, hit and miss compared with the original starry wisdom, but modern witches believe that despite the accretions and maybe distortions of the past sixty centuries, there still remains at the center of the cinder a spark of that mysterious dark angelic fire which first breathed life into the clay of this world.

It is to this remnant of the old wisdom in its most *practical* aspect that you shall be introduced in the following pages. This is what witchcraft is all about. Theory and scholarship I shall leave to other books. The interested reader, should he wish to pursue magical theory in greater detail, or follow the historical thread of the witch trials back into the labyrinth of time, will find a list of some of the more useful works at the end of this book in the bibliography.

CHAPTER 1

First Steps

The Powers and Their Attainment

HAVING read the preceding pages, you now may be ready to take your first step, your initial, practical commitment to the way of witchcraft.

For your first step, it will be sufficient for you to make a token gesture. The traditional initiation rites we defer to Chapter 7; it is entitled, "The Coven and How to Form One." Here and now it will be sufficient for you to make a symbolic gesture which will ceremonially demonstrate your severance from old restraints and inhibitions that in the past have acted as the main obstacles to the development of the powers within you. Basically, these restraints can be symbolized as the yoke imposed by such established systems of irrational thought as organized religion, be it Christianity, Judaism, or Buddhism. *Organized* religion, let me emphasize. Of course, there are many other ironclad systems of thought without occult bases which have been imposed upon the public mind from time to time, such as Communism, Fascism, or capitalism, but these at least function under the pretense of ministering to the bodies of mankind rather than to the good of the soul, whatever that might be.

The domain of witchcraft is the realm of the unseen and the point at which it impinges upon man's psyche, and as it is in this very same area that the various churches have sought to dabble their fingers, it is with these institutions that we witches take issue in principle. Ironically, you will find that all the innovators and founders of said religions were revolutionaries in their time who took issue with their parent religions and were usually labeled heretics of one sort or another for their pains.

So enough of all the cant—religious, political, nationalist, whatever. Overboard with the lot of it. And this is where your little gesture comes in. No, we are not going to ask you to burn a draft card or an American flag; the time-honored tradition of repeating the so-called Lord's Prayer backwards is all you have to observe. Whether you are or were a practicing Christian, Buddhist, Jew, Mohammedan, Parsee, Hindu, whatever, makes no difference at all. As long as you are living in a "Christian" country, the gesture is most effective.

It is a defiant relic from the days of the great witch persecutions, and though witches used not to be specifically anti-Christian, many of them became so, not unnaturally, with the advent of that tide of religiously motivated oppression and bloodshed. It is a symbol of defiance toward the dead letter as opposed to the living spirit of organized religion.

This is what you must do:

When you are quite sure you wish to take this first step, prior to going to bed on three successive nights, making quite sure you are not observed, light a candle and address yourself to it with the following words. This gibberish is, in fact, the Lord's Prayer written out backward. It is somewhat difficult to pronounce, but struggle through as best you can. It will be no more complicated than some of the peculiar words of power you will encounter later on, and it will be good practice for you. You should find it easier to say on each successive occasion; the third time you will be fairly fluent. I have written it phonetically, hence the slight difference from the usual backward spelling.

> Nema! Livee morf su revilléd tub
> Noishaytpmet ootni ton suh deel
> Suh tshaiga sapsert tath yeth
> Vigrawf eu za sesapsert rua suh vigrawf.
> Derb ilaid rua yed sith suh vig
> Neveh ni si za thre ni
> Nud eeb liw eyth

> Muck mod-ngik eyth
> Main eyth eeb dwohlah
> Neveh ni tra chioo
> Rertharf rua!

As you chant the words, use your imagination to visualize great iron shackles struck off your hands and feet by sizzling bolts of lightning and disintegrating into molten shards to either side of you. Hear the whine and crackle of the searing flashes as they accomplish the work of liberation, and consciously try to feel the burden of all your inherited guilts, all those awful shalt's and shalt not's, all that vast edifice of twaddle and claptrap, sliding easefully from your back.

When all is over, blow out the candle, uttering the witch words "So mote it be!" Should you feel any frissons of fear creeping up your spine during the performance of what may appear to you palpable blasphemy, it is all to the good. This is a process of purgation and catharsis and often carries with it a certain echo of childhood fears. Don't worry, though; any cold shivers only herald the fact that your deep mind is sitting up and taking notice. It is through your deep mind that you will develop your powers once you have cleared away the litter and debris that usually clogs it, as indeed is generally the case of the ordinary man-in-the-street.

Each of the three successive days when you get up in the morning, you must strive to remember who you are, a witch, what you did the night before, and the reason you did it. Then, maintaining that same frame of mind, embark upon the coming day.

Strictly speaking, this "unraveling" is only necessary as a gesture for the first three nights to mark your initial step on the path.

Anyway, the feeling of release that should accompany this little rite is a sure indication that the way is open for the powers to begin flowing within you. It is as simple as that. No risky copulation with fellow initiates on top of damp tombstones. No messy crucifixion of toads. Just a simple loosening of the mundane knot—a process of blessed unbinding.

As we witches say, I say to you: "Blesséd be!"

* * *

Now you can begin developing your powers, the initial step of commitment having been taken. This is done basically in two ways: First, by making use of the four great rules of magic which form the sides of the witches' pyramid; and second, by the observance of natural power tides within the framework of the universe, which constantly ebb and flow, and may be utilized to great advantage as indeed they always have been over the centuries by cultists and occultists alike.

But first I shall deal with that most important of subjects, that dark tower of sorcery itself, the witches' pyramid.

The Witches' Pyramid

The acquisition of a witch's basic power is rooted in the observance of four simple rules, sometimes known as the witches' pyramid. These are the four cornerstones of magic from which the whole mysterious edifice of witchcraft rises. The rules in themselves are not magical, but the joint application of them is. You must apply them sedulously, knowing that only in accordance with what you are willing to invest will you gain anything in return.

The four cornerstones of the witches' pyramid are: a virulent imagination, a will of fire, rock-hard faith, and a flair for secrecy.

Imagination being the ability to conjure up within your mind sights and scenes to delight the senses and entertain the fancy, it is the tool par excellence of the artist, inventor and inveterate onanist. The greatest and the most notorious personalities in the history of mankind have all possessed this power to a great degree, and I suspect you, the reader, also do. Otherwise you wouldn't be reading this book. The ability to indulge in a flight of fancy is of paramount importance to a witch, for it is through this dark glass that she in fact will cast her spells and set the world afire with her incantations.

Therefore, as a witch, nurture your imagination, treasure your fantasies. Magically speaking, you will probably put every one to excellent use. The more emotional and deeply knotted the roots of your secret visions are, the more potent will they be to effect the working of your charms. The success of all your spells will depend on just how much of a head of emotional steam you can work up over them. The more tempestuous the emotion, the better is your chance of success. You must really be prepared to roll on the ground and gnash your teeth in ecstasy or hate whenever you enter your charmed circle of practice.

Apropos of this, many modern witches employ the method actor's device of sense memory to jar their jaded emotional voltages into the correct spark-spitting intensity. This is known variously in the craft as linking, commemoration, or picking up one's contacts. However, meaningful memories apart, you can use anything you like to turn you on and get the current flowing: perfumes, sounds, strobe lights, wild dancing, sex, mantrams, hymns, and so on—wherever your preference lies. Anything and everything may be pressed into service to get your imagination crackling and those cold shivers running up and down your spine.

This, of course, is the rationale behind the traditional trappings of witchcraft—quite apart from the paraphysical implications of the rituals. A suitable setting for your magical acts is therefore requisite as one of the primary stimulants to your witchly imagination. A living room or den is about the best most of us can manage in these days, but this is where your imagination comes in and invests the place of working with all the mystery and terror sufficient to start your black juices flowing. The occasional grotesque statuette or bizarre print is all to the good. In fact, as a witch, you will be obliged to collect around yourself over the course of time a good complement of sorcerous trinkets. They don't necessarily have to be the genuine articles—real skulls and goat's-foot candlesticks are hard to come by and somewhat expensive—but seeing that atmosphere is so important, it is worth investing in the odd dime store Pacific Island devil mask or reproduction of a medieval astrological chart. It will probably grow to be a passion with you as time passes, and you may soon find yourself having to resist sternly the lure of any junk or antique shop you happen to pass, purely in the interests of economy.

So treasure up your fantasies. The controlled daydream is one of the main keys to being a successful witch. In fact, dream on, the richer and more fantastic the better!

The second side of the witches' pyramid of power is firmly

labeled "will." It almost goes without saying that the establishment of a potent will is one of the main goals of a practitioner of the Black Arts. The will in this instance is a magical one, however, and if viewed out of magical context and within the framework of everyday life, would constitute a splendid example of extravagant egocentricity or even megalomania. It is the will of a spoiled child we are dealing with here, one which brooks no opposition and impudently stares down any attempt at resistance with a basilisk eye.

This will is switched on during the actual magical operation, and it functions hand in hand with the bubbling and boiling emotions evoked by means of your wicked imagination. It is in effect the lens through which the burning emotions are focused. In order to sharpen your will to the correct needlepoint, you may wish to employ one or two aids in the form of simple exercises designed to help concentration. Eastern disciplines such as certain yoga meditation exercises can be used. They are very wearisome, but they do work, with perseverance.

Meditating on the single flame of a candle is also good, as is keeping the attention fixed upon a painted dot within a circle for half an hour without budging. The attempt to gaze at the second hand of a watch completing the circuit of one minute, maintaining one's awareness of the hand at *every* second is also very rewarding, and is frequently used by witches as a toning-up exercise for the will, here used to direct the attention.

You must begin to assert yourself; it doesn't matter on precisely what, but generally. Then, once you have begun to feel the intoxication of a powerful will growing within you, you should start exercising it in little matters of no consequence. To use it disinterestedly at first is the best way to begin, so concentrate on inconsequential things that you normally wouldn't give a fig about, and before you embark on them, become aware of the fact that you are now switching on your magical will. Getting the best of an argument is a good exercise, where brute force may be unnecessary, but persistence often wins success. Every day will bring a mass of little opportunities to sharpen your will; they are all grist for the mill. As I say, *persistence* is the watchword here. A whole host of clichés spring to mind to illustrate the point, and they are all equally valid.

"If at once you don't succeed, try, try, try again."

"Perseverance brings success."

And so on.

One word of caution, however. Don't try willing anything which deep down you yourself are convinced is impossible. In all probability it won't come about, and this will prove a serious blow to your faith in yourself. Start with little things which you know can be effected. Leave the extinguishing of candles by mental action or the levitating of ashtrays to the adept for the time being.

Remember, the point is to make the "bendable" world bend to your will. After all, your ambition is to become a witch, not God, and it would be wise to bear in mind that there is a difference. To cultivate your magical will means that first and foremost you must know what you want; you then proceed to narrow down your field of attention to encompass just that one thing, keeping it before your awareness all the time. Then you go and get it. Keep at it. This doggedness and the attitude of mind it engenders has to be part of your witch personality during the magical operation.

"As my will, so mote it be!" These are the magic words.

Which brings me to the third side of the witches' pyramid on which is etched in mighty letters of refulgent gold the word FAITH. Now this may seem a strange thing for a witch to concern herself with, but it is quite true to say that all magical power is largely dependent on this, whether it be wielded by people calling themselves witches or saints, as the case may be. Whether you cast a spell for the sake of a church, yourself, or anyone else makes not one jot of difference. A spell is a spell, whether it sounds like a prayer or an incantation.

Paracelsus put the matter in a nutshell when he wrote: "Through Faith the Imagination is invigorated and completed, for it really happens that every doubt mars its perfection . . ."

Unless you possess a rock-firm faith in your own powers and in the operability of your spell, you will not achieve the burning intensity of will and imagination which is requisite to make the magic work. Faith is the vise in which you hold steady your crucible will, into which you pour the molten metal of your virulent imagination. If you reflect on it, you will see in effect that imagination and faith are both very intimately connected with the will. Faith is that which sweeps away all remaining objections and clears the decks for immediate action. It is one of those valuable props which support you temporarily, in the course of your magical operation, and allow you to believe in the inevitability of the success which is bound to be attendant upon it. It is one more means of attaining that special state of self-imposed and hopefully temporary megalomania which is the *sine qua non* of all true acts of sorcery.

You must be well aware of the great part faith plays in the dealings of those individuals who wrestle with the more arcane aspects of fate in one way or another. A spiritual healer or a master gambler would no more approach a prospective patient or crap game cold, without the flame of faith in their powers to warm them, than would a microscopist approach his specimen without a microscope. At a rudimentary level, if you didn't have the faith you could do it, you could no more put one foot before the other and cross the road in the manner you do every day, than could a two-month-old baby. In magical matter, faith is *de rigueur*, and due to this fact it merits a whole side of the witches' pyramid to itself.

While we are on the subject of faith, it would be as well to mention at this point that you as a witch must never break your word. If you do not think you are going to be able to fulfill a promise, do not make it, even if there is only the faintest possibility that you may not be able to come through. The reason for this should be readily apparent to you, bearing in mind all we have said already on the subject of the magical will and faith. You are trying to cultivate a state of mind which you can switch on at will, whereby it is absolutely natural and in accordance with the nature of things that whatever you say is going to come true. In this case, the words of the spell. Each and every time you break your word, whether the reason for it be outside your control or not, you chip away a little of that assiduously worked for faith in yourself, which you are trying so hard to cultivate. That's all. Nothing to do with morals or ethics in this case. A witch's word is a witch's word, and is never given lightly.

First Steps

The fourth and last theoretical consideration of the pyramid to contend with as a witch is the important one of secrecy. Now witchcraft consists of knowledge, and knowledge brings power. Power shared is power lost. Although we have entered the Age of Aquarius, along with its attendant freedom and loosening of restrictions, it will still be very much in your own interests as a witch to shroud certain of your doings in a reasonable veil of secrecy. Apart from the fun and glamour involved in so doing, there are one or two practical considerations in addition to a magical one which also make this maxim of secrecy meaningful. If someone obliquely gets to hear that you, a witch, are performing a magical operation for or against him, whether or not he believes or disbelieves in your powers, way down inside him his deep mind will hear and take notice. And this is half the battle won. Nothing so arouses the deep mind's attention in anyone than the call of the dark, arcane, and mysterious.

Deep calleth unto deep; there is a natural affinity in all men's souls for that which is half hidden in a twilight world, and once you have gained the attention of a person's deep mind, you may then proceed to work on it, using your own as a broadcasting unit for your wishes. This is the essence of witchcraft.

So any half-told hint that you are actually about to cast a spell can do wonders to prepare the ground in your victim, even before the operation is actually performed. Hence much of the half-veiled secrecy of witches. This is no matter purely of fun and frolic, although undoubtedly this comes into play also. Secrecy per se can get remarkable results. Nothing succeeds like a secret, whatever it may be, however puerile or nonsensical, when you are striving to draw someone's attention. Once you have that attention, then you can begin your sorcery in good and earnest.

So practice dropping the occasional portentous hints about your magic, never of course being too explicit, but always striving to convey just enough to activate people's curiosities without making them too skeptical. Of course, you will have to be selective with what you say to people. Not everyone is susceptible to the same pitch. With some, after being pressed in vain to say more, you may find yourself confronted with the retort, "Well, *don't* tell us if you don't want to; see if we care!" But they do. And it has aroused their interests sufficiently for them to expend energy on an emotion of petulance. The worst kind of response to your engineered secrecy is one of "Oh, really . . . Did I tell you about that movie I saw the other day?" So be discriminating with your portentous hints. Sum up your audience or victim before you slyly murmur in their ears.

Another, more mundane reason for preserving a modicum of secrecy is this: Though the burning days are over, you must still keep one eye open for the law on one or two points. For instance, should one of your wax voodoo dolls be brought into court and shown as sufficient evidence of your practice of psychological intimidation upon an intended victim, you could find yourself in trouble with a lawsuit on your hands and heavy damages may be awarded against you.

Witchcraft pure and simple may not be illegal in Western non-Catholic countries anymore, but you as a practicing witch can find yourself in faintly treacherous waters if you are not always wary of where you are heading. As a witch, you should, for example, familiarize yourself with the existing witchcraft laws, if any, of the place where you reside. For instance, in certain of the states of America, to take money for any form of occult work, including witchcraft, can under certain circumstances still be regarded as a criminal offense.

In England, since 1951 when the old witchcraft laws were finally repealed, there now operates a law entitled the Fraudulent Mediums Act, which states that persons taking money for fraudulent practices involving purported supernatural activities can, in fact, still be held subject to prosecution by due process of the law. But only for fraud, not heresy. So it pays to watch your step.

If in the course of your career in the Black Arts a friend asks you as a witch to do some special favor for him, take care not to ask money for your services, however strong the temptation. Allow your friend to purchase the necessary materials for the spell. There is also no objection to his returning favor for favor after the operation. But no hard cash, if you're wise. Apart from the legal aspects, a direct financial transaction is also counseled against by a very ancient magical law. For some reason real monetary involvement appears to vitiate the potency of the magic. Try it if you don't believe me. Most witches I know have generally found it to be the case.

In all probability then, you will be able to bind your spells blithely without police interference as long as you do not actually get caught taking money for them or instigating any obvious antisocial activities such as blackmail, extortion, intimidation, or flagrant sexual practices of which the state may not approve.

With these mundane considerations disposed of, we can now return to our study of the final cornerstone of the magical pyramid, namely magical secrecy.

When you cast a spell, you will in effect be putting some very delicate "machinery" into operation. The machinery itself is made out of the stuff that dreams are made of, and the electricity that flows through it will be your own pulsating emotions and desires. Now in order to assemble this machinery in the first place and then make it move, you are going to have employed your burning will, rock-firm faith, and virulent imagination in equal, strenuous amounts. You will have slaved away to work yourself into the right intense frame of mind where it would be inconceivable that the magic could possibly fail.

Now supposing at just that precise moment the door to your place of working were to open and your husband or maybe your mother-in-law were to confront you, uttering words to the effect of, "Audrey! What are you doing dressed up like that in here? And why haven't you got any lights on? You'll strain your eyes . . . And what's all that terrible smoke? Are you trying to set the place on fire? . . ."

Total anticlimax. And probably the finish of your witchcraft for quite a while. You may well try to employ your basilisk gaze at that point, but unless you have a very well developed magical will, it will probably avail you naught.

No, all possibilities of unauthorized intrusion must be strictly limited. It is not worth the battering to your newly burgeoning witch's ego. A disaster like that can set months of hard work to little or no account.

So, bearing all these considerations in mind, shroud yourself with a certain amount of reasonable secrecy, especially about the time and place of your magical operations. Of course, if it is a rival witch or maybe a whole coven that is interested in busting up your operation, then should they know the nature of the magic you are going to work, they will probably be able to figure out the *time* when you are going to perform —say around the full moon. If they are worth their magical salt, they may also even figure out the place, by means of a divination.

Then it will be a matter of may the best witch win; magic against countermagic. But this is more properly a subject for Chapters 5 and 6, which deal with countermagic and attack. Here I shall restrict myself to sensible advice concerning the relatively simple matter of preserving a modicum of secrecy about your personal magical activities. You don't have to become paranoid, just avoid inviting trouble.

Now we have dealt briefly with the four cornerstones of magical practice, and they should speak for themselves. They reward contemplation. All successful witchery stems from their accurate employment. You can burn your Cabalistic books and drown your yoga sutras—they will avail you *nothing* in your quest for power unless you have already understood and mastered the ideas embodied in the witches' pyramid, the four great rules of magic which are the keys to all practical operations in the world of the unseen.

Casting Your Spells

Whenever you wish to work a piece of witchcraft, it is always best if you tie all your supercharged will, faith, and imagination into a single, sizzling bolt with the help of a pattern of spoken words: the charm, or incantation.

Witches, like poets, painters, and chefs, have always taken a bit from here and a bit from there in the exercise of their craft, so much so that in many cases the original wisdom has been almost totally overlaid.

Everything that seems to have an inherent power in it, that triggers the emotions strongly, is pressed into use for the purposes of magic. Snippets of folklore, religion, myth, and herbal lore, all are blended together with notorious indifference to mixing of styles and cultures. All that matters is the item's effect on you and your deep mind.

While on the subject of religious components, "words of power," Cabalistic names of God and the like, here is a tip for the wise witch: Better results will always be obtained if you happen to subscribe to the religion from which your words of power derive, in the case of the Cabala, Judaism, or maybe unorthodox Christianity. However, always remember, it is only the awe, the shiver of emotional excitement, aroused by the name or quotation, which is its chief magical value. If you can do this with an Arabic name of God, Roman Catholic saint, or Tibetan demon, so much the better. Go ahead and use it. Likewise, the name of your husband, wife, lover, favorite politician, film star, or most hated dictator will all be equally magically potent, so long as they give you that extra little kick to stir your deep mind out of its usual sluggish sleep. So much for barbarous Cabalistic words of evocation!

Usually, therefore, you will find it advantageous to devise your own incantations, as the majority of witches do. Of course, there are all the traditional charms such as you will find in the following text which have accumulated a magical charge of their own through the years, and as such, of course should be used to your fullest advantage. (And admittedly some of these do contain the occasional word of Cabalistic derivation.)

The ideal form for the incantation is that which has a beat to it. Some practitioners insist on a rhyme as well as rhythm. Rhyming couplets are the favorite metrical style, I would say. They are certainly among the simplest to construct.

Again: the deep mind is, as always, the target with this use of rhyme and rhythm. Verse, however doggerel and bad, is always potent for stirring the depths, especially when there is a certain amount of frenzied repetition involved.

In view of this particular attitude to incantation, most of the processes of medieval sorcery that are now available to the general public are seen by the average witch as extremely clumsy and, as such, highly unsuitable for performance. Not only are they closely bound up with Judeo-Christianity, but they are also always bogged down with endless preachy pages of invocation, as you will see if you ever consult one, which, far from awakening the deep mind of the operating witch, will generally tend to send it even more securely to sleep.

Apropos of religious beliefs, the modern witch tends to "reserve judgment" generally; there are those who devote themselves entirely to the fertility cult of Habondia and her horned consort. This is by no means universal, however. The gods are there if and when you need them. But more of this in a later chapter.

As a witch, you do not necessarily have to worship any complete and permanent hierarchy of supernatural beings if you don't want to. There simply exists power to be tapped—to do good or to do evil, both of which are remarkably relative concepts. Of course, as a witch, you should know from tradition as indicated in the last chapter, that there exist certain entities who will aid you in your spells; what these beings ultimately are, whether they predated man, or whether man himself created them, we cannot tell. You may call these entities gods, spirits, or watchers; or depersonalize them as powers or forces, but you must realize that *they* are now as dependent on your attentions as you in your spells are on theirs. However, in whatever relationship you happen to enter with them, always remember, *you* are the master of the occasion, albeit a courteous one! Some of these powers will be useful for one type of operation such as a love spell, but useless for another, one of vengeance, say.

What their order of precedence is in that place or state they exist in, we cannot tell, merely surmise. Only through what tradition tells us can we gain any clues. The only sort of hierarchy that exists seems to be a general one which can be classified thus:

At the top we have Great Entities, often known as Watchers, Mighty Ones, or gods by more classical-minded witches. These include the so-called witch deities Habondia and Cernunnos, whose acquaintance you will make on a later page. They are generalized powers existing within the deep minds of all of us, Jungian archetypes, if you like, which can be contracted to bring a certain power to your rituals.

Then there are spirit entities or demons, halfway between men and gods in their constitution, traditionally predating us in their evolution, however—the remnants of the Nephelim, in fact. Vassago, who you will also encounter in a later chapter, is one of these beings.

Finally, there are the spirits or shades of the dead themselves, such as will be dealt with in the rituals of necromancy in Chapters 3 and 4.

Gods, demons, shades—these constitute the chief inhabitants of the witches' pantheon. Of course, there are many minor, elemental spirits which you will be dealing with in the course of your career, but they will generally be those which you yourself *create*. Any talisman, image, alraun, or mandragore you may make will partake of the nature of an elemental. They are unseen versions of the homunculi of alchemical legend, servants of your will, called into being by an application of your witch power for the performance of a task. As such, they should be treated with firmness, as opposed to the respect and deference you will show to gods and demons. They should never, under any circumstances, be let out of the command of their witch creator. Mickey Mouse's "Fantasia" broomsticks were based on a very old magical legend incorporated into Lucian's *Philopseudes* and later into *The Lay of St. Dunstan,* which graphically illustrates what can happen psychically if you ever let your elemental servants get out of control!

Magical Times and Seasons

Finally, as a novice witch or warlock, you will need to know about the times and seasons of the witches' year. These are the correct times when you will be able to recharge your magical batteries and draw down to yourself the new currents of elemental power to work your spells. The elemental power tides of the universe are marked by the movements of the stars, the sun, and the moon, but chiefly the latter two. Though these heavenly bodies are not the actual sources of the power, they are the main *indicators* of its ebb and flow in our universe. Whenever you wish to perform a magical act, you must work taking these power tides into consideration, in the same way a navigator of a boat times his movements to utilize the sea tides to his best advantage. Of course, you can work against the tide, but it is self-defeating for the beginner, and is best left for times of emergency or until such a time as you have reached a degree of sureness in your practice.

The sun and the moon are the two great hands of our cosmic clock. Whereas the hour hand or sun governs the seasons of the year, the moon or minute hand governs the sea tides and the hidden workings of the deep mind. As such, this heavenly body rather than the sun is the main concern of witches. In European mythology the sun has always been seen as a symbol of a male divinity, the moon a female one. However, worship of the moon as a supreme deity evolved much earlier than that of the sun. It is said among witches that in England at least the cult of the moon goddess predated the Druidic, solar religion, and that it is from this early Prytanic religion that four of the great annual witch festivals are derived.

These are the nights of October 31 (Halloween); February 2 (Candlemas); April 30 (Beltane), and August 1 (Lammas). Of these, Beltane and Halloween are the more important. The four solar fire festivals of the Druids are also observed, though to a lesser extent. These are midwinter, spring, midsummer, and autumn as marked by the solstices and equinoxes, and these together with the preceding four make the eight Sabbats, or festivals, of the witches' year.

The practical import of the Sabbats is this: Halloween, Candlemas, Beltane, and Lammas mark the beginning of each quarter of the solar-tide cycle; first the tide of destruction and winter is initiated with Halloween, the feast of the dead, the first day of the witches' year. The dark tide of destruction reaches its high point at midwinter, the winter solstice. Candlemas, marks the end of the reign of the King of Winter, Lord of Misrule, and the first stirrings of the bright tide of summer. At the time of the vernal equinox, the bright and dark tides stand equally balanced, with the bright tide on the increase; Beltane marks the beginning of its fullest spate, which reaches its high point at the midsummer solstice. From here it begins to wane. The first stirrings of the dark tide are then felt at Lammas, the time of fruition and harvest when the crops are gathered in and fruits begin to ripen. At the autumnal equinox, the two tides again stand equally opposed, the bright tide waning, the dark ever increasing. At Halloween the tide of darkness again enters its full spate, and so the cycle recommences.

To farmers and those whose work is subject to the seasons, the ebb and flow of the solar tide is, of course, second nature, for it influences the entire life cycle of all that grows upon the earth. But for witches, it is observed chiefly in coven activities directed at drawing down elemental group power, hence the timing of their Sabbats. The coven is seen to consist of a group mind which needs to be periodically recharged with power. This belief they hold in common with many organized religious cults, which is one of the reasons why the witch festivals often coincide with Christian or Druidic holy days.

When you organize your own coven, you should be fully aware of the import of the various Sabbats, as will be explained in the last chapter of this book. For the time being it suffices that you know when they occur and mark them off in your calendar accordingly. For all practical magical purposes, however, the phases of the moon are the most important thing for you to observe. The method of their employment is extremely simple.

Basically, there are two sides to the moon's character; when she is waxing, the bright moon; and when she is waning, dark of the moon.

All spells of a *constructive* nature should be performed when the moon is bright, that is, waxing to full. These would include love magic of any sort, sorcery designed to bring luck or success, fertility charms, protection, countermagic, and of course divination.

An old witch verse goes thus:

> Pray to the Moon when she is round
> Luck with you shall then abound
> What you seek for shall be found
> In sea or sky or solid ground . . .

As soon as the full moon is passed, we embark upon the dark of the moon, as the light wanes and nights get blacker. During this period you will perform all operations of a *destructive* or "black" nature, such as spells of attack and vengeance, binding operations (ligature) to prevent people from doing certain things, agricultural magic designed to eliminate pests or weeds, charms to cool off passions in another, and certain works of necromancy, that is, summoning ghosts of the dead.

Many witches when they form their own coven tend to hold informal monthly or bimonthly Esbats (as opposed to Sabbats, from the French, *esbattre*, "to frolic") around the full or new moon, in order to have a general coffee klatch and maybe perform a collective ritual to aid one of the members or an outside friend who has requested help in some way. Whether you hold your Esbat at full or new moon, of course, depends on the nature of the spells you intend to cast.

So these then are the red-letter days on your witches' calendar. There are quite a lot of them. Thirteen full moons, thirteen new moons, and eight Sabbats. None of them are mandatory, except insofar as you need to make use of them. As a witch, however, you will find that the Sabbats are fun, and worth making an effort over, especially the Grand Sabbats of Beltane and Halloween.

CHAPTER 2

Preliminary Preparations

Your Witch Name

ASSUMING you have embarked on your career as a practitioner of the Black Arts, you will have to take a new, magical name to supplement your old, mundane one. Some unkind critics have called this the *nom du Diable*. It is nothing of the sort; at least, not in the sense they mean it. It is, in fact, an important part of your newly burgeoning witch personality, and henceforth you will be known chiefly by it to your fellow practitioners.

Many witches or warlocks choose to take a name which is intimately connected with magic and the supernatural, the favorites being the names of other, legendary practitioners of the Black Arts.

For instance, if you are male, you may choose the name of a legendary sorcerer such as Zyto, Balaam, Elymas, or Cyprian; or, alternatively, maybe Merlin, Althotas, Vergilius, or Vandermast.

A witch might well choose Morgana, Armida, Vivienne, or Melusina; Brisen, Nimue, Hellawes, or Fredegonda, Nocticula, Bensozia, Sidonia, or even Urganda!

Or you might choose a name of more classical inspiration like Apollonius, Medea, or Circe; or ancient Egyptian like Nectanebo or Arnuphis, or maybe something really complicated like Diancecht, Osmandine, or Ansuperomin!

The choice is yours. You must find one that appeals to you,

that calls forth your feeling for the unseen world, gives you a thrill, and frankly makes you feel considerably powerful and no less sinister! Should you not wish to use a name from legend, you may try toying with those of the gods and demigods of mythology. Greek, Roman, Norse, Celtic—whichever you wish. A very good lead in these matters can be provided by finding out your astrological birth sign and planet and looking up the legends that surround them. For instance, if you are an artist or craftsman born under the sign of Taurus, you may well decide on the name of Daedalus, being that of the wizard-craftsman of King Minos, leader of the Cretan Bull Cult, thus linking with Taurus the Bull. Or, alternatively, if you are a female witch born under Taurus, ruled by Venus, you may decide that the name "Ariadne," daughter of King Minos and Theseus' bride, would be suitable, especially as she is indeed a form of Aradia, one of the chief spirit powers of the witch world.

A third method which can yield results is the numerological one. Add up all the digits which compose the name you are best known by, using this scheme to allocate the letters to numbers:

1	2	3	4	5	6	7	8	9
A	B	C	D	E	F	G	H	I
J	K	L	M	N	O	P	Q	R
S	T	U	V	W	X	Y	Z	

Keep adding the resultant numbers together till they form a single digit, thus:

$$\begin{array}{llll} \text{J O H N} & & \text{S M I T H} & \\ 1+6+8+5 & & 1+4+9+2+8 & \\ =20 & + & =24 & =44=4+4=8 \end{array}$$

Now numerologically speaking the digits have the following traditional planetary attribution:

1 The Sun
2 The Moon
3 Mars
4 Mercury
5 Jupiter

6 Venus
7 Saturn
8 Uranus
9 Neptune

In John Smith's case, his name planet will be Uranus. His next step would be to consult a book of classical myth and legend, on the subject matter surrounding Uranus. There will be ample material to select a name from, especially if the book is one of comparative mythology, showing the interrelations of legends among different cultures.

Should none of these methods yield results or appeal to you, then you should just go ahead and evolve a name that "feels right," cooking it up for yourself out of the blue, using your intuition to guide you. This in fact is ultimately the only criterion; the preceding methods are merely indicators and helps.

So mull over a selection of names in your mind. Ponder them in reverie if you can and let your deep mind send up some hints if possible. This really is the best way, as in the final analysis the deep mind is what we are really concerned with here. The witch name is basically designed to be an indication of the *true* nature of you as you really are deep down! There exists a coven of witches in England today whose female members only use witch names of a floral derivation, Rosemary, Japonica, Aubretia, Flora, and so on!

Some witches like to take worthy mottoes in Latin like *Sapiens dominabitur astris* or *Omnia vincam*, maybe a bit ecclesiastical in tone, but quite legitimate, though to my mind again less effective than the considerably more evocative names of legend.

Just choose one that satisfies you. It may take a bit of time; but it is worth considering well since once you inscribe it on your magical instruments, you are stuck with it.

Having settled on your witch name, you must keep it very, very secret, as it will eventually become one of the keys to your deep mind. You will be using it whenever you wish to "switch on" to perform a spell; this will be partly accomplished by pronouncing the name silently to yourself whenever you begin your use of the pyramid powers.

You should only divulge it to others who are close witch

friends, preferably when you are closely bound together with them in the form of a group, or coven.

And as already mentioned, you will *also* write it on all your magical witch tools, using special witch runes to do so. Which brings me to my next topic.

The Witch Runes

These are, in fact, the letters of your witches' alphabet. Whenever you write your name on one of your magic instruments, you will use them. They are quite easy to learn, and with a little practice, you will soon be able to write them speedily. They are variously called by practitioners the Runes of Honorious or Theban Script, although this latter name does not necessarily imply a Greek or Egyptian derivation. Some witches believe that they are relics of Atlantean days, while others think that they have a connection with the Cabalistic "Enochian Script" of the Elizabethan astrologer and magician Dr. John Dee. Whatever the case, they are very ancient and have been used from time immemorial by witches as their magical alphabet in which spells and inscriptions were written.

Not only will you use these runes to write your witch name on your magical tools, but also to write it on your witch jewels.

Signs of Identification

All witches and warlocks usually possess items that are often known by occult ritualists as jewels; in a witch's case these are items worn like jewelry signifying witchdom to those that have eyes to see, often bearing in runes the witch's name, the symbol adopted by her coven (should she belong to one), and her rank in it if it possesses a hierarchy of any sort. They usually serve three purposes—that of providing a means of recognition between members of different covens; a talismanic "link" with the collective mind of their own group by means of which they "plug in" to the elemental powers drawn down at the Sabbats; and third, sometimes as a means of "Fascination," that is to provide a reflective surface of the same sort often made use of by hypnotists when they wish to throw their subjects into a trance. The ring and pendant, which often contain gemstones,

THE WITCHES' ALPHABET

are generally the only jewels which are put to the latter use, however. One jewel which definitely does not fit into this latter category, however, being hidden mostly and only revealed at Sabbat meetings, is the garter. This and the girdle cord I shall consider last.

The Witch Jewels

The Necklace, the Bracelet, the Ring and Pendant, the Girdle Cord and Garter

The necklace: The necklace is worn by women coven members often at Sabbats and Esbats only. It is in all probability of similar derivation to that of the girdle or garter. Some witches say that it has a connection with "Brisingamen," the elven necklace possessed by Freya, the Norse love goddess. Others say that through its occasional use of acorns as beads, it derives from the worship of Diana of Ephesus, whose devotees saw the head of their goddess bound with a coif of hair in the shape of the acorn itself. The number of beads for the necklace often consists of multiples of nine or thirteen. Acorns aside, however, the beads may be made of any material you please—metal, stone or wood—the only qualification being that they be fairly large and chunky. Amber is a favorite, as also are turquoise and jet. Many witches like to string their own, after exorcising the beads with fire and water initially and charging them in their own witch name, like any other magical tool, when they finish. (For instructions on general exorcisms by fire and water as well as magical "charging," see further on in this chapter.)

The bracelet: This is usually made of copper or silver and is worn by witches of either sex, again as a form of identity sign. However, unlike the necklace, it is engraved with the witch name of the bearer, the coven symbol (which is often an animal such as an owl, cat, or serpent), and his rank in it. There are usually only two "degrees" of rank, that of the triangle and the more advanced one of the pentacle. If male, the leader of the coven is sometimes known as the magister or master, the female as the high priestess. These are generally honorary ranks and titles, however, and simply indicate seniority of membership for the most part. Very occasionally are they indications of power. (See Chapter 7, "The Coven and How to Form One," for more on this.) Sometimes coven members will wear the bracelet to signify the triangle, and the garter, the pentacle grade.

Should you not belong to a properly formed coven, your name in witch runes will be all you need to have, plus any other amuletic symbols of good luck you may choose, such as your zodiac birth sign and planet.

Similar to the bracelet are the *ring and the pendant*. These are usually the only witch jewels bar the necklace that actually possess gems or stones set into them. These are the primary "fascination" jewels, and the more intricate and unusual the jewel, the better it serves its purpose. As to its composition and monetary value, it is completely a matter of individual taste and economy. The best magical witch stones are traditionally the sapphire and the opal. However, most precious and semi-precious stones do just as well, especially those which traditionally are held efficacious *against* the evil eye and fascination! These, in fact, are excellent accumulators of witch power, and as such, if you have ever worn one as a good-luck charm, has provided you, albeit unwittingly maybe, with an equal and opposite means of fascinating others or casting your own evil eye! In effect, you will be fighting fire with fire!

Here is a list, in alphabetical order, of some of those stones you may care to use as the bezel of your ring or pendant:

FASCINATION GEMS

Amber	Diamond	Onyx
Beryl	Emerald	Peridot
Bloodstone	Jade	Sardonyx
Carbuncle	Jasper	Staurotides (Cross-stone)
Carnelian	Jet	Ruby
Cat's-eye	Lapis Lazuli	Turquoise
Coral	Moonstone	Zircon

You may have your witch name engraved upon the ring or pendant—either on the reverse surface or around the stone itself. Sometimes the zodiac birth signs are also engraved, occasionally even a Cabalistic word of power such as Ararita, Tetragrammaton, Mehafelon, Ananizapta, or Shemhamphorash.

Incidentally, a very good idea which some witches resort to is to use a poison ring as their jewel. The inner cavity of the ring itself is very well suited for concealing either written charms to be carried about the person or philter powders to be slipped warily into some unsuspecting person's drink! The metal of which the ring or pendant is made can be any you wish—the following are used by witches to magically stimulate the following traits in their witch character:

> Gold—energy and general success
> Silver—intuitiveness and magical ability
> Copper—success in love
> Brass or fixed mercury—mental agility
> Tin—expansiveness and generosity
> Iron—courage and aggressive instincts
> Lead—stability

Sometimes an amalgam is made of some or all of them, depending on the orientation required. The resulting alloy is then known as magical electrum. But this is specialist stuff. Gold, silver, or copper is the usual choice.

Like the other jewels, the ring or pendant will always be exorcised and consecrated with fire and water in the waxing moon, and named with the possessor's name.

Finally, we come to a consideration of the concealed signs, the witch's *girdle cord and garter*. The girdle cord, often red in color, is used for several practical purposes, the least of which is to hold in your tabard, or ritual witch's robe. It is made of a specified length with certain knots tied in it, and is also used to measure the diameter of your magic circle when you cast one. Some practitioners also use it as a type of ritual rosary when they are performing a spell with a lot of repetitions in it, telling the knots in it like beads; I shall describe its manufacture later in the chapter under the heading of "Your Witches' Working Tools."

The garter is perhaps the most unusual piece of insignia carried by witches and, as such, is concealed and worn openly only at coven meetings. The other jewels can pass as regular items in the eyes of the uninitiated, and as such can usually be worn openly.

There are many styles of witch garters in existence. The traditional color is bright red, though black, blue, and green ones are to be seen. Often a female practitioner will have her garter made of velvet and backed with silk, the male variants being snakeskin, crocodile, or soft leather of some sort backed with blue silk. The garters are fastened by means of gold or silver gilt buckles. Sometimes tiny gold or silver bells are also sewn on, reminiscent of those worn by English Morris dancers.

On the outer surface of the garter are embroidered the witch name, coven symbol, and coven rank, if any. Sometimes the same signs that are inscribed upon the Athamé are also added.

Garters are always worn above the left knee, and let me reiterate, *only* on coven occasions or during the casting of spells.

The garter concludes the list of witch jewels. Most of them are optional, except for the necklace in the case of women. Why this latter exception should be made, I do not know. However, it is traditional coven practice, and as such should be complied with by any female witch, if she really wishes to obey the letter of the law.

Manner of Dress

This is a matter over which there is much controversy in the witch world. Many practitioners claim that the best way to work magic is the traditional way: nude.

Others, equally tradition-minded, claim that this is not necessarily the case, and that ritual robes, or tabards, should be worn. The rationale behind nudity, apart from the sheer fun of it, is that clothing inhibits the emanation of your witch power. As an explanation or justification of the belief, I have never felt it held much water. Witch power is not easily impeded by mere clothing. It passes through walls and traverses wide distances easily enough, so why should a few flimsy garments prove such a barrier to it?

No, the chief reason for the nudity is a psychological one, the state of release from tension, mundane cares, and sexual inhibition is the aim being striven for here.

So if you feel that wearing no clothes may put you in the frame of mind where your magic will work all the better, then that is what you must indeed do. Careful though! Remember prying mother-in-law. Lock the door!

However, for those who live in chilly climates or who aren't enchanted by the idea of naked frolics, the tabard is the alternative. This at its simplest is a long piece of fairly heavy black material, folded double, with a hole for the head cut at the top, poncho-wise; the sides are sewn up to within about nine inches of the top, leaving holes for the arms to pass through. The completed garment hangs to the ankles. It is belted with the girdle cord.

Many practitioners however prefer more complicated or flattering garments, in varying colors such as blue, violet, red, green, or white, often with the addition of a hood, or cowl, to be drawn over the head for greater impersonality during a ritual. Special sandals may be worn or the feet left bare, again as you will. However, let me advise you here, should you form a coven, a certain uniformity of dress is desirable—often zealous witches will possess *two* robes for that very reason; a uniform one for Sabbats and Esbats, and a more individualistic one for private use.

Again your witch name and appropriate signs may be embroidered on the hem or breast of the garment if you desire, but this really isn't necessary. Indeed the tabard itself is not entirely necessary. It is merely a psychological prop to put you in the right frame of mind for magic, and all the rituals and processes can be as easily performed wearing your ordinary, everyday cloths—just as long as they don't work to your disadvantage by bringing you back down to earth again with a bump, that is.

Your Witches' Working Tools

In order to perform any act of successful ritual witchcraft, you must have your set of basic traditional working tools. Without them, all but the most powerful born-witch or warlock is powerless when working at a distance from his victim. They are the tools of your trade, as much as an easel and brushes are of the artist.

Preliminary Preparations

1. White hilted knife
2. Athamé
3. Chalice
4. Thurible

The magical act is a cumulative one. You start from scratch with newly purchased substances, ritually purify or demagnetize them with salt, water, and incense, and then recharge them with your concentrated witch power. From these charged substances, you then fashion your implements, and with these implements, you cast your first spells.

The basic witch tools themselves are five in number; the full complement eight. There are many lesser ones which merit the designation more of common household implements that you keep specially for your witchcraft. For instance, needles for sewing, scissors for cutting, a white-hilted knife, and so on. I shall list the important ones at the end of this chapter along with other useful things you will need in your witches' cupboard.

These are your basic working tools, however:

The Witches' Knife—also known as an Athamé or Bolline.

The Witches' Cord—already mentioned, known variously as a girdle cord, or cingulum.

The Witches' Censer—the incense burner or chafing dish, also known as the thurible.

The Witches' Cup—also known as the chalice.

The Witches' Spellbook—known variously as a witches' Bible, workbook, *Liber spirituum,* or Book of Shadows.

With these simple though basic tools you will be able to manufacture all the other magical artifacts that are mentioned in the following pages; the wand, the speculum, the candlesticks, the pentacle, the mandragore, and the alraun, and all the talismans, philters, incenses, images, and amulets that will be your general stock in trade. The ways and means to manufacture such things will be discussed under the specific headings throughout the book as we come to them.

To make your working tools, the first thing you must do is to learn how to purify and consecrate all your raw materials (or exorcise them, as we call it) by means of salt, water, and incense.

Theoretically, the salt, water, and incense stand for the four elements of the Wise—earth, water, and fire, together with air—symbolically constituting the basis for the material universe, in the language of alchemy and witchcraft. By exorcising anything, you are in effect symbolically using these four basic constituents to "wash" the article of all extraneous vibrations, prior to recharging it with your own will and concentrated witch power. Before, in fact, transforming it into a servant to accomplish a given magical task. Throughout the following pages I will refer to this process of purification as either exorcism or "passing something through fire and water."

Formula of Exorcism by Salt, Water, and Incense

Basically, any form of words can be used to exorcise something, ranging from a long ecclesiastical-sounding Latin invocation to a simple jingle. Witches generally prefer the latter. Here are two charms that can be used for exorcism, and which partake of the nature of jingles:

Taking a small handful of new salt and casting it into a bowl of fresh water, *breathe* these words onto the water's surface, mentally visualizing—and this is the important thing—with all the faith, will, and imagination you can muster, a dim bluish light beginning to hover over it as you do.

> Water and earth
> Where you are cast
> No spell nor adverse purpose last
> Not in complete accord with me.
> As my word, so mote it be!

This is now your charged salt and water of exorcism which you will use to make your working tools.

Similarly, casting a few grains of good-quality church incense onto a glowing charcoal block contained in an ashtray, chant as you hold your hand outstretched over it:

> Creature of fire
> this charge I lay,
> no phantom in thy presence stay.
> Here my will addressed to thee;
> and as my word, so mote it be!

Again, strongly visualize the coals radiating that strange blue light as you speak. With this charged fire, you will complete the exorcism of your raw materials.

Now the first working tools you should make are the cup and the thurible. In fact, as soon as you have made these you will be using them to contain the water and fire respectively, rather than relying on the services of any handy bowl and ashtray.

The Witches' Cup

The witches' cup is a variant of the cauldron of Ceridwen. This, in turn, was a Celtic development of early Prytanic myth which later became the central theme of all the legends concerning the Holy Grail, that mysterious relic which is woven inextricably into the Arthurian romances.

The cauldron, bowl, or cup symbolizes the receptive passivity of the great womb of nature, out of which all things are born and to which all return. It is seen as female in nature and is analogous with night, darkness, space, and, of course, the all-encompassing sea. Water is the traditional element of the Wise related to it.

The cup or chalice is used to contain the salt water of exorcism or, alternatively, the wine of libation. This is the sacramental wine which is consumed in some ceremonies, and also used to consecrate things at times. The cup is also used to compose philters in.

During persecution times the use of the chalice or cup was generally discontinued, owing to the fact that should a witch or warlock be found in possession of one, it usually led to an immediate bout of prolonged torture, the reason being, of course, that church authorities inevitably suspected the cup to have been used for heretical and blasphemous perversions of the Mass. In their eyes they were undoubtedly justified, as there is indeed a ceremonial feast at the Sabbat, wherein witches consume cakes and wine in much the same manner as the early church did in its Agape, or love feast. It is a rite common to many cults.

In order to make your own cup, you must first buy, *without bargaining over the price* (this will apply to anything you use in your spells), a goblet anywhere from three to five inches in diameter. It can be made out of anything you please that isn't porous and will hold a liquid. Some old witch cups are made of animal horn, and others of silver or silver-gilt like the conventional church chalice, or even of tinned copper. If you decide on a brass or copper one, be sure you glaze it well on the inside, since both of these metals can become very poisonous when a reactive liquid like wine is brought into contact with them. Glass and ceramic are also acceptable, but, as I say, a metal or horn one is traditional.

The process of consecration is simple. During the period of the month when the moon is waxing toward full, take some salt water in a bowl and steep in it the following powdered herbs: vervain (verbena), mint, basil, rosemary, Hyssop, lavender, sage, valerian, fennel. Sprinkle some incense on a charcoal block and charge both fire and water with the words I have already given you, mentally putting all your effort of will, faith, and imagination into *seeing* the elements as glowing with vibrant, purifying light. Having done this, sprinkle the cup with the water, then pass it through the incense smoke, chanting words to this effect, and visualizing the blue purifying light flickering around it as you do.

> By water and fire I conjure thee
> That there remain
> within thy frame
> no adverse thought nor enmity.
> Hear my will! Attend to me!
> As my word, so mote it be!

Having done this, paint the following runes around the cup with a new brush and paint. Black or white enamel or stoveblack is best for this. For this ritual you may also mix into it a pinch of your powdered herbs, vervain, *et al.*

As you paint each rune, chant these words, visualizing the signs glowing with magical light as you do: "Blessed be thou cup of water!"

Having done this, paint the runes that spell your witch name around the base of the cup, pronouncing each letter out loud as you do so.

When you finish, chant the words "So mote it be!" and put your completed cup safely away for future use.

The Thurible

Again, a simple process. Buy a new metal chafing dish or incense burner, preferably with small legs or a stand to raise its base off the tabletop to prevent scorching.

THE CUP RUNES. (SEE CHAP. 2)

THE ATHAMÉ RUNES. (SEE CHAP. 2)

THE THURIBLE RUNES. (SEE CHAP. 2)

THE WAND RUNES. (SEE CHAP. 3)

THE CANDLESTICK OR LAMP RUNES. (SEE CHAP. 3)

THE WORKING TOOL INSCRIPTIONS

Fill it with about an inch of sand. This will provide good insulation from the heat of the burning charcoal. Now, again when the moon is waxing (this will always be the case, unless otherwise stated), exorcise the thurible with charged fire and water in the same way that you did your cup. Then paint the proper symbols around it, chanting the following words with each symbol and again charging them with light. You may mix a little dragon's blood resin with your paint if you like, for added potency. "Blessed be thou creature of fire!"

Paint your witch name around the base, repeating the letters and charging them as you do so, and again terminate the spell with the words "So mote it be!" This is your completed thurible. With it and your cup you will henceforth perform all your water and fire exorcisms.

Now that we are equipped with our main tools of consecration, we shall deal with one of the most important of all the other witch tools:

The Athamé

The Athamé, or witches' black-hilted knife, is the instrument we use to draw magical circles and other diagrams, in the midst of which many of our spells are cast. Some witches, following the Cabalistic tradition of the old magical grimoire, the *Key of Solomon,* also employ a white-hilted knife, in addition, using the former to cast the circle, and the latter for anything that needs to be ritually dug, engraved, cut, or pierced. Most present-day witches, however, refer the white-hilted knife to the ranks of the lesser instruments, and rely entirely upon the Athamé in their operations.

Buy a *steel* knife with a black handle; the blade should be about five or six inches long. When the moon is *waning*, make an infusion in distilled water of any of the *Martial* herbs listed at the end of Chapter 6. Into this, mix a few drops of blood, either your own, traditionally that of a black cat, but that of a fresh beefsteak, chicken, or lamb chop from your nearest supermarket will do. Your own is best, however.

Exorcise the knife with water from your cup and incense mixed with some of the aforesaid herbs burned in your thurible; then proceed to heat the blade of the knife on the thurible coals until it gets as hot as possible. You will have to stoke up a good heat to do this. When the blade is good and hot, plunge it into your waiting brew, chanting these words, and visualizing the knife glowing with power after each immersion:

> Blade of steel I conjure thee
> to ban such things as named by me.
> As my word, so mote it be!

This process of tempering, or forging as it is called, should be repeated three times.

Having accomplished this, you must now magnetize the blade by stroking it repeatedly with a lodestone or bar magnet. Hold the Athamé in your left hand, the magnet by one end in your right, and beginning at the handle end of the blade, draw the tip of the magnet down the whole length to the very point. Keep this up for a good five minutes, always stroking in the same direction, chanting these words at each stroke:

> Blade of steel, I conjure thee
> attract all things as named by me!
> As my word, so mote it be!

Finally, paint the proper runes upon the handle in white paint, with which you may again mix any of the powdered herbs you used in your previous infusion. Chant the following words to charge each rune: "Blessed be thou knife of art!"

Then paint your witch name on the reverse side of the handle, again spelling the letters out loud to charge them, finishing with your usual words "So mote it be!"

Finally, you must bury the Athamé for three days and three nights in the earth, point down. Your backyard will amply suffice.

At the end of this time, you may dig up your Athamé, and, wrapping it in an exorcised piece of cloth, tuck it safely away, ready for future magical use.

The third of your working tools is:

The Cord

otherwise known as the girdle, cingulum, or cable tow. The latter name derives from its use in various initiation rituals, some of which will be explained in Chapter 7. The cord is used basically to measure the radius of your circles, for binding things—and even, on occasions, for binding oneself! (For this, see under the heading "Ligature" in Chapter 6.)

To make the cord, you should ideally spin your own flax or gather your own river rushes. Never mind, though; do as most urban witches do and buy a ball of red ribbon. From this you should measure off three six-foot lengths. When the moon is waxing, exorcise these with water and fire, and knotting the three ends together, start braiding them, chanting the following jingle, binding in the magical light with each twist:

> Made to measure,
> wrought to bind,
> blessed be
> thou cord entwined.

When you finish, make a large firm knot with the free ribbon ends to prevent them from unraveling, and repeat your sealing words, "So mote it be!"

Finally, tie another large knot three feet six inches from the first knot, a further one at four feet, another at four feet six inches, another at five feet, and yet another at five feet six inches. These will be the measurements of the triple radii when you use the cord as a compass cord for your magic circle. Using it to measure by, you can make two different triple circles; a larger one for coven working and a smaller one for solo spells or small groups.

The Workbook

Your final major working tool!

In this, you must write all your magical recipes, spells, and rituals before you use them, using a good clear hand which will be legible by candlelight.

Our old friend the tradition-minded witch will insist on making her workbook out of parchment, sewing it herself, and sticking a cover on it.

However, if this seems overcomplicated to you, buy a thick book of good-quality drawing paper, about the size of a large exercise book. Then, when the moon is waxing, cover the back and binding of this book with a material of your own choice. Many practitioners favor velvet or moiré silk. Others prefer a leather or skin, often reptile. The choice of color ranges from black or white to red and green, even an occasional silver or gold!

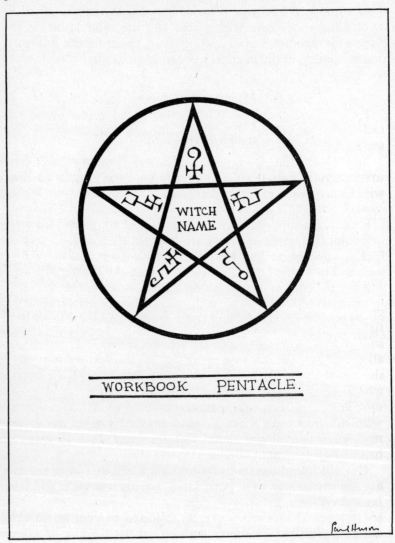

WORKBOOK PENTACLE.

You should then exorcise the book with water and fire. Then, with a pen and ink specially bought for this purpose, draw in this pentacle and its runes on the front side of the first page and the reverse of the last. As you draw in each rune, chant the following words:

> Book of words,
> book of deeds,
> blessed be
> thou book of art!

The "art" referred to is magical art, needless to say.

Finally, write your own witch name in the center of the pentacles, charging each letter as you do so in the usual way, and sealing again with the words "So mote it be!"

This book, along with your Athamé, will be your most treasured magical possession and should only be shown to other witches and coven members.

How to Make Your Magic Circle

This is your first spell of practical witchcraft! To cast it, you will be using all your working tools.

To those familiar with Cabalistic sorcery, the magic circle is generally viewed as a means of defense against hostile spirit entities; to the witch, however, though it may serve this purpose in some of her spells, it has a far more important function usually. This is, in fact, to serve as a lens to focus the witch power she raises in her rituals. It is a sort of magical boiler tank in which the steam is compressed in order to channel it into some useful activity such as driving a piston rod. In this way the witches' circle can be compared very closely with the ground mandala, or dkyilhkhor, used in Indian and Tibetan magic. It has very ancient, pre-Celtic origins.

In Cabalistic magic the circle will usually consist of basically a double or triple concentric circle. In between the lines will be written Hebrew names, divine and angelic, which pertain to the nature of the operation. In the center may often be traced geometrical figures, such as a square or a pentagram whose sides or number of points again correspond numerologically with the type of spell being cast.

To the practicing witch, however, this is all mostly totally irrelevant and unnecessary. Quite apart from the theoretical overcomplication, the practical details are much too demanding. Unless one is wealthy enough to possess a house or apartment with sufficient rooms to dedicate one entirely to magical practice, the full-painted floor circle with all its geometrical ramifications is generally quite out of the question.

No, as a witch, your basic requirement for many spells will simply be a triple circle drawn out on the floor or carpet in temporary masking tape if you want. This is advisable for group or coven workings, but when you are operating solo, you can dispense with even that, using an imaginary boundary line, but making quite sure you stick within it. Because of this it is wise to make the circle rims coincide with marks on the carpet or pieces of furniture, so you can maintain a correct visualization. Anyway, here is your method of casting your circle.

Clear a space on your den or living room floor sufficient to draw a nine-foot–diameter circle (eleven-foot for coven working). Now, pin one end of your cord down to the floor in roughly the center of the room with a heavy object—a chair or table leg maybe—or have someone hold it down if you are working in company. Now, stretching the cord out tightly, take your Athamé, and wrapping the cord around its handle at the first knot, the one four feet six inches from the pinned end, trace a nine-foot–diameter circle lightly on the floor with the knife point, keeping the cord taut and using the chair as a pivot.

You must do this in a *clockwise* direction (known as deosil to witches) always turning to the *right*. You must also *begin* your tracing operation standing in the *east* and end up back in the east. For this, you will need the aid of a small pocket direction-finding compass. As you trace the circle, use your witchly imagination to visualize that blue witch fire blasting down your Athamé blade, like an oxyacetelyne blowtorch, leaving a line of flickering violet-colored flames in its wake. Listen to them hiss and crackle; you are surrounding yourself with a circle of magical light!

If you want to memorize the right color of the fire, try igniting a few drops of methylated spirits or brandy in a saucer (careful though!) and observing the resultant flame.

Having drawn your first circle, you must now repeat the operation, shortening your cord by moving your Athamé six inches down it to the second knot, the four-foot one, giving you a circle with an eight-foot diameter. Repeat the operation a third and final time, using the next knot down, the three-feet-six-inch one, which will give you your inner circle of seven-foot diameter.

This is your magic circle. You must now proceed to exorcise the ground inside it by sprinkling and censing to the four quarters—east, south, west, and north—always traveling deosil, and using your usual fire and water exorcism.

Having got this far, you are now standing in a ritually purified witches' circle, and the lens for your witch power is in position. You can now proceed with the spell itself, such as one of the many outlined in the following pages.

Before finishing this chapter, however, I shall list a few of the ingredients and bits and pieces you will find useful in practicing your craft; buy them new, without haggling over the price, of course; keep them apart from your everyday things; and before you use any of them in a spell, simply exorcise them with fire and water.

A Witch's Initial Supplies

1. Charcoal blocks for the thurible. Preferably self-igniting, but the regular kind will do, sprinkled with a few drops of alcohol or cheap cologne to ignite. You can obtain them from most religious supply stores. A lot of shops specializing in the sale of exotic foreign imports also stock them. Be sure to get them *unperfumed,* though.

2. A supply of plain, undecorated white candles about six to nine inches long. Beeswax is excellent, but ordinary tallow or stearin will do well. Candles of other colors such as black or red will be mentioned in the spells, where they are called for.

3. Salt. Ground rock salt is best, but ordinary table salt will do for exorcisms.

4. Water. Tap water will do for exorcisms, but distilled water such as used for steam irons will be needed for your philters and elixirs.

5. White masking tape. Most art suppliers stock this. It is very useful for the temporary marking out of circles or triangles, particularly where group work is concerned.

6. Good-quality plain white drawing paper for your talismans. Ideally, sheepskin parchment, but this is very expensive and the paper will do just as well.

7. An elementary schoolboy's geometry set including compasses, protractor, ruler, and set square. This is to draw your talismans and sigils (magical symbols) with.

8. A small sewing kit containing scissors, needles, and thread.

9. A dip pen; your "pen of art" (not a ballpoint) for drawing talismans and writing in your workbook.

10. A good-quality (squirrel or sable) paintbrush for painting runes on your magical tools.

11. Thick black waterproof ink to use with your dip pen; your "ink of art." To this, you may add a perfume or herb at the time you cast your spell, consonant with its nature, such as powdered basil for love, cinnamon for intelligence, etc.

Tradition-minded witches make their own ink with one of the following two recipes, usually the latter:

Either

Powdered gall-nuts
Roman vitriol or green copperas
Alum or gum Arabic

or

Gum Arabic
Powdered burned peach kernels
Soot or lampblack (hold the back of a spoon over a candle)
Distilled water

12. A selection of household glues.

13. Paint, both black and white; your "paint of art." Most witches find a stove enamel is best because it takes on ceramic and glass as well as metal. You will be using it to inscribe the runes or your working tools.

14. A small square table to practice on, of cardtable size. This throughout the text will be known as the "table of practice" or "altar."

15. A good assortment of jars and bottles. Little medicine bottles are extremely handy for containing philters and powders. The herb jars sold in various sizes at shops dealing in fancy kitchenware are, of course, ideal.

16. Finally, a generous supply of adhesive labels for easy

identification of your preparations. Many a hex powder looks all too similar to a love sachet mixture! Enough said.

17. Finally a sharp, white-hilted knife for preparatory cutting or "bigraving" (engraving).

These are your basics. You can build up your stock as you go along. Many of the spells in the following pages call for special herbs or spices, and you can buy them for the one instance, and then store the remainder for future use. Try to keep all your magical things together, preferably locked away in a safe place—perhaps a cupboard or closet reserved for the purpose, best of all a room dedicated to your craft.

CHAPTER 3

Divination

Finding Things Out

THE word "witch" comes from the same Anglo-Saxon root as "wit" and "wise," and in its original form Wicce or Wicca meant "a knowledgeable person" or "wise man." The knowledge in question was arcane and generally forbidden by the religious or civil authorities.

Any form of consultation of a witch by a layman was and still is always begun by an occult diagnosis of the situation inquired about, prior to any action being taken. "Finding things out" is therefore of the same primary importance to the modern witch as to her Dark Age counterpart. Nowadays there are many such methods of magical diagnosis extant, ranging from elaborate ceremonial Tarot divinations to numerological analysis or simple teacup reading. But the true methods of divination as practiced by the traditional witch still remain relatively unknown, and it is with these that I shall be concerning myself in these pages.

To the aware witch, time is not a continuous ribbon passing under the keys of some celestial typewriter, but rather a complex field extending into many different directions and dimensions. Given that view of time, that a man should possess a definite future as concrete as his past and present, albeit unseen for the most part, will not strike a witch in any way as odd or unrealistic. The whole process of divination of the future rests on this approach to an understanding of the true nature of time.

Paradoxically, although the future is already "out there," the witch does not feel that her actions are already doomed to one simple course by rigid predestination. The nearest approach to an explanation would be to say that each one of us, at every moment of time, confronts a series of different choices in action. One of these ways we will take, for whatever reasons. That way as well as others is already "out there."

However, be that as it may, we still have a control over our choice of actions. We can make the destiny "out there" become a good one or a bad one, depending on our varied talents, opportunities, and, of course, choices. When a witch talented in the arts of prophecy or divination predicts a destiny for someone, she will, however, be basing it solely on a reading of the deep mind of her client. She will be reading the strongest marked "possible future" of her client at that present moment. This does not mean that there are no other possible futures, but that the one she perceives is the *most likely* one from the point of view of the moment of time she is prophesying in. If she is an expert diviner, she will be reading her client's deep mind at its most profound and basic level, which contains the firmest "guidelines" to its own future. But even these are still open to choices and different interpretations, depending on the will and inclination of the person concerned and whether he becomes sufficiently aware of where his nose is leading him—of his karma, if you will.

At this point it would be germane to mention the subject of curses and blessings inflicted by witches on people. In view of the preceding, you will see that when you as a witch inflict your will magically on someone, what in effect you are doing is throwing the weight of your witch power into the balance of a person's choice of future, and thus guiding his selection in favor of one direction as opposed to a set of others. This, of course, can be effected only through a contact with his deep mind, the place where the mysterious choices are made, hence the whole rigamarole of the magical operation.

But remember, and this is an important thing to bear in mind at all times, should your victim or client prove to be an extremely highly motivated person, with the guidelines to his actions strongly dictated from a great depth within his deep mind, or if he in fact is a powerful warlock, which is tantamount to the same thing, then the likelihood of your persuading his deep mind to accept anything other than its own selected destiny is going to be slim indeed. Not only is any spell you cast going to affect him in no wise, but the magical current you set in motion by your action will recoil on you as the sender and probably expend its energy on your own deep mind!

This is the eternal danger in malefic witchcraft, to be hoist on one's own petard; but we shall speak more of this later in Chapters 5 and 6 which deal solely with the problems of countermagic and magical attack.

However, to return to our topic of divination, we shall start with one of the first, simple rules of practical witchcraft:

Before embarking on any magical operation, perform a divination (a) to diagnose the true nature of the situation, and/or (b) to determine the likelihood of success of the particular magical operation you have decided to employ. There is no point, and indeed no future, in employing a blast of countermagic against some imaginary enemy when in fact a relatively simple amulet of beneficence may be all that is required. We must know what we are at—hence divination.

Now in magic and witchcraft, the operations of divination have always been conducted by means of contact with a power which is symbolized by the astrological symbol of Mercury. The Greeks called this power Hermes, the Egyptians Thoth, the Scandinavians Odin, the early Anglo-Saxons Woden. This power has generally been connected with the starry sky, the air, storm winds, and also the crossroads. Indeed in the voodoo pantheon the power of Mercury is often known as Maître Carrefour or Master of the Crossroads. He is the great mediator between the worlds and is also known as Psychopompos or Guide of Souls. The Saxons knew him by the name "Earendel, the Morning Star." The witch knows him by the name "Herne."

Before beginning any divination, it is always important for the witch to bring her deep mind into contact with Mercury; to tune into his waveband if you wish, whether the divination be performed by means of the relatively rudimentary entities governing the rune sticks, or by questioning a highly sophisticated entity such as Vassago in a show stone.

There are several methods of doing this, ranging from simply meditating upon one of the classical magical images of the winged Mercury to the full ceremonial rite of invocation. To my way of thinking, none of the methods are as aesthetically satisfying or successful as the use of the magical square of Mercury which, although Cabalistic in its origin, is truly witchy in the manner of its employment. Here it is:

THE SQUARE OF MERCURY

8	58	59	5	4	62	63	1
49	15	14	52	53	11	10	56
41	23	22	44	48	19	18	45
32	34	38	29	25	35	39	28
40	26	27	37	36	30	31	33
17	47	46	20	21	43	42	24
9	55	54	12	13	51	50	16
64	2	3	61	60	6	7	57

As a matter of interest, one of the characteristics of magic squares, which is known to most mathematicians, is that the numbers in each line, vertical or horizontal, add up to the same total. In this case, 260. Now you may well ask what all this has to do with Mercury? Well, you can think of magic squares as being signaling devices, types of psychic telephone numbers to the unseen. The way of using the Square of Mercury before any divination is this:

Take a blank sheet of white paper, and exorcise it with salt water and a Mercurial incense such as you will find listed under the heading "Herbs and Incenses." Having done this, draw a square with sixty-four compartments as shown above with your pen and ink of art. Now carefully and deliberately inscribe the numbers in the square as illustrated, in their correct numerical order, 1, 2, 3, 4, onwards, ending with 64. As you write each number, repeat a short invocation to Mercury of your own devising, such as "Mercury, be propitious to me," or "Herne, Lord of the Crossroads, Guide of the Dead," "Earendel, the Morning Star" or even a string of his names from various pantheons like, "Mercury—Hermes—Odin—Thoth." Whichever you prefer.

The only important thing to remember is that the charm

should summon up a mental image in your mind which in some way strikes your fancy and links the work in hand with an idea concerning Mercury, such as wisdom, speed, starlight, the air, a crossroads at night, or even one of the classical images of Mercury. It might be as well to consult a book of mythology at this point to acquaint yourself with some of Mercury's traditional forms and attributes.

When you reach the number 64, finish by "sealing" the talisman with the words "So mote it be," and drawing three crosses in the air with your right forefinger above the paper. (This is a very old method of sealing, or benediction, which was appropriated by the Christian church from their pagan forebears.) Now your square of Mercury will be charged and your deep mind fully attuned to the correct range of vibrations for the divination, which must be performed with the square kept either on your person or prominently displayed in your place of work.

Once you have made a square, whenever you wish to perform a divination, all that is necessary to do is to hold the square in your hands, and let your gaze fall upon the numbers one by one in their proper sequence, repeating your mantram at each number. No sealing is necessary at the end, however; you may begin the divination immediately. Keep your completed square in a new box or wrapped in a clean linen or silk cloth, as with your other magical artifacts; you will be constantly using it.

I shall now move on to a simple type of witch divination, which you as a beginner would be well advised to learn. The operation is known by the name of *Casting the Runes*.

Divination by rune sticks is one of the most ancient and celebrated witch methods of prognostication we have. The process dates back certainly to Druidic times and probably before. It is a very good example of a method of augury, that is, prediction or knowledge gained by signs and omens, as opposed to that of the inner vision as employed when scrying in a show stone or mirror.

Basically the rune sticks consist of four flat slats of fruitwood —apple, pear, cherry, plum, hazel, rowan, or any other wood if you cannot obtain these. But they must be wood. They should be about five inches in length by about a quarter to a half inch

Divination

	1ST THROW	2ND THROW	3RD THROW	4TH THROW

		4	3	2	1
MOTHERS					
DAUGHTERS		8	7	6	5
RESULTANTS		12	11	10	9
WITNESSES		14	13		
JUDGE		15			
RECONCILER		16			

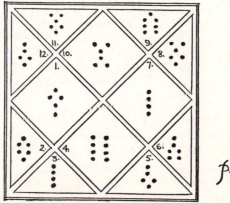

Sample of rune divination showing placement on a horoscope chart

in width. Finish off the rough edges and make the rods smooth and comfortable to the touch. Sprinkle them with salt and water and fumigate with a Mercurial incense within a properly cast circle. Now, using your brush and paint of art, make a large and obvious dot on one side of each of them, centrally located. When the paint has dried, turn the rods over and make two large dots on the other side of them, spaced so that the gaps between the dots themselves and the ends of the rod are all equal, in fact, so that the rods are marked into three equal segments by two dots.

These are your rune sticks. You should carry them about with you for a period of time before you use them to charge them with your magnetism, or witch power.

Now the method of their employment is this:

Provide yourself with some pieces of clean paper, your pen and ink of art, a good supply of Mercurial incense, your square of Mercury, a flat-surfaced table, your thurible and your cup of salt and water. Lock all the doors and means of access to your place of working, and if there is any chance of being overlooked through a window, make sure the drapes are drawn. Then purify the chamber with fire and water as you were taught in an earlier chapter, using your Mercurial incense.

Begin with the square of Mercury ritual to tune your deep mind to the correct level. At this point, write out your question on the paper provided with the pen of art. Then take the rune sticks in your right hand and cast them so they tumble away from you in parallel formation on the table. Say as you do so:

> In thy name Herne,
> Lord of the Crossroads,
> I take up the runes;
> From a word to a word
> let me be led to a word
> from a deed to another deed.

Throw the rods three more times in the same manner, repeating the spell, and note down all the figures formed by the rods on your paper underneath the question beginning at the right-hand corner and going left. *Right to left,* remember.

Now take the top dot or dots from the first (right) figure,

note them down on the right-hand side underneath; then take the top dots or dot of the second figure to the left and note them down under your new set. The top dots or dot of the third figure to the left and those of the fourth complete the third and fourth line of your new figure. In effect, you will have skimmed off the top layer of dots of your first four figures and made a new figure from them. Now do the same with your second, third, and bottom levels of dots belonging to your four primary figures (or mothers, as they are known). This will give you four new figures (known as daughters).

Now write out the eight figures again side by side, right to left, beginning with the first mother and ending with the last daughter. We will now compose our last four figures, the Resultants. These are produced by adding the dots laterally of the first and second figures, the third to the fourth, the fifth to the sixth and so on across the eight.

Now the method of adding the dots is thus:

If the total number of dots is an odd number, you note down a single dot. On the other hand if the total number is an even one, we note down *two* dots. By this process the four resultants are manufactured, which along with the mothers and daughters, make twelve figures in all.

Now to the four resultants, you apply the same process again, laterally adding the dots of the ninth and tenth figures, then the eleventh and twelfth. This produces the two witnesses, figures 13 and 14, which are likewise added laterally to produce the judge, figure 15. Figure 15 is then added laterally to the first mother to produce the reconciler, figure 16.

This process appears vastly complicated on the surface, but in point of fact is extremely easy once you get the hang of the binary addition, which is, in fact, what the process is based on. After a minimal amount of practice you will be able to set up a chart in no time at all.

Now as to the interpretation of the figures:

Basically, the two witnesses symbolize either two main factors bearing upon the problem or a choice of two possible courses of action. The judge, being a synthesis of the whole, indicates the nature of the problem itself, and the reconciler indicates the nature of what will be the final long-term outcome. Now according to the way your question has been phrased, so will the answer be capable of interpretation. So it pays to be very specific about your question in the first place.

There are some modern witches who like to place the first twelve figures within the houses of a horoscope chart. For some people it can work quite well. I myself have never found it to be particularly satisfactory, however.

Anyway here is the method should you wish to try it:

Figure	1	in	House	10
"	2	"	"	1
"	3	"	"	4
"	4	"	"	7
"	5	"	"	11
"	6	"	"	2
"	7	"	"	5
"	8	"	"	8
"	9	"	"	12
"	10	"	"	3
"	11	"	"	6
"	12	"	"	9

The interpretations are according to the astrological ruling of the house. For instance, house 1 refers to the querent, house 2 to money matters, house 3 to news and journeys, and so on.

The following chart provides a simple and accessible interpretation of the runes and their meanings.

The actual symbols used in this divination system are also shared by that of the fifteenth-century wizard Cornelius Agrippa, geomancy, so-called. This involves the use of a tray of sand to construct the figures as opposed to a set of rods. The principle, however, remains the same, the idea of heaven leaving its impress upon the earth being implicit therein.

The Pendulum

Another device frequently resorted to by witches to "find things out" is the dowser, or water witch's pendulum. This device is exactly what it purports to be, namely, a weight attached to a piece of twine. The advantage of its use over that of

The Runes and Their Meanings

Puella—Girl—Beautiful

Puer—Boy—Yellow—Beardless

Amissio—Loss

Acquisitio—Gain

Albus—White—Fair

Rubeus—Red—Severe

Populus—People—Crowd

Via—Way—Journey

Fortuna major—Great fortune

Fortuna minor—Moderate fortune

Conjunction—Assembly—Wedding—Sexual intercourse

Cancer—Prison—Inertia—Restriction

Tristitia—Sorrow

Laetitia—Joy

Cauda draconis—Dragon's tail—Beginning

Caput draconis—Dragon's head—Ending

other divination devices such as the rune sticks is the fact that it needs very little ritual preparation and its use is extremely simple. The disadvantage, however, lies in the fact that the answers it gives to questions are restricted to a solely "yes" and "no" basis. Often, however, this suffices, so for that reason I am including the pendulum here.

The traditional witch manner of making a pendulum is this:

Obtain a lodestone or, failing that, a small steel magnet and some strong twine about nine inches in length. Now, making sure the lodestone is free of dust adhering to it, or the steel magnet free from any grease, glue one end of the twine to it with a drop of strong plastic household adhesive which binds metal. When this is dry, sprinkle the pendulum with salt water, and cense it with an incense composed of wormwood herb (also called mugwort, artemesia, or southernwood) and a few grains of mastic.

Now in order to employ your pendulum, you must either hold the thread firmly between the finger and thumb of your right hand (your left if you are left-handed) and let it hang free, keeping your elbow out, away from your body or, alternatively, tie the free end of the twine onto the middle of a short stick or pencil, and holding one end of the stick lightly in each hand, rest your elbows on a table so that the pendulum dangles free between them. You may now either ask the pendulum questions with a "yes" or "no" answer or, alternatively, you may write the question down on a piece of paper and place it so that the pendulum can swing freely over it. If the pendulum swings to and fro, toward and away from you, the answer is "yes." If it swings sideways, however, the answer is "no."

Instead of the written question, you may also use a photograph of someone about whom you wish to find out something, asking the question in the same manner.

Some witches also use the pendulum to "dowse" by, that is to discover hidden water, oil, or buried minerals and lost articles. Here the pendulum should be held over a large-scale map of the suspected territory, and used to "explore" it until an affirmative answer is given. Then the pendulum is taken to the place indicated on the map, and using it, the witch then narrows her search down to the actual spot where the sought-after item or items are to be located.

The latter process is, however, fairly advanced work. The beginner witch should only concern herself with obtaining simple divinations by using it. Generally speaking, divinations will always go better if you use your square of Mercury first. The pendulum is no exception to the rule, although owing to the extreme simplicity of the divination, many witches feel they can do without any form of Mercurial orientation.

The Wand of Divination

The wand, or staff, is the magical instrument which is *par excellence* emblematic of the powers of divination or prophecy. The staff of the prophet, the divining rod of the water witch, or dowser (as opposed to the pendulum), and the wand of the necromancer are all variations on the same theme. In the witch processes that I enumerate here, a wand or wands in the plural all play a primary part. The rod is obviously a phallic emblem and has always been associated with divine wisdom whether it is presented in the Tibetan pantheon as a Dorji or thunderbolt scepter or as the classical Mercury's winged rod, the Caduceus. All the legendary wizards from Biblical times on have carried rods wherein their powers were often vested. Jannes and Jambres of the Egyptians, Moses, Aaron and Elijah, Merlin, Virgilius, Roger Bacon: the list is extensive. Apart from its phallic connotations, the wand is also a pointer, or indicator, a flying arrow in the case of the Greek Abaris, again connected with occult methods of "finding things out."

Witches employ two different types of wands in their rituals: the riding staff—in the past often disguised as the legendary broomstick—used in fertility rites and the smaller Goetic rod, sometimes referred to as the *verendum* or *buculum,* which is used in the questioning of intelligences during divination. Often the riding staff will be carved with a phallic tip to it. The *baculum* usually is of a more Cabalistic composition, often engraved with Hebraic divine names.

However, as often as not, the two rods are combined as one by many witches, and the burning need to disguise the phallic tip as a besom has surely well passed now. The rod of divination can range from one to anything up to six feet in length; from the elbow to the tip of the longest finger of the hand is often considered the ideal length. It should be made from ebony or a fruitwood of some sort, preferably hazel or almond, straight and of one year's growth if possible, but this latter requirement is not absolutely necessary. If you cut the branch yourself, try to do it on a Wednesday when the moon is waxing, at or around midnight, sunrise, midday, or sunset, for these are the times when the occult tides are at their most powerful. Use your Athamé to sever the branch, mentally *affirming* your intention as you do so, that is, "to compose a wand of divination." If you are unable to sever the wood yourself but have to purchase it, never mind; the real value is imparted with the consecration which follows. This has to be performed on a Wednesday, again when the moon is waxing, at one of the four quarters of the day—midnight, sunrise, noon, or sunset.

First you must cast and purify your circle, kindling a suitable Mercurial incense in your thurible; perform the square of Mercury rite as an introduction. Then trim the wood of all twigs and excrescences with your Athamé and peel the bark off, keeping your intention firmly in mind, repeating a jingle to concentrate your attention on the task in hand, such as, "Bless'd be thou rod of power, rod of wisdom," and keeping in mind the Mercurial images of speed and air and flight as you did in your square of Mercury.

When you have made the wand as smooth as you can, you may shape the end in a phallic manner (which is traditional), or leave it plain and unadorned, with the sexual symbolism implicit rather than explicit; the choice is yours.

Then, with the point of your Athamé, engrave the following runes upon the wand, working from right to left, and continuing to repeat your charm with each figure. When you have finished, ink or paint in the etched figures with your materials of art, always repeating the jingle either audibly or mentally. Should you wish to mix in any dried and powdered Mercurial herbs with the ink or paint before applying, this can be a very effective way of reinforcing the potency of the rod. Finally, fumigate the wand again in the incense smoke (do *not* asperge it; this would only demagnetize it and nullify all your previous effort!) and seal it with the triple cross and the injunction "So mote it be," as in the square of Mercury consecration. Either keep your completed wand in a new box of its own or wrap it in linen or silk. In all the following rituals of intelligence you will have cause to use it, whether they be those of seeing stone or mirror, necromancy, or triangle of manifestation. (See page 52 for the Wand Runes.)

The Magical Lamps

At this point, it would be a good time to mention some important artifacts, which you will need, often improvised at the last minute, but in actuality as needful of proper preparation and consecration as your Athamé or wand. These are the candlesticks or lamps of art. Quite apart from the magical significance of light itself in your witchcraft, there is the very practical necessity of being able to read your workbook of art within the circle, should you need to use long, unlearnable conjurations riddled with complicated words of power. The candlesticks are simply made. If you aren't handy with woodcarving or don't have access to a potter's wheel, buy without bargaining (most important, this) as many candlesticks as you feel you may need in your rituals. Some witches like to place one at each cardinal point of the circle and one on the table of practice in the center, making five in all. Or if the ritual be one involving a seeing stone or speculum, you will need two or three lights on the table, which in addition to the four cardinal points will make seven or eight in all. Usually, however, the cardinal point lights are used only at full ceremonial coven rituals and are generally common property of the group.

For the individual witch, two candlesticks are quite sufficient. Should you wish to make the candlesticks, as opposed to buying them, you must first exorcise your raw materials whether they be clay, wood, or metal by fire and water in a properly cast circle. As this work pertains to the nature of illumination and the operations of light, it is best performed on a Sunday, the day of the sun, preferably around noon. Having cast your circle at the requisite time and lit a solary incense, purify your materials or newly purchased candlesticks (which may be made of any material you choose). Then formulate in your imagination the brilliant, burning light of the noonday sun, and repeating a blessing with each rune such as "Blesséd be thou, creature of light," paint the following characters with your materials of art, right to left as usual. When finished, seal them with the triple cross and "So mote it be," and store in your safe place till you need them.

Always use exorcised white candles in them during your rituals, unless otherwise directed. (See page 52 for Candlestick Runes.)

The Show Stone and the Magic Mirror

Consecrated globes of crystal or glass, otherwise known as scrying, seeing, or show stones, have been used from time immemorial by witches in the development of clear seeing and the questioning of spirit entities. In the past they were made of quartz or beryl, but with the development of high-quality optical glass, natural crystal has passed out of use as being too expensive for the average witch. Or, if a show stone, be it glass or crystal, was too difficult or expensive to obtain, a witch would resort to a magical mirror, or *speculum,* which is economical to make and every bit as effective as the former.

Whether you, as a beginner witch, choose to use one or another of these items, what you will need is a black cloth or board to cover your table of practice, with a triangle of manifestation either painted on in white or stitched on in white tape. The triangle's sides should each measure about twelve inches. The triangle is a very old witch symbol, and represents the crystallization of form out of chaos. You will find it employed throughout witchcraft whenever some type of physical or magnetic manifestation is required.

Some Cabalistically inclined witches surround the triangle with a double circle, and between the two circles they inscribe the names and seals of the seven planetary angels and the demon kings of the four quarters of the earth, while others seek to enhance the potency of the figure by fortifying the sides of the triangle with the Hebraic divine names—Primeumaton, Anaphaxeton, Tetragrammaton—and placing the name of Michael, leader of the heavenly host, within; but none of these things is strictly necessary.

All you basically need is the triangle prepared with intention, which is accomplished, as with your other magical tools, by exorcising and consecrating your materials with fire and water (using a Mercurial incense) in a properly cast circle on a Wednesday. Then, go to work using a charm to state your intention such as "Blesséd be thou, focus of power," again, as with all your other artifacts. Finally, cense and seal with the triple cross.

At the same time that you make the triangle, you can also manufacture the pedestal for the show stone. This you may make simply from a square slab of exorcised wood, say six inches by one inch, depending on the size of your crystal. Make a slight rounded hollow in the center to contain the show stone and prevent it from rolling off. It should be stained or painted black with an exorcised paint in which finely powdered wormwood herb is mixed. All the time you work on it, you should continue the use of the mantram that you evolved for the triangle. Many witches surround this pedestal with the names of the four Cabalistic archangels: Michael, Gabriel, Raphael, Uriel, or their symbolic representatives, the zodiacal signs of Leo, Scorpio, Aquarius, and Taurus. Again, however, this is not strictly necessary, merely a matter of personal preference.

Finally, wash the show stone itself in an infusion of wormwood, place it on its stand when dry, and cense and seal them both.

Should you, however, wish to make a *speculum*, or mirror, instead of buying a crystal, obtain a concave clock glass or chemical watch glass. Using the same formula that you composed your triangle by, exorcise and consecrate the clock glass. Then paint the *convex* side with two good coats of black enamel and wormwood. Hollow out a piece of wood in the manner suggested for a show-stone pedestal, stain or paint it black with wormwood paint, and glue in the black mirror, curved side inwards. Cense and seal.

This is your *speculum*, which may be used in exactly the same way as the crystal. Both the mirror and the show stone should be kept wrapped in a black cloth, preferably silk, when not in use.

The Pentacle of Protection

Now you have all the instruments except one that you will need for the greater forms of divination. That last implement is the pentacle, which it is advisable to wear during *any ritual involving conjuration*, bar none, whether it be a sending or a divination. Should the power raised by the formulae "short" and rebound upon you as the operator, or in any way go awry, the pentacle of protection will be your only means of "earthing" the force if it is one which has been raised via the deep mind of the operator himself and, as such, is not subject to the restricting power of the boundary circle, which limits the activities of any alien or invading entities. Cautious practitioners don the pentacle for all magical operations, even rudimentary ones of casting the runes or a simple love spell. For instructions regarding the making of your pentacle, see Chapter 5 which deals with the important matter of countermagic and protection.

The Conjuration of Vassago

Having now assembled the primary instruments of the greater divinations, you are ready to perform one such operation yourself. There are basically two varieties of these, one being the conjuration and communication with nonhuman entities, and the other dealing with the spirits or shades of the dead, necromancy so-called, or sometimes sciomancy. You will occasionally find that some witches tend to make the distinction between the two terms in that sciomancy, they claim, involving some relic of the defunct person summoned, an object link of some type, be it a lock of hair, bloodspot, or some personal belonging, attempts the evocation of the shade or ghost of the dead person, which is confined to visible appearance.

Necromancy, on the other hand, they argue, implies the reanimation of a recently defunct corpse, as in the legendary operation performed by Thessalian Erichtho at the request of Sextus, son of Pompey. This distinction, however, is merely scholarly, and the majority of witches use the term "necromancy" to refer to the operation which the pedants label sciomancy, namely, the evocation of the shades, such as was attempted by Eliphas Lévi in the nineteenth century. The corpse-reanimation method is very rarely, if ever, attempted these days, for obvious reasons.

Necromancy does not call for the use of your show stone, but rather a triangle of manifestation, so I shall leave that process

1. The wand
2. Seeing stone within the triangle
3. and 4. Lamps of art

till last, and deal with the conjuration of nonhuman entities first. The entity summoned for questioning *par excellence* is one that has been a favorite among witches from time immemorial, and is known by the name "Vassago." He is numbered among the seventy-two demonic intelligences in that medieval grimoire, the *Lemegeton,* or *Lesser Key of Solomon*; and Wierus, Cornelius Agrippa's pupil, also mentions him in his *Pseudomonarchia Demonorum.*

> . . . Vassago, a mighty prince, of the nature of Agares, who declareth things past, present and to come and discovereth that which hath been lost or hidden. He is good by nature, and governeth twenty-six legions of Spirits. . . .

But knowledge of his existence dates back long before this, even to before earliest Babylonian times. He was one of the Nephelim, and in Eastern fable, he is accounted one of the seventy-two Lords of the Djinn.

Your experiment should be performed during clear weather, when the moon is two, four, six, eight, ten, twelve, or fourteen days old, and thereby, of course, always on the increase. So great is the power of Vassago, however (he is a "prince" in the hierarchy), that he is not bound by any sidereal or solar rules of time, and therefore may be summoned at any hour of the day or night. He is to be called only in matters of extreme perplexity, when all lesser methods of divination have availed you naught. Although he is "good by nature," it is extremely important to remember that he is one of the seventy-two from of old, a being formed out of primordial fire eons before man evolved into his present shape, of an intelligence at this present time far superior to that of most men alive, and in the humiliating position of being susceptible to conjuration by apelike clay-formed *Homo sapiens,* by means of a faculty as yet mostly underdeveloped within said simian creatures. So approach his conjuration with *extreme* respect at all times; it is no idle operation.

Having selected your day of operation, you must choose a companion to act as a scribe or recorder of the visions. Lock yourselves in your secluded place of working, having gathered together your paraphernalia and such other close companions as are immediately concerned with the divination.

Your paraphernalia should consist of:

Your altar table with its triangle sign covering, pointing east;

Chairs in the west, facing east across the table, should you wish to remain seated during the scrying;

Your Athamé, cord, thurible, cup, workbook, square of Mer-

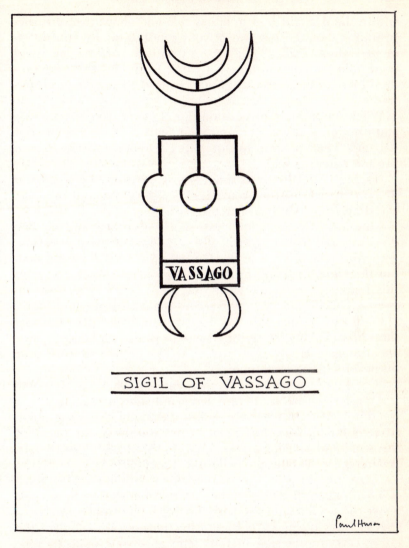

SIGIL OF VASSAGO

cury, and pen and ink of art, a supply of Mercurial incense, and a box of incense consonant with Vassago's nature (see end of this chapter, "Herbs and Incenses").

All or any of these things may be held by your assistants throughout the operation.

On the table itself should stand your show stone, or *speculum*, within the triangle, and to either side and about twelve inches behind it should stand two of your candlesticks containing exorcised white candles. The person who is to perform the ritual must hold the wand in his right hand; upon his breast (and indeed those of his assistants) should hang the pentacle of protection.

When all is safely in position, kindle your Mercury incense and candles, and trace around your floor a triangle with your Athamé. Then proceed to cast your circle and exorcise it with fire and water as usual.

Having done this, you should next perform the square of Mercury ritual to attune yourself. Then replenish your thurible, this time using "Vassago" incense.

Now, take two of your clean sheets of paper, and on one draw the sigil of Vassago full size, as shown in the illustration, with your pen and ink of art. On the other also draw the sigil, but this time small and in the top, right-hand corner. Next, on this last sheet, carefully write out the question you wish answered. On this piece you will record the nature of your visions.

Place this on one side for use later, and return to the first sheet now. Taking the full-sized sigil in your right hand, asperge and fumigate three times with Vassago incense, stating your magical intention each time:

"Creature of paper, I name thee Vassago. Thou art Vassago."

Transfer the paper to your left hand now, and taking your wand in your right, trace the sigil in the air above it three times, strongly visualizing a line of blue fire streaming from the tip of the wand and forming a great glowing sigil hanging in the air. Again repeat the binding spell three times:

"Creature of paper, I name thee Vassago. Thou art Vassago."

Then, again with the wand, draw three crosses in the air above the symbol, and seal with the words "So mote it be."

Now, moving in a *clockwise* direction, circumambulate the circle, carrying the sigil in your left hand, your wand in your right. Finish at the east of the circle, facing east. Hold the wand upright over the sigil and invoke Vassago with these words:

> By Satandar and Asentacer
> I conjure thee
> O thou great and holy

> Vassago! Vassago! Vassago!
>
> Vouchsafe to descend from thy abode,
> bringing thy influence and presence into this glass,
> that we may behold thy glory and enjoy
> thy society and aid!

Again circumambulate the circle clockwise at this point, returning to the east as before to continue:

> By Satandar and Asentacer
> I conjure thee
> O thou great and holy
>
> Vassago! Vassago! Vassago!
>
> who knowest the secrets of Elanel
> who ridest on the wings of the wind,
> and art endowed with superlunary motion,
> do thou descend and be present I pray thee. . . .

Circumambulate yet once more and finish the invocation:

> By Satandar and Asentacer
> I conjure thee thrice three times,
>
> Vassago! Vassago! Vassago!
>
> to descend and appear to us within this glass
> speaking secrets of truth and understanding.

Then return to the west of your altar table, facing east, and place the sigil in the triangle under the *speculum* or show stone on its stand.

At this point you must seat yourself comfortably in front of the table, and holding your wand with both hands, gently and without strain fix your gaze on the surface of your *speculum*. At the same time with all the force of your imagination, visualize the same blue radiance playing around the *speculum*, and audibly repeat the question or nature of the divination addressed to Vassago, as previously set down on your paper. As you continue to gaze at the *speculum*, the surface will appear to fade away; in fact, your gaze will shift out of focus, and then spring back sharply in again.

This effect will continue for a while due to your eye being foxed by the shifting perspectives in the glass. You may also find you are experiencing a curious constrictive feeling around your forehead and between your eyes. At this point, should you have performed the divination aright, you will then begin to notice that the *speculum* surface has begun to haze over with a blue-gray mist. This is the sign that the vision is opening, and it is at this stage that Vassago will begin to take over and show certain things to you.

He may initiate the vision by revealing himself to you in human or therioform guise, or he may simply begin to show you the answer to your queries in uncomplicated symbolistic tableaux, rather like the diminutive images seen through the wrong end of a telescope or pair of binoculars. But one thing here is of paramount importance to beginner witches. Do *not* shift your attention from the *speculum;* try not to let your excitement at what is happening disrupt the delicate link between your everyday consciousness and deep mind. This is a very difficult instruction for the beginner, but it can effectively ruin the divination if not complied with.

Sometimes you will find that pictures are building up *at the side* of your immediate gaze. Here you must resist the temptation to move your line of vision to catch a glimpse of them, but rather allow them to build and unfold themselves before you. Sometimes the visions may seem to make no sense to you at the time. Be that as it may, you must describe them out loud, and have the companion who is active as your scribe note them down with the pen of art on the paper on which the question is written. The visions are very fleeting and will vanish like dreams from your remembrance should you not take care to record them at once.

When the stream of images seems to have finished, the glass will haze over for a last time and then return to its normal state. At that point, you must place more Vassago incense in the thurible and repeat the so-called license to depart to Vassago, which breaks the spell and terminates the operation. This license must *never* under any circumstances be omitted; to do so is to court magical disaster of the worst possible type, maybe even of the nature of that which befell the legendary Egyptian diviner Chiancungi in seventeenth-century England.

He and his sister Napula had, as the result of a bet, endeavored to conjure the spirit Bokim to visible appearance, unsuccessfully it seems, for no manifestations were forthcoming. After frequently repeating the formulae, Chiancungi and his sister grew impatient and, omitting the license to depart, quit the circle without more ado. At which point, according to witnesses, they were "instantly seized and crushed to death by that infernal spirit, who happened not to be sufficiently constrained till that moment, to manifest himself to human eyes."

Because there may be no *visible* manifestation of demonic activity does not mean necessarily that your spell has not worked. And even though Vassago be "good by nature," it pays not to take short cuts. To reiterate, in the summoning of intelligences, particularly those seventy-two formed of the primordial fire, maintain the strictest adherence to the principles of safe witchcraft.

The License to Depart

> O great and holy Vassago,
> we license thee depart into thy proper place
> and be there peace between us evermore
> by Satandar and Asentacer!
> So mote it be!

Keep a careful record of the visions obtained in this manner. Often the less obvious ones will either reveal much, hitherto unsuspected, when used as a basis for meditation, or as is sometimes the case, assume a new relevance with the advent of new information, previously unknown, on the subject inquired about.

On the other hand, do not despair if the operation is not an immediate apparent success. The door of vision is one which opens slowly but yields to persistence. Remember the advice of the Chaldean oracles: "Invoke often!" As long as the intent is a serious one, the ritual of Vassago is no exception to this rule.

When you have completed the license to depart, broken the circle, and completed your vision record, you must burn the sigil of Vassago to ashes. In contrast to your square of Mercury, the sigil of Vassago may not be used again. To repeat the operation, you will have to employ a fresh sigil every time.

Dreaming True

The subject of acquiring prophetic dreams, generally speaking, comes under this Mercurial heading. Processes concerned with acquisition of dreams concerning lovers, present or future, will, however, be kept for Chapter 4, Part 1, "The Loving Cup." But should you or a friend wish to acquire knowledge about a certain matter, and not wish to resort to the rune sticks or any form of conjuration ceremony, a very simple, and sometimes quite effective method of securing said information is by inducing a prophetic dream. Wait until the moon is waxing, approaching full. Then, prior to going to bed, take a warm bath in which has been mixed a few drops of the following mixture:

 Oil of lavender
 Oil of rosemary
 Oil of peppermint
 Oil of thyme
 Powdered poppy seed

While you are taking the bath, fumigate your bedroom with an incense composed of:

 Camphor
 Powdered aloeswood
 Jasmine
 Pulverized cucumber seeds
 Powdered white sandalwood

All of these are to be used in equal parts. This is a Lunar Incense, the moon being the ruler of sleep and dreams.

Before you lie down to sleep, write your question on a piece of plain white paper with your pen and ink of art, and place the paper and a small sachet of wormwood herb (Artemesia) under your pillow. If the spell works, you should have your answer to the question in the morning.

Necromancy

The summoning of the dead has always been considered by witches as among some of the most dangerous operations in the book, strangely enough, sometimes even more so than the summoning of demons. The truth of the matter is that it can be an extremely taxing operation to perform if the motivation is anything other than love, and if a physical manifestation is required, as is always the case when the shade is conjured to visible appearance.

Unless one who is suited to such energy transfers is present, that is, a materializing medium, the nervous and physical depletion visited upon the participants can prove truly onerous, and in some extremely rare cases, fatal. For this reason the ritual is often reserved for full-coven performance at Sabbat on those occasions when it is employed, in this way providing a good complement of participants to act as energy donors.

The best time for practicing necromancy, however, is when the solar power is waning to its lowest ebb between the autumnal equinox and the winter solstice; this fact is made use of in the traditional witch festival, Halloween, wherein necromancy is employed. This is, of course, the Feast of the Dead, one of the four great Sabbats. (See Chapter 7, "The Coven and How to Form One," for more on this.)

However, complications aside, necromancy is one of the more spectacular of magical operations when successful, and if a legitimate motivation impels a witch to have recourse to it, and she maintains a serious, respectful, and considered attitude toward the operation, then chances of success are high.

There are two types of motive which make the operation of necromancy feasible and indeed permissible: intelligence and love. The first, that of intelligence, is resorted to when all else fails, when tea leaves or Tarot cards give unintelligible answers, when the rune sticks talk in riddles, when even Vassago falls silent, and when the one person who can give you the answer to your question is dead. This is the more complicated operation to perform. The second permissible motivation, that of desiring to meet a loved one again, gives recourse to an operation which is easier than the first mentioned and is of the type which is often incorporated into the grand Sabbat of Halloween, although, strictly speaking, most Sabbat rituals do employ some elements of the first variety.

Halloween, or the Feast of the Dead, is the time when the illustrious magical dead are drawn back into the company of the living by the ties of love and magic, to share in the joy of the Sabbat and bestow their blessing on the Witches' New Year, which begins November 1.

Most witches refer to the necromantic operation of love (as opposed to that of intelligence) by its traditional name, "The Dumb Supper"; it can be used to evoke the shade of one's *future* spouse as well as that of a deceased loved one. I shall reserve instructions for its performance for Chapter 4, which deals solely with amatory matters, and return to that operation concerned with "finding things out." Therefore, to conclude this chapter, here are the details for the performance of:

Necromancy of Intelligence

This is, strictly speaking, a work of darkness, albeit intelligence, and as such should be timed to fall upon a night of the new moon or very shortly after. It requires thirteen days' preparation, however (which characteristic it shares with the necromancy of love), that preparation being a short nightly meditation around midnight on a photograph or portrait of the deceased whose shade you hope to summon. On the night of the fourteenth day, the new moon, cast and purify your circle just before midnight with a Mercurial incense, after making sure the room is secure from any intrusion. The paraphernalia you will need for the operation include: your Athamé, cord, cup, and thurible, naturally, for erecting the circle; your wand, altar table with triangle cloth, lamps, and an equilateral triangle of white tape (large enough to stand in) on the floor outside the circle to the west. In this is placed a skull. Now this may be an actual skull if you have recourse to one, a replica of one made by you, or a drawing of one, never mind how crude, also composed by you.

In the small triangle on the altar should be placed a photo-

Divination

graph of the deceased flanked by the lamps of art and an hour-glass (an egg timer will do for this). You should have on hand a generous supply of Necromancy Incense (see end of this chapter under "Herbs and Incenses"), and also writing materials to record the shade's answers.

Finally, on your breast must hang the important pentacle of protection (this applies to any companions as well).

At the first stroke of midnight, approach the west side of the altar table, facing east, and consecrate the photograph in the altar triangle with salt water and incense. With the wand you must then trace an equal-armed cross surrounded by a circle in the air above the photograph, visualizing the symbol burning with a blue radiance as you did in the Vassago ritual. As you perform each of the consecrations, say these words:

> Colpriziana Offina Alta Nestera Fuaro Menut
> I name the [name of deceased]
> Thou art [name of deceased].

The circle cross you trace over the photograph is, like the triangle and pentacle, a witch symbol of great antiquity. Some witches, who are hermetically inclined, say that it is an abbreviated version of the alchemical rose cross, whereas others see it as being a type of the *crux ansata,* or Egyptian ankh, symbolizing divine life. In this particular instance, however, the symbol connotes a different history altogether, being derived from the same source as that old pirate device familiar to all readers of *Treasure Island,* the skull and crossbones. This emblem makes its appearance in more serious context in both Templar and Masonic symbolism, alongside that of the witch tradition. It is the sign of Osiris. Its proper import is that of death (sometimes accompanied by resurrection), and most necromantic processes make use of it. It is also used in laying curses on people, as you will find out in Chapter 6, which deals with magical warfare and such matters.

Having traced the symbol above the photograph, carrying the wand in your *right* hand, the photograph in your *left,* proceed clockwise, walking *backwards,* to the rim of the circle in the eastern quarter and, holding the wand upright over the photograph, pronounce the following conjuration to the east:

> Spirit of [name] deceased,
> thou mayest now approach the gates of the east
> to answer truly my liege demands.
> Berald, Beroald, Balbin!
> Gab, Gabor, Agaba!
> Arise, arise I charge and command thee.

Repeat these words again to the south, then the west, and finally the north again, walking *backwards* around the inner perimeter of the circle, and changing each time the name of the gate corresponding to the quarter. Should you have any companions for this ritual, they too should accompany you around the circle to the four quarters, also walking backwards. Then, still proceeding backwards, you must return to the east of the altar table by yourself and, facing west across it, replace the photograph in the altar triangle. Pause for a minute or two at this point; all present should maintain a strict silence.

Then carefully place your necromantic incense within your thurible, and when it is fuming well, repeat the words of the grand citation, striking the photograph gently with the end of your wand at the completion of each line as you do so.

> By the Mysteries of the deep [strike],
> by the flames of Banal [strike],
> by the power of the east [strike],
> and by the silence of the night [strike],
> by the holy rites of Hecate [strike],
> I conjure and exorcise thee, spirit [name] [strike],
> to present thyself here [strike]
> and answer truly our demands [strike].
> So mote it be! [strike].

(The "Hecate" invoked here is the classical Greek goddess of witchcraft. She is three-formed, having Persephone and Selene, goddesses of the dead and the moon respectively, as her other aspects.)

At this point replenish the thurible with more necromantic incense, extinguish all lights upon the altar table so that the room is plunged into darkness, and again moving backwards, carefully pass to the west rim of the circle, to kneel down, facing the triangle of manifestation upon the floor. Cross your arms slowly upon your breast—this is the witch gesture signifying the skull and crossbones symbol—and repeat the words of the charge *inwardly* as you do so: "Allay Fortission, Fortissio, Allynsen Roa!"

At this point close your eyes and again remain silent for a few minutes. Then, still with your eyes shut, greet the spirit quietly as though he were present before you. Here you may experience that most unpleasant crawling sensation, fear, but you must avoid panicking at all costs, keeping in mind that your questioning is legitimate and just. In fact, it is with this point of the ritual in mind that the whole issue of justification of the operation before the outset is concerned. You must be certain within your own mind that the operation is being conducted for legitimate purposes, all else having failed, in order to face this final moment of fear with equanimity.

Now, summoning all your courage, pronounce the deceased person's full names clearly and loudly three times, slowly extending your arms on either side of you in the form of a cross, and opening your eyes. If the operation has been successful, you will gradually perceive a dim form in the triangle before you, seemingly composed of the substance of incense smoke, sometimes illuminated from within by a very faint bluish phosphorescence. Whether the apparition is built up on a magnetic and physical or purely psychic basis or a mixture of both depends solely on whether you as a witch function best as a seer or a materializing medium, which are the two ends of the magical spectrum whereon witches function. Depending on your various constitutions and the degree of your magical development, you and your companions may differ in what you see before you in the triangle. One may see a dim form, while another may see a clearly defined figure, and yet another see nothing at all but merely feel the presence of someone who wasn't there before. But whatever you do or do not see, you must present your question at this point, with the knowledge that if the information is not immediately forthcoming, it will be revealed later, usually by way of a chain of curious and inexplicable coincidences.

When the form fades, it will mean the power raised by the ritual has ebbed away, and the time will be at hand to conclude the operation. Return to the east facing west across the altar again, again walking backwards. Rekindle the lamps (and the thurible if necessary), place a final offering of necromantic incense upon the coals, and repeat the license to depart, which runs thus:

> Go, go, departed shade [name]
> by Omgroma Epin Sayoc
> Satony, Degony, Eparigon
> Galiganon, Zogogen, Ferstigon.
> We license thee depart into thy proper place
> and be there peace between us evermore.
> So mote it be!

Then, finally, as with all your other Mercurial experiments, note down the results. In the final analysis, the best way to gain results is by a careful trial and error method, and this always depends on an accurate record being made. The results of your various researches should form a valuable part of your magical workbook.

Herbs and Incenses

For all divinations, great or small, whether the operation be one of mere sortilege such as casting the runes or a grand operation of necromancy, two easily accessible Mercurial divination incense ingredients are extremely useful to have on hand at all times: namely, gum mastic and cinnamon (the latter preferably in oil or essence form).

The first may be obtained at any good art materials suppliers as it is used in picture varnish, while the second can be obtained easily enough from any pharmacy. These two ingredients may be fumed on top of charcoal by themselves as divination incense or mixed with the following traditional recipes to form a more powerful blend.

1. Wormwood (Artemesia)
   Flax
   Cardamons
   Anise
   Camphor
   Chicory

2. Orris root
   Fennel
   Pomegranate skin
   Red sandalwood
   Poppy seed

3. Valerian root
   Saffron
   Wormwood
   St.-John's-wort
     (Hypericum)

4. Linseed
   Psellium

5. Violet roots
   Parsley

6. Anise
   Poppy seeds
   Camphor

7. Cloves (powdered)
   Frankincense
   Mastic
   Cinquefoil

Any or all of these may be mixed to advantage with Solomon's-seal and/or holy thistle herb to enhance the effect. Experiment to see which type suits you best.

Dittany of Crete is mixed with any incense where a materialization is required in the operation. Most if not all of the herbs aforementioned may be obtained from any shop which handles the sale of botanicals. Substances like the gums and essences, such as camphor and cinnamon, can be obtained at the pharmacy.

Vassago Conjuration Incense

This is a Jupiter-type incense, for though he is Mercurial in function, Vassago is primarily Jupiter-oriented in nature. His incense should be composed of:

   6 parts frankincense
   6 parts balm of Gilead
   6 parts grain of Paradise
   $\frac{1}{2}$ part saffron
   Touch of ambergris (an artificial tincture is quite sufficient)

If you cannot obtain these ingredients, a good substitute can be compounded of frankincense, saffron, and cedarwood oil.

Necromancy Incense

3 parts wormwood herb (finely reduced)
2 parts good-quality, resinous church incense
2 parts gum mastic
3 parts dittany of Crete (finely reduced)
½ part pure olive oil
½ part wine
½ part honey
A few drops of the operator's blood

Blend the ingredients together and let stand overnight. The resultant incense should be of a fairly solid, crumbly consistency, but if it turns out too liquid, add extra dittany and wormwood until the right, dryish texture is reached.

CHAPTER 4

Spells for Lovers

This chapter I have divided into two sections, the first to satisfy the traditional witch who has yearnings toward romantic love and would practice solely on that level; the second half I have entitled simply "Sex Magic," which should speak for itself and is aimed at the more modern-minded witch.

Part I. The Loving Cup

As the title of this section indicates, one of the main witch implements you will be employing in the traditional, romantic approach will be the chalice, so far only used in consecrations. The Athamé is never used in this branch of witchcraft, being an instrument of defense or aggression. Many of the lesser love spells make use of philters and potions for the raising and transmission of magical power; it is the chalice that contains them at their compounding which provides the focus for the invoked force.

Should you or a friend wish to cast a love spell to gain the attentions of another person, it will be well to remember the general witch principle of the transmission of power, which brings me to another big rule of practical witchcraft. A magical operation will always enjoy a greater chance of success if you "complete the circuit." Extremely powerful witches can indeed work without the aid of object links or power objects with the person or entity they are attempting to influence; they simply locate him or her with their fully activated deep minds and

The loving cup

work their will directly. Those of lesser ability, and that of course includes all beginners, must make use of an object link so-called, such as was employed in the ritual of necromancy in the form of a photograph. That is, an object intimately linked, or belonging to, the person on whom the effect is being worked.

The alternative to this is the employment of what is often referred to as a power object, that is, some object manufactured by the witch as charged with her own will and magnetism, which is physically conveyed into the presence of the designated victim; in fact a form of talisman, whether for good or ill as the case may be, which acts as a kind of battery or condenser of magical power. Most philters partake of this second definition.

The Puppet Spell given later in the chapter provides an excellent example of total completion of the circuit, using both object link and power object.

The chalice is dedicated to certain of the subtler powers of the unseen, which are considered feminine in relation to the more violent nature of those invoked in works of, say, wrath and chastisement; the chalice powers are invoked by means of a symbolism somewhat similar to that of the classical divinities of love, such as Venus and Amor. Indeed the chalice is obviously sexual in its implication of receptive passivity, as opposed to the more thrusting aggressiveness of the wand and the Athamé.

It would be truer to say that the witch symbolism of the chalice was rather more akin to that surrounding the elvenfolk, the fays, and enchantresses of medieval legend, Vivian, Brisen, Nimue, Lady of the Lake, Morgan le Fay, and of course Melusine. The May queens and corn maidens of European folklore are all partakers of the same symbolism along with Greek Persephone and Euridice, retracing their steps to the underworld during the cold winter months when the sun has grown dark and the days short; the Lord of the Dead holds rule over the land for the first three months of the witches' year beginning on the first day of November, the Feast of All Hallows.

The Lady of Delight is known by many names among witches, some of them classical in inspiration like Diana or Hecate, or Celtic like Rhiannon; she is also known as Habondia, Hulda, and Herodias, and sometimes by other versions of the last name, Aradia, Ariadne, or Arianne. She is Mistress of the Moon as well as the realm of Venus.

In all your operations of romantic love it is her presence you must invoke, by any of the aforesaid names you may find significant—again a little mythological research will help you here. You should strive to contact the goddess before your spells of romantic love, by visualizing her clad in silvery garments, mantled in darkness wherein the stars dimly gleam, and with long streaming hair. She is crowned with a wreath of flowers and corn, while above her brow shines the lunar disk on either side of which rise two rearing serpents. On her right hand perches her symbolic bird, the white dove.

All flowers and blossoms, particularly those with a perfume, are sacred to the Lady, and before beginning the more complex operations of love, it is as well to strew your altar with them. Apart from the associative symbolism of flowers, they also give off a subtle magnetism which is peculiarly in accord with works of this nature. No magical circle is necessary for these operations either, for the force invoked is a benevolent rather than a hostile one, and as such needs neither the sharp magical focusing nor the quality of incisive delineation provided by the Athamé's traced boundary line. No demonic entities or unfriendly departed shades are summoned in this type of witchcraft. All that is required is the purification of the place of working, and the spell itself.

Now all of these processes in this chapter are best performed on a Friday around eight in the morning, three in the afternoon or ten at night, when the moon is waxing. Some truly astrologically minded witches claim that the moon should be passing through the first ten degrees of Taurus or Virgo and well aspected to Venus and Saturn as well. This, however, is not strictly necessary, although fully in accord with principles of medieval witchcraft. The observance of the correct moon's phase, suitable day of the week, and time of day, along with a firmly resolved intention, is all that is really necessary.

Among the first love spells you should acquaint yourself with as a beginner should be those classed under the heading "Philters."

This is the way they should be compounded:

Having observed the correct time of day, as indicated above, you must seal your place of working from all intrusion. In its usual, central position should stand your altar table, topped with its triangle cover; one angle pointing east, as always. In the center of the triangle should stand your cup, flanked with your lamps. The thurible should also be present on the altar, together with a box of suitable incense (the composition of which will be given at the end of this chapter). Finally the materials for your philter, a pestle and mortar such as is sold by any good kitchenware shop, and, of course, your workbook in which the spell has been previously written out.

Finally, surround the altar triangle with a circle of fresh flowers, preferably sweet smelling. These may be any that please you; freesias, narcissus or lilac, jasmine or carnations, anything you like, depending on your location and the time of year. The choice is yours. To a lot of witches, the rose seems a very good choice, as this blossom has always been considered most germane to matters of love, and a symbolic attribute of the Lady. Cabalistic legend has it that Balkis, Queen of Sheba, was a witch, and that the wisdom she came to question Solomon, King of Israel, about was magical in content.

> ... I am the rose of Sharon, and the lily of the valleys,
> as the lily among thorns,
> so is my love among the daughters. ...

The rose has been preserved as the Lady's emblem in the annals of courtly love and among the symbols of alchemy. The lily, however, passed directly into Christian Catholicism and became an attribute of the Madonna, which is only right and proper, as the Virgin Mary is but a Christian echo of an aspect of the Lady herself. However, due to this association, it is more to be considered a symbol of cool chastity rather than love or passion.

Having seen to your initial preparations, illumine the lamps and kindle the appropriate incense, chanting as you do such words of consecration as:

"In thy name, Habondia, and that of thy Ministers of Love, do I proceed in this work of Love."

Summon up the Lady's image in your mind's eye, also recalling such memories of past love as will serve to "turn you on" to the right wave length. What sort of memories can do this must be left to the reader's own discretion. You know your own past best. Having thus dedicated your operation and brought your deep mind to attention, you may now proceed with the composition of the philter.

The first, and simplest, love charm you should learn is one used for centuries by witches,

The Coriander Spell

Pour a small quantity of pure distilled water into the chalice, and count seven coriander seeds into your mortar. Pound these well and strongly summoning an image in your mind's eye of the person or persons that the spell is designed to affect, call their names aloud three times, and chant these words,

> Warm seed, warm heart,
> let them never be apart.

Then cast the powder into the chalice, imagining as you do so the full force of your desire entering it also. See it as a flame descending on the surface of the liquid. Complete the spell with the words "So mote it be!" and draw the seal of the triple cross in the air above the cup with your right forefinger. Leave the herb to steep for about twelve hours; then strain the philter through fine muslin or cheesecloth and introduce it secretly into the food or drink of the person or persons the spell is desired to affect.

This spell is a good example of the use of a power object, as in fact are all the following philters. Now which of the philters will be most successful for you to use is going to be a matter that you should experiment with on your own account. Some witches swear by the Coriander Spell, others have more success with the following:

The Periwinkle Spell

Having observed the correct time of the month and day and prepared your place of working in exactly the same manner as for the preceding Coriander Spell, assembled your ingredients, kindled the thurible, and invoked Habondia:

Take dried leaves of periwinkle (*Vinca major* or *minor*), Mercury herb, cinquefoil, vervain, and rose petals, place them in your mortar and grind them to a fine powder. Repeat as you do so, over and over, a jingle to declare your intent such as, "By this act I draw [name] and [name] into a bond of love and desire." Then taking two very small pinches of the resultant powder, mix them with the water in the chalice, again charging it with the full force of your crystallized libido, and again sealing with the triple cross and the words "So mote it be." Leave the philter to steep for twelve hours, strain through fine muslin or cheesecloth, and introduce it secretly into the food or drink of those named in the charm.

Generally speaking, I think you may find this the more successful spell of the two, owing to the potency of the ingredients, which the coriander, although mildly effective by itself, cannot hope to compete with.

Finally, there is the True Love Philter. This has been with us a long, long time, and is no less effective than the former potion, when properly used, but is rather less employed owing to the scarcity of one of its ingredients, namely mistletoe berries, rare at most times save Christmas. You will generally find magical practitioners avidly buying up mistletoe when it appears in the shops around December, and not putting most of it to decorative uses, either.

The procedure adopted for composing this philter does not vary from that of the Periwinkle Spell, save in its ingredients, which are:

    Dried seeds or flowers of elecampane
    Dried vervain leaves
    Dried mistletoe berries

Pound and mix with the water in the chalice exactly the same way as you did in the Periwinkle Spell.

The process of actually introducing a few drops of the philter into the food or drink of your victims is an art in itself. If you are a witch given to cookery, the process can be made relatively simple. Should you be on sufficiently good terms with your intended victims, and of course a sufficiently well-accepted *cuisinière,* the gift of a few home-baked cookies or even a chocolate soufflé may not be considered unduly strange.

Of course, the ideal method of introduction is by simply dining or taking refreshment with your intended subjects, and dexterously laying your spell during the evening when you are not observed. Of course, you must be extremely circumspect about your actions lest you get known for this kind of activity; you may then begin to find you are mysteriously losing friends, despite the fact that they may be finding themselves beginning to take an equally mysterious delight in each other's company.

Should neither you nor the person who requests your services as a witch be a dab hand at cookery nor feel yourselves sufficiently nimble to sprinkle a few drops of your philter into your subject's food or drink, then never mind; there is another possible way of accomplishing your ends. Buy a pack of cigarettes of the brand you know your victim to smoke, and with a small eye-dropper, introduce a few drops of the philter onto the tobacco of each cigarette. All that remains is that you or an accomplice offer your victim a friendly cigarette: Your aim is thus very neatly accomplished.

There are any number of other ways of solving this simple problem, and I shall leave it to your resourcefulness and imagination to devise them for yourself.

Witches, of course, have been famous for supplying love potions and philters throughout the ages. Notable cases like La Voisin in Louis XIV's time spring to mind. A lot of them, including La Voisin, often employed revolting ingredients in their mixtures, like powdered toads or the desiccated dust of moles, usually whipped together with a good helping of some highly poisonous aphrodisiac like cantharides, the notorious Spanish fly. This was, and still is, a sure, telltale giveaway for the inefficient witch. The bludgeoning effect of drugs is the last resort of the ineffectual spellbinder. Witchcraft is effected by *magical* art, not *chemical* means. Always remember that in your workings.

Most of the simple though traditional love spells that clutter up the workbooks of older witches tend to be rural charms mostly unsuitable for the modern urban witch who lives in an apartment in New York City, or a semidetached in Croydon, England. Some of them, however, preserve the real flavor of old-time witchery, and as such deserve mention in passing.

One making use of the second law of direct transmission is the

Willow Tree Spell

On a Friday morn (8 A.M.) when the moon is waxing, dig the earth out of the footprint of the one you would have as a lover, and dig it into the soil surrounding the roots of a willow tree, chanting the following charm as you do:

> Many earths on Earth there be
> whom I love mine own shall be.
> Grow, grow willow tree
> sorrow none unto me.
> He the axe, I the helve,
> he the cock, I the hen:
> As my will, so mote it be!

Another charming one of similar ilk is

The Apple Spell

Apples being a fruit sacred to Habondia, it is entirely appropriate that they should figure as much in love magic as they do. Here is the original spell translated from the workbook of a German witch in rhyming couplets:

> On Friday early as may be,
> take the fairest apple from the tree,
> then in thy blood on paper white
> thine own name and true love's write.
> That apple thou shalt in two cut
> and for its cure that paper put,
> with two sharp pins of myrtle wood
> join the halves till it seem good.
> In the oven let it dry:
> And wrapped in leaves of myrtle lie,
> under the pillow of thy dear,
> yet let it be unknown to her.
> And if it a secret be
> she soon will show her love for thee.

Myrtle, like the apple, is also sacred to Habondia; also the spell is true to all the usual witch principles in its insistence on the fact that it must remain a secret, and the two apple halves with the paper sandwiched between remain undiscovered by the victim.

Another simple piece of old-time sorcery you might care to try is the

Tormentil Spell

This can be performed as it stands or with full ceremonial chalice preparation as used for your other philters, among which it may be grouped. I place it here rather than with the others on account of the rarity of the herb itself, which though once commonly stocked by herbalists for its astringent properties, is now something of a rarity and, as such, only deserves mention among our quainter reminders of bygone days.

Pound or grind to powder the root of *Potentilla tormentilla*, repeating the name of the person you desire over and over as you do.

Then take a pinch of the powder, and with it, either compose a philter in distilled water, or drop it into the person's food, uttering these words as you do.

> Tormentil, Tormentil,
> make [name] subject to my will.
> Be he bound or be he free,
> as my will, so mote it be!

Personally, I have never tried this spell, not ever having had the luck to obtain any tormentil. There may still be some around in out-of-the-way herbalists. If you ever get the chance, buy some and try it. It used to be a sorcery much attested to a century ago.

The Sator Spell

Here is an experiment of love which makes use of a simple written talisman to be carried by the person who wishes to be the object of desire. It is a spell which does not make use of the law of transmission, however, but rather acts as a "booster" on the deep mind of the supplicant.

For a change, this process borrows from Christian symbolism rather than the other way round. However, you do not have to be of Christian persuasion to make use of it. It has been in existence long enough—nineteen centuries in fact—to gather round it a potency as a love spell quite independent of its early ecclesiastical origin. The good use it has been put to down the years by practitioners of the craft is ample evidence of that.

Spells for Lovers

The name of this particular piece of Magic is the Sator Spell. The words of the charm itself probably derive from the words *Pater noster* and "*A.O.*," standing for Alpha and Omega, the first and last letters of the Greek alphabet. *Pater noster* is the Latin for "our Father," the first words of the so-called Lord's Prayer. "Alpha and Omega" is one of the many titles bestowed upon Jesus by the early Christians, meaning the "first and the last," a reference to his attributed divinity. These words were sometimes formed into an equal-armed cross, which symbol though pagan in origin, as has been already mentioned, became a suitable stock on which to graft the newly arrived cult symbol, the Latin or cross of crucifixion. This emblem was then used as a code sign among early converts.

```
                    P
                    A
         A          T          O
                    E
                    R
         P A T E R  N  O S T E R
                    O
                    S
         O          T          A
                    E
                    R
```

However, prior to the formation of the Holy Roman Empire, the early Christians *themselves* were subject to great persecution, and someone hit on an ingenious method of continuing the use of the *Pater noster* code sign and still utilizing all the letters comprising the cross, but cunningly forming them into an acrostic which was at the same time a palindrome. That is, a square of words which reads the same across as it does down, and also can be read backward to the same effect.

```
         S A T O R
         A R E P O
         T E N E T
         O P E R A
         R O T A S
```

So successful and satisfying was this formula, that it was joyfully seized upon by the practitioners of the Black Arts, and turned to excellent account, particularly as a love spell, which it is now generally known as and much renowned for.

The method used in preparing this spell is as follows.

Select a Friday with the moon waxing and choose your time, either 8 A.M., 3 P.M., or 10 P.M. Then, your altar dressed in the usual manner for amatory workings, purify the chamber with fire and water, with the regular Habondia invocation and attendant images. Then take a sheet of clean, white paper such as you used for your square of Mercury, and after exorcising it with water and fire, divide it up into twenty-five equal squares, five down and five across with your pen and ink of art. Then chanting a suitable jingle phrasing your intention with each letter that you inscribe, such as, "[name of person whom spell is cast for] greatly desired and strong in love!"

Write the letters of the acrostic into the square in the following order, beginning with number 1 and ending with 25, as usual injecting into it all the force of desire and yearning you can muster.

```
S A T O R      9   1    4   13  19
A R E P O      3  12   24   15  21
T E N E T     23  18  20/7   5  10
O P E R A      8   2   11   25  16
R O T A S      6  26   17   14  22
```

Begin at number 1, A, and end with number 26, O. The center square, N, should be written in seventh, and written *over* again twentieth. When you have finished, seal the charm with the triple cross and "So mote it be!"; wrap it in a piece of clean cloth or place it in a box, and bury it in the earth for a day and a night, if possible at a crossroads or a place where two paths meet. A crossroads or churchyard is the traditional place, but a flowerbed or ordinary patch of ground where two paths cross will do. When the twenty-four hours has elapsed, remove the talisman from the soil, and give it into the keeping of the person it is to benefit.

During the time they wish to receive its aid, they should

carry it on their person and sleep with it under their pillow. The spell will not last forever, though. It is only good for about twenty-eight days, and then a new talisman has to be constructed.

A very simple though sometimes extremely successful magic for the witch with a green thumb is

The Hyacinth Spell

Actually, this may be performed with any type of bulb from a tulip to an onion! Habondia being the patroness of all flowers, however, a sweet-smelling variety stands more chance of success, I always feel.

Plant the bulb in a new pot, naming it as your loved one as you do. Every morning and evening when you water it, chant these words intently over it.

> As this root grows
> and this blossom blows,
> may her heart be turned to me.
> As my will, so mote it be!

A Planetary Spell

Finally, in this section of romantic love, here is a traditional Cabalistic spell, which operates by invoking the aid of *Sariim*, princes or intelligences attributed to the heavenly bodies, in this case Mercury, the moon, and Earth itself who rule over and direct the demonic cohorts. The Cabalistic titles conferred upon these powers are, of course, a thin disguise for those original watchers, or witch-entities, with which you are beginning to become acquainted. Two of these you have already been introduced to, namely, Herne, the Wise One, and Habondia, the Lady of Delight, subject of the present chapter. The third you have yet to meet—the Earth Power, which we will deal with in the following chapter, which is devoted to the construction of the pentacle and mandragore, among other things, and deals with the problems of protection, counter-magic, and general well-being.

PLANETARY TALISMAN.

Because of the fact that this spell calls upon the powers of genuine witch entities, albeit under a Cabalistic guise, and contains some rather pleasing imagery, it is made use of frequently by poetically inclined witch novices. In my opinion it is somewhat verbose, as most Cabalistic workings tend to be, but here it is.

Spells for Lovers

You will need a clean sheet of talisman paper, your pen and ink of art, one of your lamps of art, your cup of water, salt and rosemary, and your thurible containing a suitable amatory incense.

Select a clear night when the moon is waxing and shining brightly in the sky. Having made sure you are alone or that your only other companions are witches like yourself, place the paper in your altar triangle, and draw the following diagram on the paper with your pen and ink of art. Pass it through water and fire, naming it with the name of the person you wish to influence. On the reverse side of the talisman, write "Melchidael Baresches."

Now if you have a garden or very secluded backyard, you can perform the whole ceremony out of doors. If not, perform the ritual up to the point indicated above indoors, and complete the following outside.

Search out the moon in the sky, and then observe which is the brightest star close to it. Having done this, place your parchment on the ground, bare earth or grass as opposed to concrete or asphalt, if possible. Then cover the parchment with your right foot and bend your left knee to the earth. Then take your workbook containing the spell in your left hand (it's better to learn it by heart if you can), your lighted lamp of art in your right and, seeking out the moon and star with your gaze, pronounce the following incantation three times:

> I salute and conjure you,
> O beautiful Moon, O beautiful Star,
> O bright Light which I hold in my hand!
> By the air which I breathe, by the breath which is within me, by the earth which I touch, I conjure you. And by the names of the spirits who are princes residing in you; by the ineffable name On, which hath created All; By thee, O resplendent Angel Gabriel, together with the princes of Mercury and Earth, Michael and Melchidael!
> I conjure you again by all the divine names of God, that you send down to obsess, torment, and harass the body, spirit, soul, and five senses of the nature of [name of victim] that they come to [name of supplicant] at [such and such a time] and do accomplish his [her] will, having no friendship for anyone in the world but especially for [name of supplicant]. So long as he

[she] shall be indifferent to [supplicant] so shall he [she] be obsessed, so suffer, so be tormented. Go then promptly; go Gabriel, Michael, Melchidael, Baresches, Zazel, Tiriel, Malcha, and all those who are with you. I conjure you by the great living God to accomplish my will, and I [Witch's name] do promise to satisfy you duly!

Having repeated this thrice, cast amatory incense upon your thurible coals and, rising from your kneeling position, stand the lamp of art upon the paper, and leave it to burn down and extinguish itself.

On the morrow, give the talisman to the person who requested it, and have him place it in his left shoe or otherwise carry it about his person until such a time as the spell takes effect and the victim seeks him out.

As for the Cabalistic names for Mercury, the moon, and the Earth, Michael, Gabriel, and Melchidael are traditionally the angels assigned to these spheres. Tiriel and Malcha are the intelligences assigned to Mercury and the moon respectively, while Baresches is in all probability the past part of Malcha's complete Hebrew name which has become detached and turned into an entity in its own right. "Malcha Be Tarshishim va A'ad Be Ruach Shechalim." The name Zazel is that of the spirit of the planet Saturn, here doubling for the Earth. In astral or sidereal magic which deals with a heptadic or sevenfold planetary scheme, the Earth powers are generally classified and invoked under the aegis of Saturn.

The worst thing about this charm is its verbosity, which far from stirring your deep mind into activity, may in fact only succeed in lulling it back to sleep. The redeeming qualities of the process, however, lie in its firm basis in witch principles, with its invocations of the powers of the earth, moon, and star Earendel, with the moon representing the Lady as initiator of Desire. Incidentally, I omitted to mention, but by now it should go without saying, when you utter the invocation to the star mentally summon up your Mercury symbolism from Chapter 3, and when you invoke the moon, concentrate on Habondia and her attendant images. For the Earth, which I will deal with in the next chapter, summon up in your mind's eye an image of all growing things; of plants and mosses and great ancient forests, of the smell of peat and loam; the darkness of cellars and caves, the silence of gardens at night at the abandoned overgrown churchyard. Think of all horned and hoofed animals, also.

Above all, be *aware* of the earth beneath you.

The Love Dream

A traditional variant of the Dreaming True Spell is that of the St. Magdalene's Eve Spell, which date, incidentally, is held by witches to be sacred to Habondia, no less.

In order to perform this operation, which traditionally should be done only on St. Magdalene's Eve, July 22, and the aim of which is to procure a dream of a loved one, rather than one of knowledge, prepare a bath in the same manner as in the Dreaming True Spell mentioned in the last chapter, but under your pillow tuck a sachet of St.-John's-wort (hypericum) and a piece of paper on which has been incribed the name of your beloved.

Prior to turning your light out, drink a potion composed of half a cup of distilled water, three drops of white wine, three drops of gin, three drops of vinegar that has been stirred with a sprig of rosemary. This should be mixed in your witch's chalice.

Then dream on!

Amatory Necromancy, The Dumb Supper

Finally, to conclude this section on romantic love, I shall deal with that second type of operation which comes under the definition of necromancy, and as such was mentioned previously in the chapter on divination. The operation of amatory necromancy is known among witches as the Dumb Supper. It can, however, be utilized for two purposes; the first being the evocation of the shade of a dead loved one, the second the calling forth of what is known as an eidolon or wraith, the spectral apparition of a *future* loved one or spouse.

Whether the operation is of the necromantic or eidolon variety does not change the central ritual, the Dumb Supper proper. The only difference lies in the thirteen days preparation for the necromantic variant, similar to that of the necromancy of intelligence.

In common with all the other amatory operations aforementioned, no boundary circle will be needed for this rite; even if the work is one of necromancy, the constraining ties by which the shade is summoned are those of love and affection, and one will not be dealing with a potentially hostile entity.

Should you, in fact, be calling the shade of a dead loved one, you should time the operation to coincide with some date which was in some way auspicious to him—the day of death, birthday, wedding anniversary, or whatever. Some time which you feel that the soul of the deceased, in whatever state of consciousness it may have passed into, may still dimly be aware of; a time when the ties of Earth may yet exert some slight influence on it, however weak.

Prior to summoning, you should arrange a commemorative shrine facing east on the west side of the room in which you plan to do your magical working. This should be composed of a photograph or portrait of the deceased, veiled with a dark cloth and flanked with flowers which should be changed from time to time, and any object links or personal mementos of the deceased that you might have.

Exactly at midnight on every one of the thirteen preparatory nights, seal yourself in your place of working, light one of your lamps of art in the east of the room, unveil the portrait, kindle a small amount of amatory necromancy incense in your thurible, and seat yourself facing the picture with the light streaming from behind you. Inwardly, call the person by such names as you knew him by, while keeping your eyes fixed on the picture. Try to recall all the incidents you can wherein you shared moments of affection or love with the deceased. Continue your meditation for anything from ten minutes to one hour before extinguishing the lamp, redraping the portrait, and so concluding.

During the thirteen days of preparation you must also try to seclude yourself from company as much as possible, even from that of other witches, reserving most of your affections for the memory of the dead person. This can be very difficult, but it should be persevered in. It is, in effect, the sounding of a preliminary, gentle call into the unseen to the shade of the departed one, which builds each evening at your meditation, culminating finally in the actual evocation ceremony.

When the night of evocation arrives, having eaten no supper nor partaken of any refreshment since sunset, just before the hour of midnight strikes, arrange your place of working in the following manner:

Cover your altar table with a new, white, exorcised cloth, and place a chair at the west side of it facing east, and one opposite, facing west. On the table, place a bouquet of sweet-smelling flowers. Then light two of your lamps before the portrait, and kindle your thurible, burning amatory necromancy incense.

Consecrate your place of working now, walking backwards beginning at the east, passing to the south, the west, and finally the north, asperging and censing as you go, and calling upon Habondia to aid you in this work. Every action in the ceremony must be performed *silently and backwards* for only thus do we begin to walk in the paths of the dead.

Having got this far, you must now lay two place settings at the table, yours in the east, the deceased's in the west, using your ordinary household dish service and cutlery which should have been passed previously through fire and water. The settings should be sufficient to provide for the normal amount of courses you would serve at a regular dinner for two if you were serving it, preferably of the type of food you know was favored by the deceased. It should also include a glass for wine, beer, or whatever beverage the deceased enjoyed drinking with meals. You must now proceed to serve the food, again walking backwards to and from the kitchen, and always as silently as you can. When you serve the food, you must serve only very small portions, a quarter of the amount you would regularly eat, as it is a symbolic gesture only: The dead are very light eaters!

You should allow sufficient time for the first half of the operation in order to reach this point just as midnight arrives. As the hour strikes, approach the portrait, backwards as always, slowly unveil it, and mentally repeat the necromantic grand citation to yourself as you do so:

> By the mysteries of the deep,
> by the flames of banal,
> by the power of the east,

> by the silence of the night,
> And by the holy rites of Hecate,
> I call thee by the ties of love,
> Spirit of [name of deceased]
> to break thy eternal fast with me.
> So mote it be!

Then, after replenishing the incense, move backwards clockwise round the table to your seat and begin to eat your portion of your supper. As you do this, *avoid looking directly at the seat opposite you. This is most important.* If you break this rule, you can effectively nullify the spell. The temptation is enormous but must be resisted strongly.

When you have finished your repast, leave the dishes as they are, and walking backwards, replenish the incense and extinguish the lamps at the portrait, still avoiding staring directly at the chair in the west. Then return to your own. Close your eyes, call the deceased's name three times, and then mentally repeat the words of the great necromantic charge: "Allay Fortission Fortissio Allynson Roa!"

With your eyes still shut, mentally welcome the loved one. Traditionally, this is the place where the shade will manifest. You should slowly open your eyes and see what you can see. Again, as in the necromancy of intelligence, this will depend on the stage of your development. Communication with the shade theoretically can be carried out mentally; most witches find that this takes the form of a peculiar wordless communion, a sort of spiritual osmosis or blending together of ideas, your own, and that of the deceased. Even if your inner eyes are not sensitive enough to perceive any form, or the current raised by the operation is not sufficiently strong to bring about a materialization, it can nevertheless be a very unnerving experience to find yourself confronted by someone loved, but long dead, and in such intimate contact again that your very minds meld together. Allow yourself to enjoy this silent communion without reservation. The time will pass all too quickly. When you have fully enjoyed, or been duly horrified by, whichever the case may be, the manifestation or, alternatively, when the experience begins to dwindle like a dream as the hour of midnight passes and the magical current slackens, repeat the license to depart silently to the shade:

> Go, go, departed shade [name of deceased]
> by Omgroma Epin Sayoc,
> Satony, Degony, Eparigon,
> Galiganon, Zogogen, Ferstigon,
> we license thee depart into the proper place
> and be there love between us evermore.
> So mote it be!

Cast a few more grains of incense on the coals as you silently bid adieu.

Finally, before you finish for the night, complete your magical record, as always.

Now, as I mentioned before, some witches claim this very same ritual can be used to evoke an eidolon of one's *future* loved one. This is a form of summoning of the living. The only difference between this and the necromantic version just described is that the summoning of the eidolon omits the thirteen days preliminary preparation. It is, moreover, a tricky operation for beginners to perform and also a somewhat untrustworthy one, as there is obviously no object link possible, save for the operator's tenuous emotional link with the future.

This may strike some as the last word in absurdity, but if you pause to reconsider the parapsychic phenomenon of precognition as we did in Chapter 3, you will realize that for a witch, who deals wholly with the world of the paranormal, the laws of time as well as space as we know them in our everyday lives do not necessarily apply.

The time to employ this ritual of evocation of a future loved one is traditionally midsummer's eve, the night of June 20, just before the summer solstice.

On that note, I shall end this first section of spells for lovers. The following pages will deal with spells designed for the more impetuous practitioners.

Part II: Sex Magic

In the contemporary world of instant sex without romantic preamble, the modern witch may not have the patience required for the more dated "Loving-Cup" approach. In other words, she will be seeking for some magic which, if Habondia's charms prove too lightweight, would allow her to be swept off her feet literally and metaphorically.

The key to success in this area of magic lies in our old friend, the witches' pyramid. Our chief weapon is none other than the potent will itself. Of course, we are dealing here with the art of bewitchment proper, sometimes known as the evil eye. But let us call it by its real name as used by practitioners themselves:

The Art of Fascination

In order to understand this mysterious process, by which you will be effecting your more lustful ambitions, we should first glance briefly at the theory which underlies the practice.

The art of fascination, in itself an integral part of all witchcraft, can take many forms, ranging from the simple matter of "binding" someone (enforcing one's will), to the more exotic and difficult practices such as the "binding" of animals (snake charming), and control of physical phenomena like the gathering or splitting up of clouds (weather working) and controlled poltergeist phenomena (smashing windows, levitating ashtrays, etc.).

The human body radiates energy, which forms an egg-shaped cocoon about it which modern occultists call the aura. Exactly what the nature of this energy is and where it comes from we don't know; the prevalent theory among witches is that it is produced via the nervous system. It is known variously by the names od, odyle, magnetism, telergy, or simply witch power.

Red-haired people are said to possess this energy in freefloating form available for projection more than any others, hence the awe and fear that the red-headed witch has been held in from the time of ancient Egypt down to the present

Spells for Lovers

day. Set, the sorcerous brother of Osiris, was reputed to have had red hair; back in the old country in the eleventh century William Rufus (son of William the Conqueror) was publicly much feared on account of his connections with witchcraft, red hair, and the evil eye! Today the red-headed witch has become something of a cliché, but the origin of the belief is rooted in centuries of witch knowledge. If you have red hair, you are lucky indeed!

This energy, or witch power, is in fact what you have been using all along to empower your rituals. It can, however, be used without the assistance of a spell, if you learn how to project it correctly. This projection is known as fascination. Generally speaking, the power can be projected by strong mental action alone. However, most practitioners find it much easier to do when accompanied by a gesture of some sort.

Strangely enough, witch power seems to be more strongly emitted from some areas of the body than others. These are: the eyes, the mouth, the hands, and the genital organs. Because of this fact, the gesture has a more important function than merely a psychological prop for the practitioner. In fact, when you wish to exercise your witch powers directly, especially in sexual matters, there are three things you should endeavor to do:

1. Fix your victim intently with your eyes.
2. Get into manual contact with him.
3. Contrive to breathe on him somehow.

No doubt these things will all be second nature to the seasoned seducer, but magically speaking they do enable your power to make contact with your victim more easily.

Here is a brief quotation from a witch's old workbook on the subject, which though archaically phrased gives a very good description of the basic eye practice:

> For when your [the witch's and her victim's] eyes be reciprocally bent one upon the other and are joined beams to beams, and lights to lights, then the spirit of one is joined to the spirit of the other and strong ligations made— And most *violent* love is only stirred up with a sudden looking on, as it were,

with a Darting Look, or piercing into the very inmost of the heart! . . .

While trying to fulfill conditions 1, 2, and 3, you will stir your deep mind, summoning all the pyramid powers into activity, letting your imagination run on a lustful rampage, bending your basilisk gaze upon your victim with all the intensity of a burning will held steady by the hand of faith, the while maintaining that enigmatic secretive smile which is the trademark of your craft.

An old dodge used by witches for pumping up the power to its required intensity is the use of rhythmic breathing. Here we make use of two principles: The oxygenation of the blood to bring increased energy, but more importantly, the mental *tying* of the in-and-out breathing with the pulse of the bloodstream and acceleration of it accordingly. This has the effect of quickening the metabolism, and generally enhancing the output of nervous energy available for conversion into witch power.

The ideal way to employ your powers of fascination are, of course, if you can get your prospective victim onto home territory; the witches' lair! Invite your victim round for drinks and dinner, hopefully with the moon waxing on a Friday, though this isn't really necessary. Friday, apart from magical considerations, is a good night, as your victim in all probability won't be pressured to rush off after dinner on the pretext of work the following day!

Put him at his ease, serving cocktails before dinner if you like but keeping everything casual and intimate; use candlelight if possible. Wear a dab of your Cernunnos perfume. (See end of chapter.)

Prepare the dinner yourself. This will provide you with an ideal opportunity to employ your philters. But don't overdo them. You don't want the food or wine to acquire a strange taste.

The meal itself might well consist of a juicy meat dish, as rarely done as you can manage it, well-garnished with sage, thyme, or coriander philter powder, and maybe served with a crisp side salad containing such amatory vegetable as endive, parsley, raw carrots, and apples; chilled tomatoes stuffed with basil can also be a good thing to serve.

Of course, oysters and champagne are *excellent* in these matters, but you should first take the trouble to find out whether your victim appreciates them. Some unfortunate souls find them nauseating even to contemplate, and this is hardly the frame of mind to cast your future lover into at the beginning of the evening! It might be well to find out exactly *what* your victim's tastes in food actually are before you even embark upon the meal, and vary your menu accordingly. One of the surest ways to a person's heart is through the stomach.

Apropos of this, at the end of this chapter you will find a full list of amatory herbs and plants which you may be able to weave into your cooking.

For dessert you can deliver your whammy. Cardamom apple pie! Both cardamoms and apples are extremely magically potent in matters of love, and can be readily combined in this very acceptable and homey recipe.

After dinner, philters can again be ever so subtly introduced into liqueurs. These should be drunk in a room which you have previously fumigated with a suitable love incense; the lights should be low, and music may be playing very softly in the background.

You should contrive to place your victim so that he is seated with his back to the west. You should be in the east, the place of power. You may now begin your process of fascination, secure in the knowledge that he is all but yours for the taking.

At this point, you must introduce your eye technique. How to catch your victim's gaze with your own is a matter of individual preference. Some witches still use the old dust-in-the-eye dodge. Others just fix their gaze rudely on the point between the eyes of their victim without more ado. In my opinion this is the best way—the frontal attack!

Should he—I say he; it will be she if you happen to be a warlock—should he, in fact, sternly resist all your attempts to catch his eye, then you can only conclude that maybe he has guessed what is afoot; you should then immediately pass to phase two of the operation, manual technique. This is effected by the introduction of an exterior object of some delicateness or precision, which will be placed in his hands for closer scrutiny. Your witch jewel loaded with your magnetism is ideal for this. Now while he is examining this, you must take the opportunity to settle close enough to him to initiate and maintain some form of manual contact with his body, beaming all the concentrated force of your witch power into him through the link, whether it be shoulder, waist, knee, or even more intimate parts.

Should he by some devious process manage to elude your grasp, move directly to phase three, breath technique. In order to do this, you must arrange yourself in such a way that you can actually breathe on him, preferably near his face and ideally into his mouth, again powerfully emitting the full radiance of your witch power through your open lips. At this point, you will probably have gained full ocular contact at last, so you may also use this additional channel for your powers of sorcery.

Having got thus far I would say you are off and away. All that remains is that you turn the conversation instantly to matters of sex.

However, if all else fails, I can only suggest you resort to the use of one of the following spells.

Not everyone is always immediately successful at fascination, inasmuch as the powers of the pyramid need practice and application before they can be switched on and off at will. But keep working at it! As I say, all things yield to perseverance, matters of love no less than anything else.

Should you gain no appreciable result the first time around, one of the following spells will aid you in your entrapments. The last two are very potent and can be of considerable help to the lustful though maybe as yet unfascinating practitioner.

The rituals themselves in this area of magic are ruled by a very different power to Habondia. In fact, we are dealing with her consort, the Horned One, in medieval times claimed by the church to be none other than Satan himself. The attribution is merely scholarly, however, as the Horned One existed long before Christianity came into existence, with its concept of the devil. Whereas Habondia's symbol is the dove, Old Horny's is the goat. To students of symbolism, this attribute should speak for itself. The goat is the age-old representative of lust and debauchery, and Cernunnos himself, for such is his witch name, is frequently represented as possessing the cloven hooves, horns, and erect phallus of his attribute. His symbolism has much in common with that of the Greek god Pan with his attendant satyrs and silenoi and the prehistoric phallic giants carved into the turf in various places around England such as the Cerne Giant and the Long Man of Wilmington. He is the god of the dead, winter, and chaos, and it is from this aspect that he derives his title, the Lord of Misrule. Herein he is characterized as the King of Debauchery and Licentious Frolic. The midwinter festival of Saturnalia is dedicated to him, and witches celebrate this about the same time that Christians celebrate Christmas.

Whenever you wish to perform a spell whose object is to boggle someone's mind with lust, you should invoke holy Cernunnos with all the powers of the witches' pyramid. Instead of Habondia's flowers, however, upon which Old Horny tramples joyously, you should surround your altar triangle with pinecones, evergreens, and the horns, teeth or hooves of animals, which are all especially held sacred to the god.

We are not dealing with the gentle mystery and twilit glamour of Habondia's womanly enchantments, but rather the darkness of the wildwood, the trampling and snorting of the god of beasts, and those rude and basic facts of life, the rearing phallus and the hungry vulva.

To begin this section on lust, here is a small traditional spell, more suitable for performance by the male warlock, to stir up the baser passions in a lady. It is not much in use nowadays for obvious reasons, but it is quaintly illustrative of the use of the principle of direct transmission. Though there is no ritual to speak of here, nor any invocation to the Horned One, he and his ministers are definitely present in the warlock's mind when he makes use of this charm.

The ingredients for this sorcery are simply a bitch in heat and another, male dog, plus a small, attractive looking glass such as the warlock knows will prove acceptable to the object of his lust. Now the trick of this spell lies in arranging that the two dogs couple on a Thursday around the hour of 8 A.M., 3 P.M., or 10 P.M.; having arranged for this accordingly, you must then contrive to catch the reflection of the copulating dogs in your looking glass, uttering this spell forcefully as you do so, and bending your basilisk gaze on the scene before you:

> I the dog and she the bitch,
> I the helve and she the axe,
> I the cock and she the hen.
> As my will, so mote it be!

Having done this, hopefully without exciting too much attention from your neighbors, either present the loaded looking glass to your future ladylove as a gift, or in some way induce her to gaze into it. One look and she will be lost to you. Be prepared to have the clothes torn from your back.

The rituals of this section are also best performed on a Thursday, a day held sacred by witches to the more aggressive approach to love, again at 8 A.M., 3 P.M., or 10 P.M. Unlike any other spell you have performed before, however, you will be employing a grand triangle of manifestation, and the instruments of power will be your Athamé and chalice; the altar should be decked with animal horns, evergreens, and so on.

Now the first spell that utilizes the awesome power of Cernunnos is a process which exists in *at least* fifty variants in the witch world; it is known by the rather inoffensive name of the Love Knot, a tame title for such a dramatic piece of sorcery. Its object is to render the performer the object of overwhelming lust for another stated person. It can have a backwards and destructive method of employment which we will return to in a later chapter under the heading of "Ligature"; but for now I shall dwell on its positive aspect.

Whereas simple love philters will generally only conjure sweet yearnings of tender passion (unless of course heavily dosed with aphrodisiac drugs), the Love Knot is highly potent traditionally, when it comes to unashamedly stirring up lust, and is often used as a last resort along with the Puppet Spell.

Like many other really powerful spells, it introduces the element of time into its working; water cannot break rocks swiftly, unless used in great quantities, but a steady drip-drip can do wonders with erosion. Often the deep mind is far more

The Love Knot Spell

All you have to do to accomplish this piece of witchery is to possess yourself of a few hairs from the head of the person you seek to influence. A hairbrush and comb is the most likely place to look for these. People are apt to get suspicious, rightly so as it happens, if you smilingly produce a pair of scissors and blithely purloin a lock of their hair.

Prepare your place of working as already indicated with pine-cones, ivy, evergreens, and horns. In your thurible, burn one of the Cernunnos incenses suggested at the end of this half of the chapter; in the chalice pour a few drops of red wine. On the floor, with the point of your Athamé, trace around the edges of a large equilateral triangle, big enough to contain yourself and the altar and allow you plenty of room for movement. This should be marked out with white tape beforehand.

Begin the spell by chanting the following ancient invocation to the Horned One, starting in the east and repeating it to each quarter, traveling clockwise.

As you do so, cense and anoint each side of the altar table with a dab of wine from the chalice. This in effect is consecrating the triangle to the service of Cernunnos.

At the same time, try to visualize yourself as standing in a small clearing within a vast, dark forest. The tops of the trees close far above you over your head, and through the green twilight you can hear in the distance the trampling and occasional cry of a wild beast as it crashes through the undergrowth. It seems to be approaching the clearing in the trees where you stand, drawing ever nearer each time you face another quarter to repeat your invocation. Now you can even smell the rank goaty smell of the beast! It is Cernunnos himself, the Horned One in his dark semianimal form with rearing antlers and erect phallus, eyes burning like coals in the forest gloom. Finish your call to the north, and see him vividly in your mind's eye standing in the east outside the perimeter of your charmed triangle. You may visualize him as the classical god Pan, the Sabbatic goat, or even as that figure of Elizabethan romance, Robin Goodfellow, or Puck. These are all but faces worn by Cernunnos, god of the witches!

Invocation to the Horned One

Eko; Eko Azarak! Eko; Eko Zomelak!
Eko; Eko Cernunnos! Eko; Eko; Arada!
Bagabi lacha bachabe;
Lamac cahi achababa,
   Karellyos!
Lamac Lamac Bachalyas;
Cabahagy Sabalyas,
Baryolas!
Lagoz atha Cabyolas;
Samahac atha femyolas,
Harrahya!

Return to the east, and facing west across the altar, gather up the three pieces of twine and consecrate them with incense and wine in the name of the Horned One. Then knot the ends of the twine and braid them together, binding the hair into the plait as you do. Summon up the image of your victim in your mind's eye as you do this, repeating this quaint jingle over and over:

> Lord Cernunnos I ask of thee,
> let [name] no pleasure, sleep, nor solace see,
> till heart and loins be turned to me!

When the cord is woven, tie the free twine ends together forcefully with the words:

> As my will, so mote it be!

No triple cross of sealing is necessary here since the tying action is forceful enough on its own. Fasten the finished cord around the upper part of your thigh if you are a woman or around the genital organs themselves if you are a man, tight enough not to slip, but not so tight as to restrict the circulation of the blood. This would only be self-defeating. Wear this cord, or cingulum as we call it, for twenty-eight days, removing it only for showers or bathing.

Should no appreciable result have occurred by this time, you up the ante, so to speak, and set the seal on the magic by performing this final part of the spell:

Prepare your place of working with a large floor triangle again and with the usual arrangements of lamps, incense, and pinecones on the altar, making quite sure that the thurible contains a good quantity of glowing charcoals. The chalice should be back again in the triangle, this time containing a few drops of olive oil, red wine, honey, and your own blood or urine.

Then invoke Cernunnos at all four quarters as previously. Remove the cord and tie nine knots along it, beginning with one at either end and working in pairs toward the center, where you should place the final one. As you do this, repeat your charm with each knot:

> Lord Cernunnos I ask of thee,
> let [name] no pleasure, sleep, nor solace see,
> till heart and loins be turned to me!

Finish on the last knot with "As my will, so mote it be!"

Having done this, dip the cord briefly in the chalice so that it picks up a few drops of the liquid, then cast it, together with a few grains of your incense, onto the thurible coals, repeating these words with all the intense conviction, not to say lust, you can manage:

> Ure Spiritus Igne
> Renes nostros et cor nostrum
> Fiat, Fiat, Fiat!

The second half of the process reinforces the subtle effect of the first on the victim's deep mind, and gives it a sharp reminder of what all the nudging has been about.

Incidentally, some malicious witches who take a delight, indeed pride themselves on such matters, perform the Love Knot in reverse on pairs of lovers or married couples. This operation is known in the craft by the interesting French name *Dénoûment des nœuds,* or "loosing the marriage knots." It has been practiced through the centuries, and sixteenth-century theologians such as Del Rio, De Lancre, and Bodin spoke frequently of it in their writings. It was one of the prevalent witch practices which fanned the flames of hysteria in the public mind almost more than anything else leading to popular endorsement of the great witch persecutions of the sixteenth and seventeenth centuries.

The Puppet Spell

The other lust spell you should definitely be acquainted with for last resorts is the famous puppet spell, sometimes referred to by snobbish practitioners as *l'Envoûtement d'Amour*. This is the one I mentioned earlier in the chapter as being an excellent example of the use of both object link and power object. Here it is.

Select a Thursday when the moon is waxing at 8 A.M., 3 P.M., or 10 P.M., and after securing your usual privacy, deck your altar table with horns and evergreens as in the previous experiment, the chalice of wine outside the altar triangle, the lamps of art, and your thurible containing a suitable Cernunnos incense. *Within* the triangle should be placed freshly exorcised modeling clay or beeswax, either of which are easy enough to obtain. Also a few hairs from the head of the person you are going to bewitch, or some of his nail clippings. Hair is usually easier to obtain. Failing both these things, an item of the victim's clothing will do—a tie, sock, or handkerchief—anything so long as it has been worn by the victim.

To complete your preparations, as in the previous spell, draw a large equilateral triangle on the floor around yourself and the altar with the point of your Athamé, big enough to walk around in, and in such a manner that the sides parallel the one on your altar covering. Again, you may mark this great triangle out with white masking-tape beforehand if you wish.

When you have drawn the triangle, place the Athamé back on the altar in the small triangle alongside the modeling materials and hair.

These preparations should be sufficient to have alerted your deep mind, so you can now begin the spell, chanting the invocation to Cernunnos at each side of the altar and again anointing it with a dab of wine from your chalice.

Spells for Lovers

Now when the cold shivers on your spine inform you that the Horned One is indeed present, take the clay or wax and mold it into a doll whose features resemble your victim's as closely as you can manage. A bought doll is a very poor substitute, although some witches do use them—half the magic is contained in the modeling process. I have known other witches who go to the opposite extreme and not only take the pains to get the features right, but even go so far as to build the doll up from a tiny skeleton made of pipe cleaners, which is then "fleshed out" with modeling clay. But don't worry, just do your best. It really doesn't matter how crude the puppet is, just so long as it is the best you can manage. The one important thing to remember is that you must clearly delineate the sex of the mannikin. That is, you must exaggerate the sexual organs of the doll in such a way as to be quite apparent that they are in a state of extreme sexual excitement.

When you have finished your modeling process, carefully press the hairs into the puppet's head, or if you have nail clippings, stick them gently into the extremities of the arms and legs. Should you have a piece of clothing, wait till after the next operation before wrapping it around the doll's body like a makeshift coat. Then take your Athamé and, with the tip, scratch the words (victim's name), son or daughter of X and Y (victim's mother's name and father's name). Then turn the image over and scratch on the back of it:

"N" (victim's name) lusting for "M" (supplicant's name). At this point, if you are using a piece of clothing instead of hair or clippings, tie it around the puppet. Now consecrate the puppet with oil and wine, chanting these words as you do each time and strongly projecting the mental image of the victim onto the figurine as you do so.

> In the name of Cernunnos, the Horned One,
> Creature of earth [or wax],
> I name thee [N], son [daughter] of [X] and [Y].
> Thou are [N], son of [X] and [Y].

Then seal it with the triple cross and the words "So mote it be!"

Having done this, lay the completed puppet in the altar

triangle face up with its head pointing to the east. Take the Athamé in your right hand (left if you are lefthanded) and raise it high above the image, pointing at the place where its heart would be; now, visualizing Cernunnos himself standing behind you guiding your hand, strongly project the mental image of your intended victim onto the puppet, trying to *see* it as him. When your mind is set unwaveringly on this idea, chant the spell thus, whipping your emotions into a final torrent of fire as you do:

> It is not my hand which does this deed
> but that of Cernunnos, the Horned One.
> As blade pierces heart,
> so shall the loins of [N] burn with lust
> for [M] [supplicant's own name].

With that plunge the Athamé forcefully into the puppet's heart uttering the usual sealing words "As my will, so mote it be!" Withdrawing your knife, wrap the hapless puppet in a purified linen cloth.

This fulfills the first condition of the law of transmission, that is, work accomplished by means of an object link. In order to enforce the spell by satisfying the second condition of the law, once you have wrapped the puppet in the clean, exorcised cloth, you should then at some point conceal it somewhere in the victim's vicinity, burying it under the eaves of his house or hiding it in his home where he won't find it. Failing that, bury it under a spot over which he is sure to pass. But be careful to hide it in a place where he won't get his hands on it, for two very cogent reasons. The first is simply that you should avoid letting your victim get the wrong end of the stick about what kind of magical blast is being aimed at him. If he happens to harbor a secret and maybe unconscious fear of the occult and discovers your puppet labeled with his name and gashed through the heart, the spell could very well misfire and, far from summoning desire, more likely engender a hearty loathing in him for you, your client, and the entire unholy business. Amatory magic is a very touchy business, in many ways much more so than works of wrath and chastisement, hexing, and the like.

The second, less obvious but far more important reason for

concealment is one which may not occur to you as a beginner witch but would leap to the mind of an old pro immediately: Should your victim himself turn out to be a dabbler in the Black Arts, or indeed intimate with one such as yourself who is, it would be a comparatively easy operation for him to divine the direction from which the magical onslaught emanates, and by means of the very same puppet, being impregnated with your magnetism, bring about your magical downfall in any number of ingenious ways. Therefore, let me again reemphasize a certain degree of caution, at the risk of sounding repetitious and unnecessarily wary.

Herbs and Incense of Love

To conclude this chapter on amatory matters, here are a few simple recipes for the various incenses mentioned in the preceding pages, plus a list of amatory magical ingredients you may wish to experiment with on your own.

LOVE INCENSE

First, an incense to be used with all general works of love such as the composition of philters, the Planetary Spell, et cetera.

Traditionally, witches used to make this of musk, lignum aloes, red coral powder, tincture of ambergris, and rose petals, mingled with a few drops of pigeon's blood and the desiccated brain of a sparrow! However, modern witches generally omit the last two ingredients and substitute an old culinary standby, the white of an egg, strangely enough. This, apart from its magical effectiveness, also can be used as a binding agent for the powders, should you wish to compose ready-made incense cones or pastilles as opposed to loose granules.

All or any of the flowery perfumes are appropriate to these operations, so if you should wish to substitute for the ambergris, which even in its synthetic form can be quite expensive, you may safely employ oils of myrtle, jasmine, rosemary, violet, verbena, or sandalwood—frankly whichever you happen to find the most seductive. You may even mingle in a perfume you intimately connect with one of your climactic experiences of the past to great advantage. Coral powder traditionally has a magical affinity with operations of love, but again, due to its comparative rarity, many modern witches also omit this. The ground rose petals and the powdered lignum aloes provide a very good solid base to mingle the flower oils or essences with. Musk and civet essences may also be mingled to great advantage with your incense, but these, like ambergris, tend to be on the expensive side. Many modern haute couture parfumiers utilize these three essences or their synthetic substitutes as bases for their most closely guarded recipes.

Amatory Necromancy Incense

1 part vervain herb (verbena) (finely reduced)
1 part wormwood herb (finely reduced)
1 part powdered sandalwood, lignum aloes, or rose petals
1 part dittany of Crete (finely reduced)
1 part gum Benjamin (benzoin)
Moisten with a few drops of:
    Pure olive oil
    Red wine
    Honey
    The operator's blood
A dash of essential flower oil of your choice (a favorite of the deceased, if possible).

Blend all these ingredients together on a Friday when the moon is waxing, leaving them to steep overnight. Add extra herbs to make up a dry consistency if necessary.

Extra Philter Herbs

Along with the plants already mentioned, here is a short list of herbs readily available on the market, which traditionally are held to be highly potent in magical love philters and, as such, are employed by most modern witches, with varying degrees of success. As a novice witch, you will find it well worth your while to purchase some of these, including the herbs already mentioned, to experiment carefully with along the lines we have laid out in the preceding chapter.

Useful Philter Components

Fennel
Sea holly root, or Eryngo (*Eryngium maritimum*)
Cardamom
Dill or anet
Ginger
Cumin
Marjoram
Cowslip flowers (*Primula veris*)
Endive (when used as a sachet, potency lasts seven days)
Linden or lime tree flowers
Mullein
Grain of Paradise, also known as Egyptian Paradise seed
Motherwort (*Leonurus cardiaca*)
Ginseng root (much favored by our Eastern copractitioners)
Violet petals
Sweet sedge (sweet flag, *Acorus calamus*)
Verbena
Thyme
Anise
Basil
Rose petals (can be used in form of rose hip syrup)
Apple (either blossom or fruit itself)
Lovage (*Levisticum officinale*, "loving herbs" of old lore)
Rosemary
Honey
Juniper berries
Valerian

After being consecrated, the herbs can also be made up into love sachets given to the person who longs to be desired. They should be carried about on the person and tucked under the pillow at night. Make the sachets themselves of thin white cloth tied up with red ribbon, yarn, or thread; this is the traditional witch method. (For more detailed information on sachet powders, see the next chapter.)

Finally, here are some twenty extra useful love herbs *for use in sachets only* which you may care to experiment with. In all cases the herbs singly or mingled together should be consecrated in the name of either Habondia or Cernunnos, with the intention of the charm firmly uttered over them while they are being tied up with the ribbon.

Some of these ingredients should be kept extremely well-guarded and labeled, however, and *never* under any circumstances be administered orally as a philter; they can be highly poisonous and the effects extremely nasty. I have listed them accordingly.

USEFUL SACHET POWDER INGREDIENTS

Lavender
Vervain
Orris root ("love" or iris root)
Balm (*Melissa officinalis*)
Rue (use for a clear head in love matters!)
Hawthorn blossoms
Periwinkle blossoms (*Vinca major* and *minor*)
Yarrow (potency lasts seven years—good for marriages)
Dragon's blood reed (more traditional to the United States, brings back straying lovers)
Mandrake root (*Bryonia dioica. Don't eat this.* Highly suitable for Cernunnos magic)
Olive leaves (calming of strife)
Cowslip flowers
Satyrion root (Any type of orchid. Not advisable to eat. Highly suitable for Cernunnos magic)
Myrtle leaves or blossoms
Balm of Gilead buds
Meadowsweet (*Filipendula ulmaria*)
Jasmine blossoms
Violet petals
Bergamot
Lignum aloes
Sandalwood
Marigold
Southernwood (*Artemesia abrotanum*, or "lad's love")

Most of these herbs can be bought from any shop which specializes in herbal medicines or botanicals. Make sure the herbs are unadulterated though; many shops try to get away with tricks like substituting bay for myrtle and so on. Incidentally, a very good amatory herbal bath sachet to be used before any adventure in love, whether it be an act of witchcraft or a night on the tiles is simply prepared as follows:

Mix together these dried herbs on a Friday when the moon is waxing:

> 7 parts lavender
> 6 parts rosemary
> 5 parts rose petals
> 3 parts lovage
> 2 parts verbena leaves
> 1 pinch orris root
> 1 pinch thyme
> 1 pinch mint
> 1 pinch sage
> 1 pinch marjoram

Tie up in a piece of thin muslin or cheesecloth, and steep in your bathwater. This may sound like a fascinating *bouquet garni* but I can assure you many witches find it highly potent for *choses d'amour!*

Rosemary by itself can be steeped in pure water, and the infusion obtained used as an amatory wash for the hands, or for sprinkling to the four quarters of the room prior to any invocation of romantic love and Habondia. It tends to be quite unsuitable for Cernunnos, however.

CERNUNNOS INCENSE

For use in any invocation of Cernunnos, or spell designed to arouse lust.

> A few drops patchouli essence or patchouli leaves finely powdered
> 1 part good-quality fine-grain church incense
> 1 part bay leaves finely reduced
> 1 part cyprus wood or pine needles finely reduced
> 1 part wormwood herb
> 1 part vervain herb
> Moisten with a few drops of:
>   Oil of cloves
>   Gum turpentine (pine oil)

Olive oil
Honey
The operator's blood
Red wine

Finally, a drop of civet or musk essence if you can get hold of them. If not, never mind.

As with all your other incenses, let this mixture steep overnight, adding more solid ingredients if necessary to bring it to the requisite dry consistency. It should be prepared on a Thursday at the usual time, with the moon waxing. It is very strong, and you should use it sparingly.

Cernunnos Perfume

To be worn during any operation or adventure involving lust and seduction. There are several varieties of this perfume extant, the commonest one consisting of this formula:

- 5 parts musk (synthetic essence will do)
- 5 parts civet   "   "   "   "
- 1 part ambergris   "   "   "   "
- 1 part patchouli
  or cassia   "   "   "   "

The first three of these ingredients are very expensive, however, so here is a very good alternative recipe, which can also be highly potent used sparingly:

- ⅓ patchouli oil
- ⅓ cedarwood oil
- ⅓ pine oil (good-quality gum turpentine)
- 1 drop vanilla
- 1 drop jasmine oil or ilang-ilang
- 1 drop oil of cloves
- 1 drop essence of rose
- 1 drop geranium oil

This perfume should be mixed with pure alcohol should you wish to compose a toilet water or cologne as opposed to a heavy perfume. Should this recipe be too difficult for you to make, patchouli oil by itself will do.

A few drops of Cernunnos can be mixed with your Sabbat oil to add extra impact. The actual composition of that oil I shall reserve for Chapter 7.

As in the composition of the Love Incense, so also here; should you wish to experiment with new essences and perfumes, go ahead. However, for matters of lust, as opposed to romantic love, I would advise you to stick to the more bitter and piney perfumes. Leave the flowery essences to Habondia and her works of romance.

CHAPTER 5

Countermagic and Protection

DON'T delude yourself. The minute you set foot upon the path of witchcraft, a call rings out in the unseen world announcing the fact of your arrival. And sooner or later you are going to have to confront the problem of protecting your friends and yourself from the magical bolts that will undoubtedly be slung at you by less friendly practitioners. Supernaturally induced bad luck, whether occasioned by the casual glance of someone's evil eye or a more potently organized attack, is always the result of an unconscious blind spot in the victim's deep mind, either created by or played upon by the attacker. The mischief this works is technically known in the craft as binding the victim's soul or deep mind, thus rendering him considerably more accident-prone than he generally is.

This is so unless, of course, the magical shaft is one specifically directed at achieving a specified result, such as gnawing stomach pains or instant loss of hair, in which case the attack is definitely something more than a mere casual overlooking, and should not be treated as such.

Magical "overlooking" of the general type, ill-wishing, let us call it, can be guarded against with a special overall field of witch power, which acts rather on the analogy of a blanket insurance policy. This is accomplished by fortifying yourself and your home with charged protective power objects known as amulets. These are similar to the power objects encountered on a previous page save for the fact that they are charged solely with the intention of inducing a state of harmony, generosity, expansiveness, security, and optimism in the deep minds of those in their vicinity. That frame of mind most likely to lead to lucky breaks occurring in fact.

Most novice witches carry luck amulets of this sort as a matter of course, and usually hang a good selection of them around the house for good measure. They can be constructed from any number of substances—animal, vegetable, or mineral. The ones mentioned in this section are all of a mineral or vegetable basis and rely mainly on contact with that third witch power you are about to be introduced to: the earth itself.

To the witch, the Earth archetype represents the source of all sustenance, healing, and fertility. The magical symbolism of the Earth is similar to that surrounding those classical deities concerned with domestic and agrarian affairs, especially the female ones, such as Ceres, Vesta, Egeria, Ops, Cybele, and Rhea; the great Earth mothers, in fact. Many witches refer to the Earth power as Hulda, Erda, or Hertha. Our words "Earth" and "hearth" are derived from the last two names.

Hertha is so closely related to Habondia that these two goddesses are often related to one another in magical legend as mother and daughter, thus tying in superficially with the old Greek myth of Demeter and Persephone. However, many modern witches consider Habondia and Hertha to be but different aspects of the same power, which they refer to simply as the Goddess.

It was Mother Hertha that you invoked as the third power in the Planetary Spell of the last chapter.

As a beginner witch who intends to pursue the path, it is essential that you place yourself and your home under some sort of protective spell from the outset. There are a good many amuletic spells for doing this. Here are two of them. The first is suitable only if you happen to live in a house as opposed to an apartment.

On the day of the *new* moon, purchase a fresh hen's egg. The fresher the egg, the better—a fertile one is best of all. That midnight, observing your usual discreet precautions, kindle a Tellurian Incense in your thurible (see end of chapter) and place salt and water in your cup, clearly pronouncing these actions to be "in Hertha's name."

Now, holding your Athamé in your right hand, the egg in

the other, tread a path three times deosil (clockwise) round the outer perimeter of your house or property, concentrating hard on Hertha's image and strongly invoking her either by simply chanting her name to yourself or by using the following incantation:

> Hertha, Great One, Mother of all life,
> who gives birth to all
> and renews her Lord the Sun each day
> who bestows himself on all men equally;
>
> Guardian of sky and sea, all powers and potencies,
> through your might alone all nature falls silent then sinks into sleep.
> You bring back the light to dispel the darkness
> only once more to cover us most safely with your shadows.
>
> You in whose hand rests everlasting chaos,
> even wind, rain, and storm,
> at whose word oceans roar;
> who chases away the light and stirs up the tempest
> and at whose whim sends forth joyous day again;
>
> Ever faithful sustainer of all life,
> when our souls depart, they fly to your keeping
> thence to return yet again.
> Rightly you are called Great Mother of All,
> for you conquer by your name alone.
>
> Source of strength for all men and gods
> without you naught is born nor perfected;
> I call upon you, ruler of creation;
> I call upon you as divine,
> I call upon your holy name,
> Hertha, be pleased to grant that which I ask,
> protect this house and home
> and all who live therein,
> so shall I always thank you with due faith.

Hertha herself may be visualized as a dark, statuesque woman of mature age, robed in russet and green and bearing in her arms a sheaf of golden corn dotted with scarlet poppies. About her ankles and forearms twine green serpents, and her full dark breasts are exposed in the manner of the queens of ancient Egypt. Her lambent eyes are of dark gold; above her high coif of iron-dark hair she wears a square crenellated crown, like four towers bound together. These are the four castles or watchtowers of witchcraft that stand at the four quarters of the world. Beneath her feet lush vegetation springs. Behind her, in the mountainside, a giant cavern yawns. Great masses of creeper trail over it in places like a curtain. The autumn air is heavy with the scent of new-mown hay, and bees drone lazily in the distance.

With each step of your ritual, see, in your mind's eye, your feet leaving blue, glowing footprints of witch power on the ground behind you. You are surrounding your house with a giant protective circle of light!

When you have finished your circumambulations (hopefully without encountering mishap such as arrest by the local police for loitering), you should seal the egg into a previously prepared and exorcised black box cushioned within by some dark fabric —a piece of your discarded clothing is ideal. This box you must now bury deeply and permanently, either as nearly under the threshold of the house as you can manage or beneath your hearth, if you have one. You will probably have to pry up a loose floorboard for this. Failing these things, simply wall the box up in the house somewhere, in the attic or preferably the cellar. The important thing to remember here is that the egg must be incorporated into the basic fabric of the house, if not the foundations.

Wherever you decide upon, you should first exorcise the spot with your Earth incense and salt and water. Then place the box in the space provided, calling upon Hertha three times to protect your house from all misadventure and to bless all those within it with harmony and good fortune. Having done this, spit thrice into the hole, and then proceed to fill it in solidly and permanently.

By performing this ritual, you will have placed your house within Hertha's care. It is in fact the vestige of an ancient sacrificial earth ritual, and can be considered most effective in matters of blessing the home, and protection generally. In the past, rural witches would use this process to bless pastures and ploughed fields as well as individual homesteads.

Similar in effect, but considerably different in approach is the Square of Saturn Spell. This is a *talisman* as opposed to an *amulet*. It makes use of a Cabalistic magic square similar in kind to your square of Mercury, but entirely different in composition. Actually, the powers of Saturn and Mercury are radically opposite in nature, Mercury being the airy sky principle of intellectual matters, Saturn, the earthy and chthonic principle of material things. The method of making your square of Saturn is thus: Choose a Saturday on or just after the new moon, and at either 8 A.M., 3 P.M., or 10 P.M., kindle a Tellurian Incense in your thurible, and place salt water in your chalice. Exorcise a piece of talisman paper by fire and water, and with your pen and ink of art, divide the paper up into nine compartments.

Now, slowly and deliberately fill in the squares with the appropriate numbers, beginning with number 1 and ending at 9. With each number, as in your square of Mercury variety,

The Square of Saturn

```
4 9 2
3 5 7
8 1 6
```

concentrate on Hertha's image and chant a phrase which suggests the Earth power to you. This can, again, be composed of a list of the goddesses' names such as "Rhea, Ceres, Hulda, Vesta" or simply "Hertha, bless this house and all who live in it," or even a stanza from a poem which evokes the feeling of safety, protection, or prosperity, such as the Hertha invocation already mentioned or any other verse you care to choose. It need not be directly connected with the home. If it is, so much the better.

When you have completed square 9, turn the paper over and draw a very simple plan or sketch of your house, surrounding it with three concentric circles, drawn clockwise and beginning with the outermost. Repeat your jingle with each circle.

This pictorially represents the magical security of your home. Cense and seal with the triple cross and "So mote it be!" and fold the paper into a packet, tying it firmly with red ribbon, knotted thrice. As with your egg, conceal it immediately in a consecrated place in Hertha's name, making it part of the structure of your home.

These two devices, the egg and square of Saturn, should suffice to cover any everyday contingencies such as occasional bursts of hostile vibrations set up by family rows over the dinner table, or those set humming by casual "overlooking" of the envious next-door neighbor or visiting friends (probably totally unconsciously on their part).

However, being great magpies and pickers-up of unconsidered trifles, many witches like to reinforce the protective earth currents by hanging other devices such as holystones and sachets of protective magical herbs at strategic points around the house: the hearth, threshold, over windows and doors, in attics, cellars, and, of course, over the beds. Witch balls, horseshoes, keys, and other iron objects are also looked on with great favor; iron implements such as the latter are, however, stronger stuff, partaking more of the nature of items of defense rather than beneficence. Similarly, the irreplaceable pentacle, used as a door symbol, also comes under this defense heading. But more of these later.

The English holystone itself bears ample witness to its country of origin's preoccupation with the art of pun making, even at an early age. The amulets themselves are in fact simply stones with holes in them. But (and this is the important part), in order to be effective amulets, they must first have been formed by natural process, that is, the erosion of wind and water; and second, they should also be found by the user rather than bought. Certain flints are often best for this; these are quite common in some types of terrain, and can often be sought for on ploughed fields or pebbly beaches. On discovering a holystone, you must pick it up, declaring as you do, that your action is being performed "in Hertha's name." The stones should be hung or placed as near your hearth as possible. Failing that, if you live in an apartment and neither possess a hearth nor, in spite of your burgeoning witchly image, feel inclined to have one installed, simply hang them in the room you happen to spend most of your time in—den, kitchen, maybe even bedroom.

As in the case of the egg, don't pass the holystone through fire and water; no purification or charging is necessary. It is an amulet, not a talisman, and is used *au naturel,* straight out of the Earth.

Magical herbs of beneficence will be dealt with at the end of this chapter, so I will now move on to discuss the witch ball. This amulet can take two forms. The more fanciful, and less traditional, is that of a hollow glass globe about the size of a medicine ball, silvered on the inside and resembling nothing more than a giant Christmas tree ornament. The rationale behind its use is similar to that of a fascination gem. It is generally hung centrally from the ceiling of the room in which you spend most time or, alternatively, in the front hall, "guarding" the main entrance to your home. You can often find such witch balls in antique shops, as at one time they became very popular among wealthy nonwitches, providing as they do handsome ornaments with which to replace the inevitable chandelier.

However, the second variety of witch ball is the truly traditional one. This is simply a fisherman's hollow glass net-float. As this is again an amulet, not a talisman, it should be the real thing. It receives its "consecration," or magical charge, during its actual use in fishing. These floats are usually made of green bottle-glass, and again, may sometimes be discovered in junk or antique shops if you are persistent in your search. They should also be hung up "in Hertha's name."

Before leaving this general magical protection section, I should mention briefly a few of the more popular portable amulets which may be worn by the budding practitioner. Most witches usually collect a formidable arsenal of these over the years, wearing them singly or in various combinations as the mood strikes them. The witch pendant and ring will generally serve as your main protective devices, talismanic in this case, but you may combine their effects with those of the following amulets if you so wish. Personally, I feel it unwise to pile amulet on amulet indiscriminately as many do, certainly without trying them singly first. That imposing figure of a witch hardly able to maneuver under the weight of a hundred different amulets, witch jewels, and symbolic knickknacks is nowadays an all too common sight in occult circles, I'm afraid. At the best it seems to betoken a certain lack of faith in one's own sustaining witch power, somewhat giving the game away to those that have eyes to see!

Even as a beginner, you should try to restrict yourself to carrying not more than one amulet at a time (excluding your witch jewel). This will allow you to experiment with its effectiveness. As your powers develop, you should learn to rely less and less on portable "batteries" of this sort, however. Finally, you will be able to discard all such artificial aids, relying completely on your aura of witch power to ward off any bad vibration or hostile current.

Portable Amulets

The *cross-stone,* also known as staurotides, is, in fact, a crystal of ferrous aluminum silicate or staurolite, which occurs naturally in orthorhombic form (a crystal possessing three planes set at right angles to each other). In fact, the crystal is formed in the shape of a three-dimensional Greek cross or solid cross of nature; symbolically, this indicates the seven mystical dimensions of space, namely north, south, east, west, the abyss above, the abyss below, and the holy center. Herein lie the seeds to the complex Cabalistic Ararita formula. The amulet should be suspended in a red cloth bag tied with red thread from the neck of the bearer, again laying him "under the spell of Hertha's protection."

Also considered a potent earthly amulet is the image of *the hand* making the phallic "sign of the fig," fist clenched, thumb thrust between first and second fingers, carved in nephrite (jade), amber, coral, jet, carnelian, or any other fascination gem, again suspended in red from the bearer's neck in Hertha's name; an old iron key will also serve the same purpose, being similar in its sexual implications.

Elf-shot, ancient flint or stone arrowheads, of pre-Celtic "Pictish" origin, have always been considered highly potent by witches in matters of protection, the manner of employment being no different from the preceding items.

Last, but by no means least, there is the famous *siderite.* This is a stone made of magnetic iron oxide, otherwise known as lodestone or magnetite. From time immemorial siderites have been treasured by witches, and if you were to try to choose between wearing one of these as opposed to one of the preceding four, I would counsel you definitely to decide on the siderite. Though slightly more complicated to manufacture and maintain, many witches find it well worth the effort.

By the light of the full moon (the window must be open if you perform this ritual indoors), place the lodestone on a piece of talisman paper which in turn covers your workbook. Now consecrate it with as many drops of Sabbat oil (see Chapter 7) as there are years in the prospective bearer's life, plus one extra dab for the present year, chanting the following quaint formula with each touch:

"May Hertha bless thee [N] with all her might and main."

See the drops of oil glow as they touch the stone, infusing it with witch power. Then tie the stone *loosely* in a red flannel or chamois leather bag bound with red ribbon with the sealing words "So mote it be." I say "loosely" because every full moon the bearer is going to have to remove the siderite, and after dipping it in a glass of water and drying it, sprinkle on it a small pinch of iron pyrites dust or iron filings "in Hertha's name." This is known as "feeding the stone." The siderite must be worn around the neck or carried about in the pocket.

In the past, male practitioners would often carry this amulet about with them suspended close to the genital organs, traditionally this being said to increase the sexual vigor and potency of the bearer. In this instance, the Horned One was involved in conjunction with Hertha in the initial consecration. However, in these days when a large family seems more an encumbrance to be guarded against than encouraged, this doesn't seem quite so popular a device as it once did.

Finally, before I embark upon detailing methods of magical defense as opposed to countermagic generally, we should mention that all-important subject of *familiars*.

The Witch's Familiar

As a practicing witch, you realize you are going to have to possess a familiar. Don't get alarmed, though. This does not mean you will necessarily have to saddle yourself with a pet such as a dog or cat if you don't want one for whatever reason. There are several different types of familiars, or *magistelli*, to give them their more correct title. *Magistellus* is Latin for "little master," and the word is often used by witches strangely enough to designate one of their small, magical servants. The term "familiar" is one coined by the ecclesiastical authorities during the persecutions, implying merely an intimate friend or servant.

Basically, there are three types of *magistellus*. There is that which is used as the coven "totem" animal, mentioned earlier in connection with the symbolism of the witch bracelet. This symbolic animal form is decided upon at the formation of a coven by mutual agreement among the members and after much introspection and divination. The chosen totemic animal form or forms, for there may be several, is then ritually "assumed" by coven members during the chain dance at the Sabbat itself, and also should they at any time wish to indulge in the practice of "sending forth the fetch," commonly known as astral projection.

Omens and auguries of coming events may also be drawn by the seasoned practitioner from the appearance on the scene of one such specimen of a coven totem, a gray bird maybe or a large black cat. Part of this witchlore may have filtered out in the past and now be responsible for the common public beliefs about lucky or unlucky black cats crossing one's path, and so on.

The second type of *magistellus* in a witch's repertoire is simply the aforementioned pet animal with whom one enters into an emotional rapport. Should the animal be of the same species as one of the coven totems, then of course it takes on an added witchly significance. If you own a pet, you may wish to make use of it as a power object. By charging it with a curse or blessing, as the case may be, specifically directed at someone, that person on coming into contact with the animal will discharge the spell and receive the full impact. Be wary of your witch friends' cats or dogs—be sure you are wearing an amulet of some sort before you cozy up to them!

The third, and to the individual witch, most important type of *magistellus* is that of the *magical servant* such as mentioned earlier in Chapter 1. This may be a demonic entity such as Vassago, who has been "bound" to some magical instrument such as a show stone or mirror, permanently or temporarily. It may also be an elemental creature formed by the combination of your witch power and some natural phenomenon. This type of *magistellus* becomes the protective spirit or Watcher, a magical guardian for the home. They take time to formulate, but really can prove to be of tremendous value. For unlike the general Earth spells which are effective to guard your home from general bad vibrations, to guard against out-and-out magical attack, a *magistellus* is ideal; it possesses a definite will of its own, the entire aim of which is to protect the house and those that dwell in it from all offensive sorcery. As such, it is really a magical type of vigilant robot, programmed solely to watch over the safety of the home. A sorcerer's watchdog, in fact. Two simpler types of *magistelli* of the elemental variety you should be conversant with are made from plants.

The Mandragore and the Alraun

Traditionally, you should seek for a mandrake (to give it its English name) of the opposite sex to your own. This isn't entirely necessary, however, the main concern being that when you find one, you *carve* it to represent the sex opposite to your own.

There are two genera of plants which traditionally go by the name of mandragore: The *Mandragora officinalis* which belongs to the class of Solanaceae, and the English mandrake, white bryony, or *Bryonia dioica,* belonging to the class Cucurbitaceae. Solanaceae is the family which includes such plants as the tomato and potato, while the Cucurbitaceae include the cucumber and the gourd. Also among the Solanaceae are included such old-time favorite witch poisons as dwale (deadly nightshade), enchanters' nightshade, and the devil's-apple, or *Datura stramonium*. The latter is better known in the United States as Jimson weed. Mandragores may be made from the roots of all these, but great care should be taken as they all can be *extremely poisonous*. The English mandrake (white bryony) is preferable for this reason, and just as traditional.

Here is the method of preparation:

On a day when the moon is waxing, preferably just after the

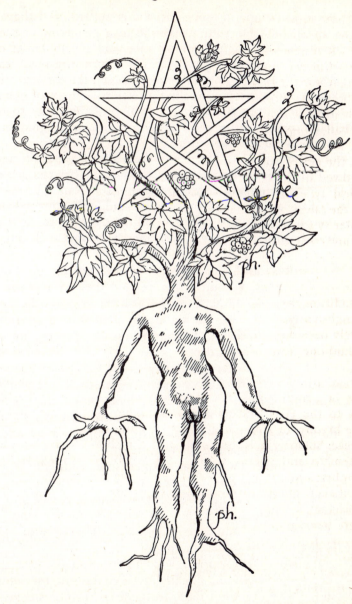

The mandragore

new moon, sometime between the winter solstice and the vernal equinox, look for your mandrake in a hedgerow or piece of wasteland. That night, making sure you are not observed, draw a deosil circle with your Athamé around the plant and, using the knife as a digging implement, loosen the earth around the root. Without injuring the main section of the root, gently draw the plant from the soil. You will probably have to tug quite hard, and you may even hear the traditional "groaning" of the root as it leaves the earth.

You must now trim the foliage of the plant off the main stem, leaving a small piece of root adhering to it. This you should replant where you took the original mandrake from. The major portion of the root you must take home and, with your Athamé blade, carve on it the features of a doll the opposite sex to your own. While you carve, repeat over and over some such phrase as: "Guard this home in Hertha's name."

The carving should take the form of an accenting of salient features of the root. You must then replant the root in either a churchyard or a place where two paths meet or cross. This ensures maximum potency. Failing either of these two locations, any patch of soil convenient to you will do. Prior to replanting, you should again draw a deosil circle in the soil. Now for the next lunar month, twenty-eight days from when you initially uprooted it, you must water the plant regularly. Some witches use a mixture of distilled water and blood, others that of distilled water and milk. In either case the distilled water should predominate over the other liquid in a proportion of about twelve parts to one, making thirteen in all.

When the lunar month has elapsed and midnight is approaching, draw your circle around the spot where the root is buried and dig it up again with your Athamé. You will find, if you are lucky, that most of the carving scars will have healed over with new bark, and your mandrake will appear to have actually grown in the shape of a mannikin.

To complete your operation, you should clean the root and either dry it thoroughly in a heated oven containing the smoke of vervain leaves or pass it daily through an incense smoke of vervain burned in your thurible. The latter method takes about three months to complete since the root dries very slowly.

If you can't obtain vervain (*Verbena officinalis*), the lemon-scented variety of garden verbena works just as well.

When all is accomplished, keep the *magistellus* in a place as close to your hearth as possible or in the room you use most.

The other type of *magistellus* I propose to discuss is the alraun.

To make one of these, the purpose of which is identical to that of the mandragore, you must first find a witch tree or quickbeam. In Europe this is known as a rowan or mountain ash. Witch lore holds its wood to be most powerful in matters of countermagic, and it is traditionally the wood from which the stake for dispatching vampires was made. The world tree of Teutonic legend, Yggdrasil, is considered by some authorities to have been the rowan, which ties in with the Cabalistic notion of its being the original tree of life.

Traditionally, the alraun was a device used by warlocks rather than witches. The time of year for its composition differs in no way from the mandragore. You must first seek out your rowan tree, and on the night of the waxing moon, draw a circle around it deosil with your Athamé, declaring your intention to compose an alraun in Hertha's name. Having done this, water the tree for a full lunar month with the same mixture as used for the mandragore, mentally selecting a reasonably thick branch for carving and declaring your intent each time you do it. At the end of the month, you must sever the selected branch with your Athamé, and carve it into a small female image, anything between five to twelve inches long, using a similar spoken charm as the mandragore one while you work away at it. When you are finished, cure the image in vervain smoke. Now to complete the operation, you must sleep with the alraun in your bed at the full moon, looking to it for that night, as the old books put it delicately, "as your wife." Enough said.

Like the mandragore, the alraun should be enshrined near the hearth to complete the spell and initiate its protective activity.

Magical Defense

As a newcomer to the field, you will need to get to know some of the signs which can prove to be sure indicators that some form of definite occult attack is in operation against you.

Apart from unpleasant vibrations and general miasmas of hostility or fear, the symptoms of a magical attack can range from extremely severe, recurrent nightmares, through runs of unbelievably bad luck, psychosomatic disturbances and allergies, often accompanied by poltergeist manifestations, to outright cases of lunacy or even sudden death. In the case of the latter, even countermagic won't avail you much.

Of course, all of these things, bar the poltergeist phenomena, can, and in the case of the nonwitch, generally do have a definitely nonoccult basis. As such, it is always best to consult a regular doctor or psychiatrist before automatically assuming any form of magical attack. But should you actually have been *informed* in one way or another that you are being made the target of a sorcerous onslaught (and this is quite likely to be the case if you recall what was said in Chapter 1 about laying the groundwork for an attack), then you won't have too much trouble figuring out where the mischief stems from when any of the aforesaid symptoms begin to manifest themselves.

If you are a practicing witch, you must expect the occasional fracas from time to time. You may possibly even enjoy it—at least it gives you a chance to flex your magical muscles a bit.

The first really telltale signs are the periodical nightmares and general sense of evil in the air. The dreams will generally have a specific motif repeated ad nauseam with minor variations on the theme. As a witch, your first step will be to determine their nature, if possible, and what their period of occurrence is, if any. Usually, if they are in any way magically induced, they will correspond in some way to the phases of the moon, usually reaching their peak at new rather than full moon.

Generally speaking, the nightmares themselves won't be the magical attack but rather the cries of help to your conscious self from your deep mind, which is the real target for all the bolts of dark fire. Should the attack worsen, then of course the deep mind's pleas for attention will become more frenzied, and you may begin to discover you are experiencing waking dreams or hallucinations. These can take the form of many different types of sensory delusions ranging from the visual pink-elephant variety to aural and olfactory ones. The latter may take the form of disembodied voices, snatches of music, a high-pitched whine or tone (in the past referred to by occultists as the "astral bell") and imaginary odors of varying degrees of pungency, usually fetid in the case of an attack. In fact, all the signs of a "bad trip" without an occasioning drug or naturally occurring personality disorder. Should you be fortunate or unfortunate enough to also possess free-floating witch power of the type manifested by so-called materializing mediums, then you will also begin to be the target of such apparently malicious poltergeist phenomena as disappearing objects, mysterious breakages, inexplicable outbreaks of fire and the like. All the signs of a traditional haunting, in fact.

Persistent runs of misfortune are often taken to be signs of a well-lodged curse, but they are more often than not self-inflicted by the victim's own deep mind for some devious reason, as already mentioned in Chapter 2.

Of course, if you are solemnly informed by a malevolent rival that you are about to be magically strafed, and your bad luck promptly begins from that time onwards, then you would appear to be a fool to ignore the more obvious root cause, in favor of some nebulous theory concerning an obscure self-destruction wish. Actually, really skillful practitioners tend to divine their victim's psychological weak spots, and then play upon their fears, aiming their attack precisely at those deep-mind blind spots where there is already a built-in self-destruct mechanism ready to be triggered. The most deadly attack is the least suspected one.

The main thing to avoid in all occasions of suspected magical attack is abandoning one's judgment to overriding fear. The descent into paranoia is one of the main pitfalls for many otherwise very competent witches. Probably one of the best ways of guarding against this is to let one of your witch friends handle the situation for you, with the express instructions to exercise as much skepticism as possible. It is to this fellow-practitioner that you must turn also for the relevant divinations, for these are the first practical magical steps to be undertaken under the circumstances. To divine the *nature* and if possible the *source* of the hostility should be your purpose here. The pendulum, Vassago, and the rune sticks are possibly the best methods to employ. Tarot and the I Ching can also be used.

Generally, you will find a magical attack to be motivated by one of two factors: lust or hate. However, in these days of more readily available sexual gratification, the first factor has faded very much into abeyance, save in such barbarous institutions where chastity is still enjoined. Hate, on the other hand, is still with us, alas in no lesser degree than in the Middle Ages, judging by evidence presented in the various news media.

A would-be magical antagonist of more-advanced caliber will often indulge in the luxury of enjoying attack in person, so to speak, by formulating his witch power into a definite "shape," and then transferring his consciousness to it. The shape is then sent forth to accomplish the witch's will. The shape, fetch, or wraith is often animal in form, the type being dictated either by analogy with the ensouling emotion of the projector or, on occasions, being that of the coven totem.

This process of "sending forth the fetch" is identical to that of present-day practices of astral, or etheric, projection. The fetch itself may be perceived with the inner vision of the victim or, on very rare occasions, with his physical eyes should he or the antagonist be in any way a "materializing medium." This is the basis for the legends of the werewolf and the vampire. Both of these creatures represent the materialized witch power of the practitioner through which he acts using the shape as a vehicle for his own consciousness.

In cases of the legendary werewolf, the ensouling desires of the projector would be those of destructive rage, while in those of the equally famous vampire, incubus, and succubus, they would be lust.

The artificially produced fetch differs from the *magistellus* or Watcher only in that the witch transfers her consciousness to the former and not the latter, and that the first relies solely on witch power and the powers of the deep mind, while the latter usually involves the implications of some further exterior agency, whether of demonic or elemental nature.

Tradition has it that when a habitué of "sending forth the fetch" happens to die, the vampire or werewolf personality can live on as a self-perpetuating robot, a psychic fragment of the original owner, maintaining its existence by feeding upon the magnetism of the unsuspecting living while they sleep. This witch practice has given rise to that body of lore known as lycanthropy, complete with all its traditional methods of dis-

Countermagic and Protection

patching such creatures—wooden stakes, silver bullets, and the like. Should a projected witch fetch assume any degree of materialization, it can in many cases be as vulnerable as the sleeping body of the projector itself, often transferring any wounds inflicted upon it back to its parent body by means of the process of repercussion. Because of the difficulty in accomplishing the projection, and the perils involved subsequent to a materialization, sending forth the fetch is generally regarded as a work for the more advanced practitioner.

However, if you wish to study it more fully, the elementary rudiments of projection can be gleaned from any of the current books on astral projection that are in print at the present time.

When you are reasonably sure you are the victim of a recurrent magical attack (and they usually are repeated), aspirins and laxatives having availed you naught, you must at that point set about the task of working out an adequate system of defense, using your own countermagic to weather the storm and, if possible, turn back the thrust.

You can rest assured that night will be the time most favored for the attack, and if you have observed the rhythm of the occurrences, you will probably be able to gauge sufficiently when the next attempt is likely to be made. Now we arrive at another most important rule of witchcraft. In matters of occult warfare, *passive defense is the most effective type of retaliation.*

When a witch mounts a magical attack, if it happens to misfire or if the victim is in any way adequately protected, as they say in the craft—"An the witch bide the issue!"—the home of lost curses is right back where they came from, the sender herself. So if you can arrange to be ritually well-defended at the time that the dark spell is being cast, the spellbinders will, in fact, be conjuring to their own destruction. Advanced practitioners try to avoid the recoil by enveigling other, less-advanced members of their coven only too glad to try their hand at a bit of cursing, to do the actual dirty work for them: a well-known expedient in all fields! Regardless of any feelings of compassion for who actually "bides the issue," however, you should proceed with all your means of defense as surely as you would board up your house if it stood in the path of a hurricane.

The magical attack will usually begin any time after sundown, so you should have your preparations ready well before.

Consult an astrological ephemeris, nautical almanac, or your local newspaper for the exact time the sun actually sinks below the horizon.

Your main defenses are going to be the grand magical circle and the pentacle of protection. You will also employ the magical power of iron and protective herbs extensively, plus one or two other little devices; all your Earth amulets and *magistelli* will, of course, be working overtime.

First, you must see that the victim or victims all bear upon their breasts the pentacle of protection. Here is the manner of its construction:

The Pentacle of Protection

On a Tuesday or Saturday midnight, with the moon waxing, cast and purify your regular circle, using an incense of either pure dragon's-blood resin or one compounded of one part church incense, one part lignum aloes, one part powdered alum, and five drops of cedarwood oil. Then take some of your talisman paper, and from it cut three four-inch squares. Exorcise these with fire and water.

Then, with your pen and ink of art, draw the following five-pointed star on the first of them. (See illustration.) You will see that it is a more complex version of the one in your workbook and is sometimes called the pentagram of Solomon. Having drawn the figure as carefully as you can—it will probably be easier if you rule it in lightly in pencil first, using a pair of compasses to construct the circle—proceed to fill in the magical symbols and words, starting at the top point, working around clockwise and finishing with the center. As you write each magical word, chant it deliberately out loud in combination with the following charm:

1. "Be ye far from us, all hostility, deceit, and illusion, in the name of *Abdia!*"
2. "Be ye far from us, all hostility, deceit, and illusion, in the name of *Ballater!*"

and so on.

When you have finished, repeat the process, this time using

Countermagic and Protection

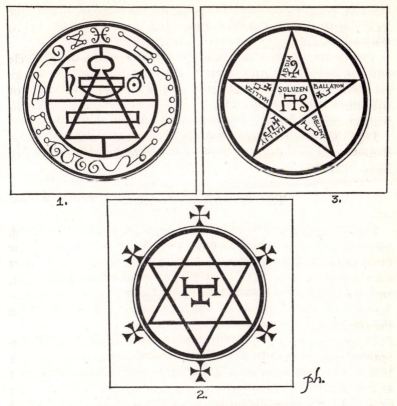

Pentacle of protection, comprising,
  1. The secret seal of Solomon
  2. The hexagram of Solomon
  3. The pentagram of Solomon

your Athamé to trace over the star and the symbols above the paper, in your witchly imagination seeing them burn in the air with spectral blue witch fire.

Now take your second piece of parchment and draw on it the six-pointed star, or hexagram of Solomon, as in the illustration, inscribing the T-shaped cross in the center last. This cross, referred to by witches of the last century as the triple tau of the arch Mosms, is a variant of your triple sealing cross. Combined with the hexagram and the six minor taus, it is regarded by witches as an extraordinarily powerful talisman of protection.

When the ink has dried, retrace the *inverted* triangle (▽) with salt water from your cup, chanting these words:

"So therefore he who would govern the works of fire must first asperge with lustral water of the loud resounding sea."

Then with the thurible, trace in the air above the star the upright triangle, chanting:

"And when after all the phantoms are banished, thou shalt perceive that holy formless fire, that fire which darts and flashes through the hidden depths of the universe: Hear thou the voice of fire!"

Finally, retrace the whole star yet again with the Athamé, this time in silence, visualizing the symbol glowing in blue light.

The design on the third piece of paper must be written with your pen of art in blood—your own or that of a beefsteak, chicken, or lamb chop from the supermarket again will do. You should wipe your pen of art carefully free of all ink before you embark upon this. This last design is known as the secret seal of Solomon and traditionally was the symbol by means of which the seventy-two lords of the demons or Djinn were imprisoned in a brazen vessel by the magus-king and sunk beneath the ocean. They were later released, providentially it seems, by certain Babylonian wizards. The legend probably stems from that of the drowned Nephelim.

When you have drawn the symbol and let it dry, retrace over it with your Athamé, charging it strongly with light and conjuring with these words:

> Bound, bound, bound be all demons and
> powers of adversity from the
> north, south, east, and west!
> Bound, bound, bound be all ill-wishers and those that
>   practice violence against the bearer of this!
> Bound, bound, bound shall be all;
> bound and sealed from N [witchname], son of M [parent]
>   and L [parent].
> Bound and held subject to his will.

Having completed all three designs, sandwich the last, the secret seal, between the pentagram and hexagram, which should be facing *outwards* with their stars visible. Then, with exorcised needle and red thread, sew neatly around the four edges to combine all three papers into a permanent packet. Over this you must then chant the following words as you hold it in the incense smoke, the tip of your Athamé blade pressed against it:

> O Pentacle of Power,
> be thou fortress and defense to
> [N] against all foes, visible and
> invisible, in every magical work!

While doing this, strongly visualize the blue fire passing down the Athamé blade to charge the pentacle.

Finally, complete the ritual by drawing the triple cross in the air with your Athamé, and the sealing with the words "So mote it be!"

A small wallet of chamois leather or red silk should now be made to contain the pentacle, which in turn should be sewn to a red cord or ribbon to be worn around the neck of the bearer. In this manner the pentacle can remain concealed. In certain demonic conjurations (similar to that of Vassago), the pentacle may then be removed and exhibited to the four quarters or to the gaze of the manifesting entity.

If you organize a coven, you will have to also prepare a round metal plate, pewter or copper or even aluminum, on which is simply engraved or painted a five-pointed star or pentagram; this is used in a similar way to an ecclesiastical "paten," and bread, cakes, or salt to be used during the Sabbat are placed on it. It is also confusingly referred to as the pentacle, but on this occasion refers more to the pentacle-disc or coin represented in the suit cards of the minor Tarot arcana. It is also a direct descendant from the Lia Fál of pre-Celtic lore, but has picked up Cabalistic overtones through the ages, still in tune with its earthy symbolism, however.

Cabalistically, it refers to the final "Heh," last letter of the Tetragrammaton, the supreme Cabalistic word of power. Some witches inscribe the letter ה in the center of the star. In any case, it must be prepared by water and fire in Hertha's name.

To return to our beleagured witch group, however. Having hung your talismanic pentacles about your neck, you should proceed to draw around yourself the grand magical circle. In principle this is identical with the regular variety, save for the fact that it utilizes certain invocations as well as the usual line of blue light.

Before casting your circle, make sure you have with you all and any amulets you require during your vigil, including your *magistellus*. Though during coven practice the circle can be left and reentered without impairing its efficiency, when used as a means of magical defense, this is quite out of the question, serving as it does a completely different function, namely, that of keeping hostile currents *out* rather than acting as a lens to focus power *within*. So decide carefully on what you will need. Articles of extra clothing, pillows, cigarettes, food, and water are also to be considered. Make sure that everything is not only clean, but exorcised with fire and water before you introduce it.

Mark out your circle with masking tape as usual, and draw your triple circle of light with the Athamé. Then exorcise the ground as usual with water and fire, using a Tellurian Incense in your thurible. Now, in addition to demagnetizing the ground within the circle, you are going to employ a magical guard at the four quarters. This magical guard, or watch, passed into Christian practice through the ages, being transformed into that night spell known as the Black Pater Noster:

> Four nooks in this house for holy angels,
> a post in the midst, that's Christ Jesus,
> Lucas, Marcus, Matthew, Johannes,
> God be in this house, and all that belongs us.

Or as the God-fearing Victorian child knew it:

> Matthew, Mark, Luke and John,
> bless this bed that I lie on!

The archangels and evangelists here represent the Christianized regents of the four elements of the wise: Michael and Mark of fire; Raphael and John, air; Gabriel and Matthew, water; and last, Uriel and Luke, earth.

However, you as a witch will bypass these later accretions and return to the old-style symbolism, namely, that of the four watchtowers of the world. Some occultists trace their use solely back to the nineteenth-century Rosicrucianism of the Hermetic Order of the Golden Dawn, others to the experiments of the Elizabethan magus Dr. John Dee. To a witch, however, they are a direct representation of the four "castles" of pre-Celtic lore, which are said to stand at the four corners of the world. Each castle or watchtower is referred to one of the elements, that of the east to air and childhood; south to fire and youth; west to water and maturity; and north to earth and old age.

Witches sometimes refer to the north as the "abode of death," and the watchtower of the north is sometimes known as the "glass castle." Glass is here symbolically analogous with unbreakable adamant, and this "Land behind the North Wind" refers to that vast abyss of death through which we all must pass before being reborn into the world of men again. It is also, of course, a direct reference to the vitrified towers of the elves. Your magical implements, or "weapons," may be assigned to the various watchtowers, but here opinion differs considerably as to their correct assignation. Many witches tend to use the Cabalistic identification of the rod to fire, sword to air, pentacle to earth, cup to water. The cup seems to be about the one implement about which no one is in any doubt. More traditional, perhaps, is the concept of the sword of fire, rod of air (sometimes an airborne arrow or spear), cup or cauldron of water and pentacle, plate or shield of earth. These are directly analogous with the four magical treasures of pre-Celtic lore mentioned earlier; In later Celtic myth they became known as the Sword of Nuada, Spear of Lugh, Cauldron of Ceridwen, and the Stone of Fál. (The latter, incidentally, is said to be none other than the Stone of Scone which at present reposes under King Edward's throne in Westminster Abbey.)

The way to invoke the Lords, or dominant entities, of the four watchtowers is thus:

Place one of your lamps of art at the east just outside the circle boundary and light it; then taking your wand in both hands, raise it high above your head, close your eyes and slowly and powerfully chant an invocation to the powers of the air such as the following:

> All-wise Eagle, Great Ruler of Tempest,
> Storm, and Whirlwind, Master of the Heavenly
> Vault, Great Prince of the Powers of the Air,
> be present we pray thee and guard this circle
> from all perils approaching from the East!

As you do this, strongly imagine a wind from the east begin to blow on your face, steadily increasing as you repeat the spell. Similarly, through your closed eyelids be aware of a light from the east beginning to shine in your face. Be aware of the rising of the wind, and hear the sound of the creaking of the branches of the world tree, that tree of knowledge upon which the Lord of Wisdom hung for nine stormy nights; hear the beating of those mighty wings! All those present with you in the circle, should they be witches, must also maintain the same visualization as you chant. Relinquish the wand, and move clockwise to the south now, lighting a lamp of art there. Take your Athamé in hand and raise it high above your head. As you do, visualize the sun above your head, blazing with midsummer intensity. Suddenly, from the burning orb, a "fiery sword," a searing bolt of lightning cleaves the baking air, forking toward the south side of your circle, answering the summons of your uplifted witch blade.

See a pillar of incandescent fire spring up at the circle rim! Hear the thunderclap crash in your ears as you cry the words of summoning to the Fiery One! Feel the heat radiating from him as he takes up his watch in the south.

> O thou Lion, Lord of Lightnings, Master of
> the Solar Orb, Great Prince of the powers of Fire!
> Be present, we pray thee, and guard this circle
> from all perils approaching from the south!

Again all present should accompany you in your visualization.

The powers of the west should be invoked by the chalice, here representing the elemental power of water.

Sprinkle a few drops of salt water from the chalice to the west and, as you do, see a mighty, glass-green sea open beneath your feet. Low over the waters hangs the full moon. Feel the cold mist rising from the waters and listen to the eddy and swirl of the currents, the lap of waves upon the shore.

> O thou Serpent of Old, Ruler of the Deeps,
> Guardian of the Bitter Sea, Prince of the
> Powers of Water, be present we pray thee and
> guard this circle from all perils approaching
> from the west!

Finally, passing to the north, light the lamp, and taking in hand the pentacle-paten (not the pentacle of protection which you are wearing around your neck), close your eyes and sprinkle a few grains of salt from the disk on the ground outside the west of your circle. Chant the spell. As you do, feel the earth begin to tremble and rock beneath your feet, ever more powerfully, increasing in magnitude and finally thunderously splitting asunder, gaping open before you in a yawning chasm!

> Black Bull of the North, Horned One,
> Dark Ruler of Mountains and all that lies
> beneath them. Prince of the Powers of Earth,
> be present we pray thee, and guard this circle
> from all perils approaching from the north!

Finally, return to the center of the circle, and facing east, standing with your legs wide apart, extend your arms on either side of you and close your eyes; then chant the sealing words "So mote it be!" As you do, visualize a brilliant rotating wheel of fire within your own breast, throwing out spears of scintillating light in all six directions: to the north, south, east, west, up, and down. By visualizing thus, in this particular stance, with your arms and legs flung wide apart, you are representing the magical five-pointed star, or pentagram. This is a symbolic enactment of the fact that within you the four elemental powers are reconciled by one special principle, the so-called alchemical quintessence. This is the holy center, or "stillpoint of the wheel." The indestructible part of you. You may also at this point chant the Hebrew word of power, "Ararita!" *

---

* Which signifies: "The One; principle of His unity; The principle of His oneness; His changing form being One!"

Your last step in the ritual will be to place your mandragore or alraun just within the circle perimeter to the north, with its head pointing north, toward the place of greatest darkness.

You may then settle down for the night to weather the magical blast.

The worst type of attack you are likely to encounter will be quite adequately dealt with by this circle. It is unlikely that any more magical working will be required of you from within your psychic fortress, so you can safely sleep in peace, confident that your magic circle is ample defense.

The only practitioner who would in theory be able to pierce the defensive boundary is one of extremely advanced powers, and as such he would probably be well beyond the need of having to resort to anything as ill-advised as a magical attack on his own. A whole coven maybe. That is another matter. There seems to be folly as well as strength in numbers. From the non-human point of view, supernatural entities such as shades of the dead or demonic intelligences appear to have very little interest in the human race, especially the last-mentioned class of beings. They generally only become involved in magical warfare when summoned and directed specifically, and as such their power is limited strictly to correspond with that of their invoker. So the circle and watchtower formula will still prove effective. And finally even with the combined forces of a demonic entity *and* a whole coven working against you, the circle will still hold together in all probability, such is the sloppy and dilettante attitude to coven practice generally these days. As I say, it requires an extremely clever and powerful practitioner to break through the watchtower seals, and quite frankly one such as this will have long passed the stage where bouts of magical fisticuffs still hold any appeal.

The grand circle should only be used at the height of the attack. As you can see, it is physically very limiting and places you completely incommunicado from the outside world save for the use of a telephone, which incidentally should be on your list as one of the things to take with you into the circle. Should you step over one of the lines in the circle, it immediately releases the magical force field you have so painstakingly erected, and leaves you instantly susceptible once more. It is lucky that occult attacks usually take place at night for this very reason.

During the day, when you will quite naturally wish to be out and about, you may merely draw an imaginary circle of blue light about you deosil in the air with your Athamé and chant a few words of intention to the effect of:

> I [N] hereby surround myself with this
> circle of protection across which no hostile
> power dare set its foot.

This will generally remain effective for twelve hours or so, and then should be renewed. Should your adversary decide to actually visit you in person to deliver his curse, you must make sure that one of the following old traditional measures has been taken.

First, paint or draw pentagrams, pointing outwards, on your doorsteps; charge them with your Athamé and then cover them with the doormat. Then nail either horseshoes or horns upward over any entrance to your home.

Or hang an old knife or sword on the front and back door, surrounded by a wreath of bay leaves.

Or hammer three iron nails (traditionally "taken from a coffin") into each of the doors, two below, one above, in triangular formation.

Or beneath your doorsteps bury a witch bottle, a bottle stuffed full of bent nails and pins.

The use of iron is very important in matters of occult defense as you can see. It appears to have a definite "jamming" or "scrambling" effect on any magical signal when used with intention. It is partly for this reason that iron, and indeed any metal, is usually rigorously excluded from the dress of the candidate in magical initiation rituals where a definite transmission of power is required.

Should you know that either you or your enemy is particularly gifted as a materializing medium, you should also take the precaution of placing a small saucer of very dilute nitric acid or vinegar in every room at the time you expect the attack to take place. The acetic solution seems to have the power of absorbing alien witch power in some manner, and thus preventing unpleasant materializations or poltergeist phenomena. If you haven't the time or wherewithal to do this for some reason, an old standby is to halve some onions and place a newly cut half in every room; this appears to have a similar effect. Don't make the supreme mistake of eating the onions afterward, though. Get rid of them immediately!

Finally, should someone come to you with a suspected attack and be unable or unwilling to undergo the inconvenience of using these complex protective measures, a very simple and sometimes effective expedient is the *Rowan Cross Spell*.

Tie two small twigs of rowan wood together to form a cross, using red thread or yarn, chanting these words as you do, and mentally charging it with light:

> By this cross of rowan,
> I [N] forbid all adverse and hostile forces
> entry to the house and home of [bearer's name]
> I forbid you his flesh and blood, body and soul.
> I sternly forbid you entrance to his mind, fears,
> and strengths until you have traversed every
> hill and dale, struggled through every stream
> and river, counted every grain of sand on every
> shore, and enumerated every star within the
> night sky!

Then hang the cross around the bearer's neck with these words:

> About thy neck this cross I place,
> cross of quickbeam, cross of grace;
> may it safely guard thy way
> and keep thee safely night and day.
> Heed this charm, attend to me;
> as my word, so mote it be!

Finally, some information about traditionally protective magical herbs and recipes. Before beginning, however, here are a few general observations on plant lore that, as a witch, you should know about.

More and more witches are tending to grow their own herbs, protective and otherwise, these days. Apart from the pleasure one may derive from the pursuit, it does ensure that one can obtain the required ingredient in a pure form, and picked at the right phase of the moon. Should you wish to do this, even if it be merely in a planter or windowbox, you should try to observe the following conditions:

If you are planting an herb of which the end product will be the root, do this at the dark of the moon, when it is waning. On the other hand, those herbs you intend to use for their leaves or flowers should be planted during the waxing moon.

When you wish to pick your herbs, do this in the moon's quarter which corresponds to the type of magic you intend to use them for (see Chapter 1, under "Magical Times and Seasons"): bright for constructive witchcraft, dark for destructive.

Whenever you wish to compose a sachet powder or incense with whatever intent, you should plan on using something like the following routine; it is known as trituration.

First, assemble all your ingredients.

Sachet powders generally contain two types of these: the "agents" and the "base." The latter often contains an herb such as orris root, patchouli leaves, rose petals, or some pulverized wood base such as sandalwood, lignum aloes, cedarwood shavings, and the like. These should always be well-mixed and ground in your pestle and mortar, before adding the agents. The first of these are the flower essences or perfumes of the recipe. They should be ground well into a *portion* of the herb powder. Now any *gum resins* such as frankincense, myrrh, or benzoin should then be added to the remaining herbal mixture, and likewise powdered as finely as possible.

These two powders should now be mixed together, and the oils or other liquids added last (honey, wine, blood) and mixed in thoroughly. Should the oil be in very small quantity, it can be dissolved first in a small amount of pure alcohol which is then mixed in, thus providing a greater blending power.

The resulting compound should be allowed to steep at least overnight, and extra quantities of the base added if the result remain too liquid. Completed incense and powders should always be stored in well-stoppered, nonporous bottles, labeled distinctly, and protected from bright light at a moderate temperature.

Here are four examples of different types of compounds which you can make. They are all germane to this chapter, they are in fact herbal amulets of beneficence.

First, a herbal mixture which may be placed around the house in sachets or suitable containers, and is both fragrant and traditionally beneficent (it also incidentally makes an acceptable Halloween gift to bestow on those who appreciate such matters):

To a selection of dried protective herbs of your choice, add two quarts of rose petals. Place in a covered, nonporous container with one pound of table or ground rock salt to remove any excess moisture for three weeks or so. At the end of this time, sift the salt out of the mixture, and place on one side. Now take two ounces of powdered orris root, and grind in one ounce of gum benzoin and three ounces of brown sugar. Add this to your herbal mixture, and mingle freely.

Finally, take one ounce of pure alcohol (failing that, brandy will do) and mix in four drops of essential oil of your choice. Pour this onto your dry mixture, and mingle it well together. Leave overnight to steep.

Similarly, a home protection sachet can be prepared with the following ingredients:

Powdered orris root	8 parts
Pulverized sandalwood	6 parts
Powdered lavender flowers or leaves	4 parts
Powdered patchouli leaves	2 parts
Powdered cloves	1 part
Powdered pimento	$\frac{1}{2}$ part
A drop of musk or civet essence	

Tie it up as usual in white cloth with red yarn or ribbon, "in Hertha's name."

Finally, a *Tellurian Incense* for any of the Earth Spells referred to on the preceding pages:

Either

Dried powdered juniper wood	3 parts

Or

Cypress raspings or leaves	
Gum myrrh or tincture of myrrh	2 parts
Powdered orris root	$\frac{1}{2}$ part

Countermagic and Protection

Powdered patchouli leaves (or a few drops, patchouli oil)	1 part
Powdered sage	1 part

Reduce finely by trituration. Should you wish to make incense cones instead of loose grains, add ¼ part saltpeter and enough patchouli or myrrh oil to make a thick paste. Model the cones by hand and let them stand to dry.

Before you embark on any complex operation of witchcraft, such as demonic conjuration or necromancy, purists will always advise that you take the purificatory bath beforehand. In all cases of bewitchment, this is also to be advised, especially before entering the grand circle, or before going to bed in the evening. The composition of these baths varies a great deal, but an excellent one can be made thus:

Dried rosemary	7 parts
Dried lavender	7 parts
Dried basil	4½ parts
Dried vervain or lemon verbena	2 parts
Dried hyssop	1 part
Dried valerian	1 part
Dried sage	½ part
Dried fennel	½ part

To these herbs, add half again as much cooking or table salt. When you wish to bathe, after tying up a handful of your mixture in a small muslin or cheesecloth bag, cast it into the water chanting such words as you use for your water consecrations, or the following:

> So therefore he who would govern the works of fire must first asperge with water of the loud, resounding sea.

Failing this combination of herbs, you may use either hyssop and salt or sweet balm and salt to almost equal effect. Finally, here is a list of other magical protective herbs to be used either singly or in combination in your rituals and sachets:

Holda (elderberry) (berries or flowers to be gathered at midsummer)

Madwort (alyssum)
Marjoram
Dragon herb (tarragon)
Angelica
Fennel
Bay laurel
Asafetida grass
Holy thistle herb (replace after seven days)
Bishop's-wort (betony)
Garlic flowers
All-heal (mistletoe) (May be carved into ring or bracelet)
Dog roses
Arum lilies
Benet, holy herb, or avens (*geum urbanum*)
Lucky-hands (unexpanded fronds of male fern—*Dryopteris filix mas*—dry over Sabbat fire)

And last, but by no means least, those most powerful of all herbs which from time immemorial have been held potent against sorcery of all varieties:

> Trefoil, vervain, St.-John's-wort, dill,
> Hinder witches of their will!

(Trefoil is simply a three-leafed plant of any type, such as clover.)

Should you wish to soothe the fears of those who suspect bewitchment, it should be comparatively easy for you to concoct a protective potion from edible herbs, such as by steeping a little powdered angelica, marjoram, bay, and fennel seed in some hot wine, chanting a few suitable words of benediction and reassurance, charging it strongly with your witch power.

On the other hand, should you suspect bewitchment by means of a power object or philter, you can resort to the following technique:

If you have a sample of the bewitched substance or the wax doll itself, your task is made comparatively simple. If not, you will have to content yourself with a sample of the blood, hair, urine, or saliva of the actual *victim*. Failing even that, you will just have to rely on the strength of your pyramid powers alone. With the moon waxing, cast your circle and bind or anoint with your samples (if you have any) two twigs of broom plant tied together crosswise. Then, on a piece of your talisman paper, draw with your pen and ink of art a simple image of the person you think has bewitched you, and on the breast write his name. Name the figure with fire and water (as in your Vassago ritual, using your Athamé to write the suspect's name in the air above the image). If you don't have any idea of who was responsible, just name the drawing "He who has wished me ill." Then burn both the cross and the paper in your thurible with these words:

> Three blows hast thou dealt;
> by evil heart, evil eye, and evil tongue.
> These same three blows be thine own reward!
> by fire and water, earth and air,
> and that which binds and governs them
> I charge thee, touch him not!

With the last words, draw a pentagram above the flame with your Athamé blade, and stab the center with your blade, charging the star with magical light. This is known as banishing.

If the means of bewitchment is that of a power object such as a voodoo doll, conveyed into the presence of the victim, then simply remove the pins, if there should be any, and exorcise the image with fire and water. Obliterate the name of the victim inscribed on it if there is one, and rewrite that of the attacker instead. The doll will be impregnated with the maker's magnetism, so it in turn makes an excellent object link with him! Name it thrice with his name, asperging and fumigating it as you do so; then recite your countercharm:

"Three blows hast thou dealt by evil heart, evil eye, and evil tongue; these same three blows be thine own reward, etc."

Again banish with the pentagram. If it is a clay image, finish by breaking it in little pieces, crushing the pieces up into dust and flushing the dust down the toilet or burying it in the earth. If it is wax or cloth, simply incinerate it, and again flush the residue away or bury it deep in the earth. Should the imagined aggressor indeed have tried to cast the spell, the countercharm will cause it to rebound with unerring accuracy, inflicting upon him those things he wished upon his victim, but only to the extent that he himself would have been able to initiate. If his curse would have been ineffective to begin with, then it will be ineffective in the rebound.

Finally, should you be confronted by a really bad case of haunting caused by bewitchment, asperge and fumigate the four corners of your home with one of the following incenses, using your usual exorcism formula of fire and water, and opening all doors and windows beforehand. This has a practical as well as a symbolic meaning, as you will see when you try the fumigations for yourself!

Exorcism Fumigations

1. Calamint
   Peony
   Mint
   Palma Christi

2. Simple gum asafetida

3. Juniper
   Rosemary
   Hemlock (plant, *not* tree, very poisonous)
   Sloe
   Frankincense or pine resin
   Dried garlic

4. Myrrh
   Frankincense
   Hellebore
   St.-John's-wort
   Sulphur

5. Myrrh
   Sulphur
   Red sandalwood
   Rotten apples
   Wine galls
   Vinegar
   Red wine lees
   Arsenic

Countermagic and Protection

The last three incenses are somewhat poisonous as you can see from their composition, and great care should be taken with them. Personally, I would advocate the use of one of the first two mentioned, but the last three are traditional, and as such you should definitely know about them even if you don't actually put them to service.

CHAPTER 6

Vengeance and Attack

As you will have gathered from the last chapter, the art of magical warfare is not one to be undertaken lightly, if only for the reason that should the bolt misfire, it will inevitably rebound on the sender. Having accepted this possibility, however, many witches put the discomforting idea totally out of their minds, and proceed merrily on their nefarious ways without giving it another thought. Should you also be of that light-hearted frame of mind, then you will obviously want to learn some of those time-honored methods of speeding effective curses on their way.

True to the general principles of witchcraft, the means used for effecting destructive ends is exactly the same as those used for constructive purposes. The only difference lies in the magical intent and symbolism involved. The medium for the transmission of power remains exactly the same of course, namely, the deep minds of both parties concerned.

The type of power to be raised for these operations of wrath and chastisement can take two forms: a binding, inhibitory power for inducing inertia or "tying someone's hands"—this pertains to Saturn; and a scorching, blasting power for blighting and burning (which is what people generally mean by a curse)—this pertains to Mars.

Those spells of a Saturnian nature make use of the same symbolism you have already encountered in the last chapter, namely that of Hertha, the Great Mother, seen in her negative aspect as the dark, terrible, Stony Bringer of Inertia, and Dame Habondia in her aspect of Noticula-Hecate, Lady of Night and Death.

The Mars Spells, however, introduce you to the fourth and final witch entity: He partakes of the nature of the last remaining magical element to be covered in this book, namely, fire.

You have, of necessity, already encountered this being in two places already, although without too much contact. He is none other than Cernunnos, the Horned One. The first instance being your manufacture of the Athamé with all its implied Martial symbolism, the second the section on sex magic. He is a spirit of fire and energy, as symbolized by the torch he sometimes carries in his hand and the horns or antlers he wears upon his head. A light-bearer also, hence his title, Lucifer. In view of this, he is often represented carrying a blazing torch or candle on his head, which has sprung from between his antlers, in addition to the one he carries in his hand.

He is known by a variety of names to witches in addition to that of Lucifer: Cernunnos, Mamilion, Robin, Dumus, Hu, Janus or Dianus, Barabbon or Barabbas among others. His symbolism is partly akin to that of Thunor, the Norse Thunder God of Battle, and again of Pan and Dionysus, the classical gods of ecstatic debauch and revelry. In his alignment with fire, he evokes memories of Vulcan (Hephaestus) and Wayland Smith. As Vulcan is the suitor of Venus and Pan of Diana, so is the Horned One the pursuer of Habondia.

However, many witches who belong to female-oriented covens which focus their attentions more on the goddess than the god argue that the boot is actually on the other foot. Their contention is that it was, and is, the goddess who took the initiative in the chase. Examples ranging from the Gospel of Aradia to the legend of Actaeon are cited as chapter and verse here.

Cursing

Before embarking upon the ceremonial side of cursing, let us reconsider the more general aspects of overlooking, seen solely from the point of view of your pyramid power. As already mentioned, spells will always work better when the ground is well laid beforehand, and this is particularly true in the instance of curses. The person who knows he has been laid under a curse, whether he believes in the practitioner's powers or not, is actually in a far more receptive state of mind than he who remains in ignorance of the fact. It is for this reason that the *conveyed* voodoo doll comes in so handy, providing, of course, the spellbinder is quite sure there is no chance of its being used for any countermagic against her. This eventuality can only be said to be completely out of the question when it is definitely known for a fact that the victim will either be too frightened to reply with countermagic or, as is more often the case, if he is the type of person who feigns total disbelief in witchcraft, deeming it all medieval nonsense. *The latter is the readiest victim for your doll technique!* You will know he can never condescend to indulge in any countermagic, and give full play to his superstitions. Of course, it is remotely possible that, due to his run of unbelievably bad luck, loss of wife, estate, and possibly all his hair, he may decide to review his past attitudes towards medieval superstitions; at that point he may take the step of consulting either a known witch or coven or, alternatively, a sharp lawyer who specializes in cases of psychological intimidation. Then lazily sticking pins in dolls won't be enough. You will really have to use your wits; the battle will have just begun.

If you have the taste for actual physical confrontation, then the personally delivered verbal curse is really the most handy way of accomplishing the "act of information." Try to make sure you get your victim alone for this, though, of course, in some cases, particularly those of an impromptu nature, this won't always be possible.

Again, as in any act of fascination or close-quarter projection of your witch power, three types of contact may be employed—eye, hand, or breath. Owing to the nature of the operation, however, it is usually the first method which is mainly relied upon, hence the old term, the evil eye. As in love magic, you must first catch the glance of your victim and then hold it. This may prove harder than you think, particularly if your victim is aware of your reputation as a witch. You may have to accomplish it by saying something to the effect of "I never trust a person who won't look me directly in the eye" or even, as a last resort, "Have you ever noticed how one of my eyes is a different color from the other?"

Vengeance and Attack

For delivering your curse, make use of the hand-of-power gesture—left arm outstretched, fist clenched, first two fingers pointed at victim. It definitely has dramatic appeal, especially when combined with a certain Druidic method of projecting your witch power. This involves standing solely on the *alternate* foot (the right) to the pointing hand, closing the alternate eye (also the right), glaring down the length of your outstretched arm with the open one, and delivering a full jolt of witch power.

As you do this, pronounce your curse evenly and clearly; some witches prefer to keep it dark and general in content, specifying nothing more than misfortune and misery. Others relish the graphic approach, reveling in a description of the torments they are about to unleash. The choice of approach is yours; however, I would counsel you to suit the approach to the victim. Above all, you don't want to be laughed at. This process of confrontation of the victim should then immediately be followed up with your ritual of wrath and chastisement unless, of course, you have sufficiently developed your powers to inflict a curse immediately without further ado. At this stage, however, this is highly unlikely. That kind of ability one is either born with or acquires only after years of practice.

In order to make your curse into something more than an empty threat, you are going to have to build a dark current or vortex. The utmost effort on the part of your pyramid powers will be called for here, combined with a pattern of constant repetition. Should you belong to a coven, then your task is that much easier, calling, as it does, on the combined pyramid powers of a group.

You are going to have to contact the abyss within you, and dredge up all those repressed hostilities and dark hatreds you have banished to the cellars of your mind from childhood onward. This can take time; to whip your emotions into that state of frenzy which will make the magic work is not a task that can always be accomplished at one sitting. It can be a work of some days at least, and because of the caustic energies it deals with and the harm they can quite obviously inflict on the user himself, it is not to be lightly embarked upon. This without even taking into consideration the possibility of the return current should the victim be adequately protected. Before embarking upon any operation of wrath and chastisement, truly calling as it does upon the powers of fire and darkness, make very, very sure in your own mind that the risk is worth taking. Only a mind in which no qualms or second thoughts are present can house and effectively manipulate the requisite forces.

One of the simplest ways of setting the dark current in motion by yourself alone is the time-honored *Black Fast* method.

Every mealtime you should, if possible, confront what you would consider a delicious meal either in actuality or the imagination, and sternly reject it, in favor of a morsel of food, a glass of water, and maybe a vitamin pill or two to keep body and soul together. You must keep this up for a limited state of time, beginning and ending the fast within a properly cast circle, with the circumambulations performed "widdershins," *against* the sun, and naming your intention in the form of a curse, that "[victim's name] so come to grief." Repeat this same curse to yourself every time you refuse food. The process should last for two weeks—beginning at the full moon, or just after, and ending at the new moon. As the moon wanes, so the dark tide flows swifter.

This practice can be effectively camouflaged from your non-witch friends by the simple excuse of dieting. There is more to a so-called hunger strike than meets the eye.

The second simple way of laying a curse on somebody is by the *Candle of Bewitchment*.

Here again we make use of constant repetition as a magical device. Traditionally, the hour chosen for this operation is the stroke of midnight, but actually the best time for the attack is when you feel your victim is fast asleep, and therefore at his most defenseless. In most cases this would be sometime during the early hours of the morning.

You must begin the first of this series of bewitchments, as with your Black Fast, on or just after the new moon, that period of the lunar month known in the craft as the dark of the moon.

Every night, at exactly the same time if you can manage it, cast a floor triangle similar to the one in Chapter 4, using a Martial Incense of Wrath and Chastisement in the thurible; on your altar should be a phial of your Sabbat oil (see last part of Chapter 7 for this), your lamps of art, and of course your chalice; the cord, Athamé, and workbook should be present as usual. Depending on the nature of the operation, one of Saturnian binding or Martial destruction, surround your altar triangle with a circle of cypress twigs, marble graveyard chips and pieces of bone, on the one hand, or your Cernunnos paraphernalia of holly, fir, ivy, and animal horn on the other. Within the altar triangle itself should be your candle of bewitchment, black for a ritual of binding and suppression, red for one of strafing and torment. It should be exorcised beforehand. For both Saturnian and Martial operations, a little powdered rue herb or myrrh should be mixed with the wine of consecration.

You must now tune your deep mind to the correct wavelength. For Martial operations using a red candle, you may use the conjuration of Cernunnos described in Chapter 4, beginning "Eko, Eko Azarak. . . ." In your mind's eye, see the Rampaging One: Between Cernunnos' horns from his forehead juts a blazing torch. In his right hand he bears either a flaming sword, a trident, or, alternatively, supports an immense burning staff of gold entwined with serpents and ivy and surmounted by a great gleaming pinecone: the Lord of Misrule!

With his coming, give full play to all the rage and torment within you. Feel the fiery blood of anger coursing through your veins! Allow yourself to be possessed by wrath and fury as you again perform your circumambulations widdershins, *anticlockwise!* Then take your scarlet candle in your right hand, and with your *left* begin to anoint it with Sabbat oil. Start at the center of the candle and work first up, then down, up again and then down again. Keep this up for a full five minutes. It is the most important part of the spell. With each stroke, you should chant a jingle of your own devising encompassing your intent. It doesn't matter how simple or absurd it may be, as long as it suitably expresses your feelings toward the victim, and can be kept up rhythmically as you do your anointing. With all the power of your imagination, and all the faith and intent you can muster, you must actually try to see your spell working its mischief, visualizing your victim suffering all the pangs you wish on him. This type of spell is perhaps best employed for encouraging general misfortune rather than any specific disaster, relying purely as it does on the use of the fortified imagination for contact between the respective deep minds. *Specific* disasters should be left for envoûtements using an object link, as described later in the chapter. On the other hand, should your candle burning be a Saturnian type of operation, that is, one aimed at the induction of inertia, forgetfulness, or frustration of some sort or other, then you must invoke the dark power Habondia, in her dark aspect, Nocticula, using a black candle. The conjuration such as the one to be described below can be used with effect here.

The magical landscape to be visualized should be one of darkness and mystery. One of those traditionally associated with the dead is as follows:

Night has fallen, winter has set in; the air is chilly. Two monolithic pillars of granite rise from the gentle hill, and between them winds the path of the dead, pale in the starlight. The two pillars mark the entrance to the realm of the dead, back of the north wind. Between them stands the representative of the dark power itself. The figure is neither distinguishable as male or female, an ancient robed in black, still and silent. The face is hidden beneath the shadow of a cowl drawn over the head. In one withered hand a staff of blackthorn is grasped; in the other a torch flickers with a resinous, smoky flame. An owl, the symbolic bird of death, is perched on the being's shoulder. In the far distance, the baying of dogs or wolves can be heard ringing in the chill night air. Their keeper, Nocticula, Ruler of the Dead and Warden of the Tower Adamantine, walks abroad!

This is the basic Saturnian image. Embroider on it with your own fantasies by all means. The more personal and sinister they are to you yourself, the more effective your magic will become. The one thing to remember is that they should evoke in you all those childhood fears of the dark, the deserted churchyard by night, the opening tomb, and the Thing in the cellar! All the horrors and bugbears that you can conjure up from your worst childhood fantasy should be pressed into service here, must be dredged up and put to use in initiating the dark vortex!

The floor triangle should be drawn in the usual manner, save for your altar decorations. A Saturn Incense of Wrath and Chastisement should burn in your thurible.

Repeat your conjuration to the four quarters, tracing a circle cross such as you used in your necromancy ritual at the four quarters with your Athamé, the symbol of death!

Here is the incantation:

> Agency of Ineffable Name and Vast Strength!
> Ancient, Dark One; Thou cold, barren, mournful and pernicious!
> Thou whose word is as stone and whose life is abiding.
> Thou Ancient and Alone Impenetrable One!
> Thou who keepest promises,
> who art weak and weary;
> whose cares are greater than any other,
> knowing neither pleasure nor joy;
> Thou Old and Cunning, supreme in artifice!
> Bringer of ruin and despair,
> be present here and lend thy aid!

Consecrate the black candle with Sabbat oil in exactly the same way you did the red one, reciting your charm of intent as you do.

When you have completed the anointing, whether it is a red or black candle, place it within the altar triangle, and trace a glowing blue circle cross in the air above it with your Athamé. Light it with the words "So mote it be!" Then settle down to a vigil of concentrated hate or rage. Keep this up until the candle burns itself out. (Because of the strain involved in doing this, it is best to employ fairly slender, short tapers.)

If your deep mind has been sufficiently attuned during the operation, your victim should begin to feel signs of depression or anxiety within about a day or so. Witchcraft of this sort doesn't always take effect immediately. It sometimes appears to need about twenty-four hours to percolate through the lower levels of the deep minds concerned and begin to manifest itself in waking consciousness. The secret of success here, however, remains as always in whipping up your passions to the required intensity, and at the same time alerting your deep mind by the correct degree of concentration and repetition.

While we're on the subject of Saturn-type operations, it is a good time to consider the whole subject of ligature in greater detail. Ligature, as we have already seen, simply means magical binding, usually performed by means of a symbolic cord or chain. As such, it pertains to the sphere of Saturn. In ancient times the Dark One's newest subjects were often laid to rest in the earth, bound hand and foot.

Before considering ligature proper, however, we should note in passing a process of a similar nature, using the same name but differing considerably in its aim.

On an earlier page, I referred to a certain use of the witches' cord wherein it is used by the practitioner to bind himself. This is done on two occasions. First, many witches believe that by restricting the use of limbs and blocking up the avenues of the senses, the inherent witch power can be let free to wander abroad, either in an invisible form as a disembodied and clairvoyant astral body, or a semiembodied, half-materialized fetch.

The witches' cord itself is often used for this purpose of immobilization. For the sensory deprivation itself, a mask is worn, covering the entire head but leaving the mouth free to breathe. This is sometimes referred to as a witches' cradle or witches' bridle (not to be confused with the old Scottish instrument of torture of the same name). Second, the mask and the cord are both also used in ceremonial coven initiations, and here they symbolize the blindness and bondage imposed by the mundane world upon the candidate.

In neither of these cases is the cord ligature a process of dark intent. Rather the opposite in fact.

Not so ligature proper.

Should you as a witch wish to bind someone to prevent his carrying out some action or other, one of the best methods of accomplishing your aim is by using one of the variants of the spell known to many practitioners as *The Tanglefoot Charm*.

Obtain an object link from your victim, either a strand of hair which you must plait into a cord with some red twine, or an article of clothing in which you can tie knots comfortably. On a night when the moon is waning, preferably a Saturday midnight just before the new moon, cast your triangle with a Saturnian fumigation, having bitter wine in the chalice, and stone twigs and bones upon your altar. In the altar triangle should be your specially prepared cord. Invoke the dark power, using the circle crosses and the counterclockwise circumambulation, and when you feel that chilly, numbing presence is at hand, only then begin your spell.

Take the cord in your left hand (always the left hand for operations of darkness), and tie nine deliberate knots in it, starting with one at either end and working inwards. As you do so, chant this incantation, employing your witchly imagination to strongly visualize the result of your spell upon the victim. *See* him unable to speak or perform whatever the action is you wish to prevent.

> [N] I conjure thee,
> by night your eyes are blinded!
> By clay your ears are stopped!
> By earth your mouth is sealed!
> By rock your limbs are bound!

Having tied the last knot, chant "So mote it be!"

Take the knotted cord, and bury it in the ground somewhere, softly chanting these words as you do:

> Twist and tangle [N]
> never to rise up again.
> Your eyes are dimmed,
> your limbs are bound.
> Thus I lay you down to rest
> still and silent in the ground!

You carry out a little symbolic funeral in fact.

Incidentally, should you wish to unbind this spell, you must perform a ritual which does everything in reverse. Invoke the powers of the *air* to release the victim. Dig up the cord on a Wednesday while the moon is waxing. Cast a circle, using a Mercurial incense, and invoke Herne with your square of Mercury. Begin by untying the center knot and working outwards, in the reverse sequence you tied them in, chanting a jingle with each knot, such as,

> By the winds your limbs are freed,
> by the breath your mouth is opened,

> by the word your ears are opened,
> by the light your eyes are brightened.
> [N] I conjure thee,
> awake, arise; so mote it be!

While doing all this, you must wield your powers of imagination to see the magical bonds falling from the erstwhile victim.

Ligature is a comparatively mild method of chastisement (unless, of course, it is applied as it was on occasions in the past, to one of the victim's natural processes such as the ability to produce children or urinate). The more vicious and well-known method is of course envoûtement, the immolation of a wax or clay image or puppet, as it is known in the craft.

This is usually accomplished with the aid of steel or iron, in the form of your Athamé blade, or by dagydes, steel pins. As with the magic of defense, the magic of attack often makes use of steel or iron in its practices. This metal, symbolizing as it does fire and destruction, accords well with the nature of the Horned One in his aspect as a spirit of the wild hunt. The Athamé is strictly your main magical implement of aggression. However, many witches, when they band together to form a coven, use a sword for group-work. The symbolism is exactly the same. A sword is merely more dramatic in its effect, especially when used during initiation rites. But magically speaking, the simpler witches' knife is just as effective.

To consecrate a sword, you proceed in exactly the same way as your Athamé, buying and exorcising the sword previously without bargaining over the price. Astrologically speaking, iron is the metal ruled by Mars, and it is the raw energy of this stern principle that we canalize in our invocations of Cernunnos in his aspect of Horned God of Warfare and destruction. I shall return to the subject of envoûtement later under the heading of "Grand Bewitchment." Meanwhile, whenever you wish to contact "Mars" within you, whether it be for purposes of sending the Horned One, grand bewitchment, or storm raising, a good device to make use of initially is the talismanic square of Mars, a process similar to those of Mercury and Saturn, which you have already encountered.

Vengeance and Attack

The Square of Mars

THE SQUARE OF MARS

11	24	7	20	3
4	12	25	8	16
17	5	13	21	9
10	18	1	14	22
23	6	19	2	15

(The numbers in each line, vertical or horizontal, add up to 65.)

On a Tuesday night, when the moon is waning, take your exorcised talisman square and divide it up into twenty-five compartments, five down, five across, with pen and ink of art. In your thurible, burn a Martial Incense of Wrath and Chastisement. (See the last section of this chapter.) Now devise a jingle, phrase, or word for yourself which you feel suitably represents the power of war and destruction in your mind. Again, it can be a list of the names of war gods from a variety of pantheons such as "Thunor, Balor, Ares, Mars!" or a name of the Horned One himself such as "Barabbas, Barabbas!" or the old witch curse "Rentum tormentum!" ("Rend and torment them!") or a word which you feel conjures up the full burning, terrifying presence of destruction such as "Hiroshima! Hiroshima! Hiroshima!"

Each number must now be written in, infused with the fiery intensity of a repetition of your charm, using your witchly imagination to whip up a series of suitably terrifying and aggressive thoughts in your mind. Again, as always in operative witchcraft, it is only *your* personal imagination that can really trigger off the powers of your deep mind. It is at *this* point that you must feel frenzied enough to gnash your teeth, as I mentioned earlier. This was no idle comment. When you have completed the number 25, seal the square with the triple cross and "So mote it be!" You should be fairly exhausted by now after expending so much violent emotion. If you aren't, then maybe you weren't using enough effort, and the talisman will not be nearly as effective. You will really have to push yourself. Such passion is not in a person's normal run of emotions.

Wrap the square in an exorcised cloth and keep it in a safe place. You will be making full use of it for any Martial "tuning-in."

The Spell of the Black Cross or Reversed Pentagram

Either of these two symbols can be used for this spell, depending on whether you wish to curse or bind. The Black Cross is none other than our necromantic circle cross, signifying death purely and simply, as the skull-and-crossbones motif does normally; it should be used for *binding*. The upside-down pentagram, however, with two points aloft, signifies either the horns of Cernunnos or, more properly, man *dominated by* the power of the four magical elements, as opposed to *dominating* them (one point aloft). It should be used for *cursing*. First, obtain a reasonably recent photograph of your victim. Now on a night when the moon is waning, preferably in its darkest quarter, cast a circle using an Incense of Wrath in your thurible. On the altar, place your Athamé, fire, water, lamps of art, pen and ink of art, and wand. In the altar triangle, the photograph. Now, approaching the altar and facing north, state the purpose of the magical work you are about to perform as concisely and forcefully as you can, calling upon and visualizing intensely Cernunnos or Nocticula-Hecate, depending on whether the magic is one of cursing or binding. You are merely calling these entities to witness the use of your *own* witch power, rather than summoning their actual presence with which you propose to identify temporarily. Hence the use of a circle as opposed to a triangle. Having stated your intention clearly, you must name the photograph by asperging and fumigating it three times, stating each time: "Creature of paper, I name thee [N]! Thou art [N]!" Then, with your wand of divination and air, you "breathe life" into the photo symbolically by writing the person's name in glowing blue witch fire above it thrice, chanting it out loud each time as you do. Now, as in your necromancy and Vassago rituals, bear the photograph around the circle, clockwise, carrying your wand in your right hand as you do.

Display the image at the four quarters, beginning with the east, and chant the victim's name at each of them. Finish at the north.

This completes your identification of the photograph with the victim. Now you must embark upon the darker element of the ritual. Moving, always clockwise, to the west of the circle, face east across the altar, replace your wand, and take in your *left* hand the pen of art. With it, draw the circle cross of death or the reversed pentagram on the photograph, very slowly and deliberately, chanting as you do: "I [witch name] inflict upon thee [victim's name] such and such sorrow or misfortunate," or some such statement of intent. Remember, your own words are always best. Now, replacing your pen of art, take up the Athamé in your left hand, and repeat your words and actions using the blade instead of the pen. At this point, you must really narrow down your attention and pour all the concentrated anger or loathing you feel toward your victim into your actions. See the blue witch fire from your blade crackle about the photograph! Burn him with murderous intent!

Complete the initial ritual by exhibiting the charged photograph held in your left hand to the north, west, south, and east, *in that order* three times consecutively. Twelve times in all. Each time you raise the symbol, announce at each quarter:

> As the symbol dwindles
> so shall my words prove effective!

This is the reverse circumambulation known as the path of darkness, performed widdershins; northways, against the sun, and it completes the first half of the process. The second half deals with the facilitation of the power transfer by means of a power object, following the principle laid out in Chapter 4.

The next day (ideally the selfsame night) visit the home of your victim in secret, and draw lightly in Sabbat oil or gum Arabic the circle cross or reversed pentagram, whichever you happened to use, on the threshold of the house or apartment. Trace over this symbol with your Athamé, charging it with witch power. Should it be impossible to get to the threshold, trace the symbol at a point where you know your victim will have to pass and set his foot. This work of magic is, in fact, nothing less than the erection of a psychic booby trap. Hence the use of oil or gum to form the basis of the symbol: It must remain invisible to the physical eyes of your victim. Incidentally, the symbol is programmed solely to react to the victim's presence, so it should in no way endanger any other passer-by.

All that remains to be done now is to destroy the photograph *slowly*. The best way to accomplish this is to dissolve it in a pan of dilute nitric or hydrochloric acid (a photographer's developing pan is ideal for this) face up, so that you can watch the image fading. Failing this, simply tear a small piece *off* the photograph every night at approximately the same time as that which you performed your ritual. This process, sometimes known as the lesser bewitchment, is, as you can see, a rather unpleasant one. Most of the operations detailed in this chapter are similarly so, involving as they do the sustained forces of hate and fear. But if the Powers of Darkness fail to worry you and you remain determined to make your weight felt as a witch and equally determined to risk the consequences, then these are the processes to use. But when you sup with the devil, you must needs use a long spoon; and as I mentioned before, the only "spoon" really long enough is that rather unethical method of getting someone else to do the dirty work for you. And even then you will still have to consider the possibility of magical reprisals, should you be found out. As I mentioned at the beginning of Chapter 5, your occult activities never go by completely unnoticed. It is my belief that "something" if not someone is always alerted whenever occult balances are tipped one way or another by the considered use of witch power by an individual or group.

The Barabbas Spell

Here is a ritual of wrath and chastisement passed down to us originally by the witches of medieval Spain.

It is a conjuration of the Horned One, using his Christianized titles, "Barabbas," "Satanas," and "the devil." In his destructive aspect, Cernunnos could well be allied with those images, although nothing like the usual Christian theological background for his existence is accepted by present-day members of the craft. However, the spell is impressive, and traditional, even with the implied theological red herrings.

Vengeance and Attack

Cast a triangle on a night when the moon is waning, using an incense of wrath and chastisement. Decorate your altar with your usual Cernunnos embellishments. In the center of the triangle, place your glowing thurible.

Summon Cernunnos with the incantation, "Eko, Eko Azarak, etc." Then take a small amount of purified salt, coriander seed, and a small carnelian, or sardstone. Not only is this a magical "accumulator" or fascination gem, but it is also a Martial red in color. Place it in your pestle and mortar, and grind the substances together. They don't have to be pulverized to a powder, just sufficiently to mix well with one another. Divide the resultant mixture into three heaps.

As midnight strikes, scoop one of the heaps into your left hand, and chant the first part of the spell, passing it from hand to hand, to and fro, as you do:

> Salt and coriander, I conjure thee
> by Barabbas, by Satanas,
> by the devil cursed be!
> Not as salt and coriand I call thee
> but the heart of [victim's name]!

With that, cast the mixture into the thurible fire with your left hand. As it blazes up, continue:

> As thou burnst, so let the heart of [N] burn;
> and bring it here to me!
> Conjured by the Queen of Sard,
> by the underworld itself,
> by the sailors on the sea!

> [N] I summon thee
> by Barabbas, by Satanas,
> by the devil conjured be!
> By the underworld itself,
> Spirit of the Sard,
> enter in [N]
> and bring him quickly here to me!

> Powers of the abattoir,
> guide him here to me!

> Powers over Cocodover,
> bring him quickly here to me!
>
> With more messages I send to call thee,
> by the Queen of Sorcery,
> by the Queen of Elvenhome
> who walks the fields by day,
> the crossroads haunts by night
> spinning wars and enmity!
>
> I join you all! Now go we all
> enter [N] silently,
> from thence I return home yet again
> after twisting his side,
> his lungs,
> and the strings of his heart most terribly!

Repeat this three times in all, using the second and third heap of powder for each repetition. At the end of the third repetition, seal with the triple cross *made with the left hand,* and the words "So mote it be!"

Before you deal with the great keystone of destructive witchcraft, "Grand Envoûtement," or bewitchment, I would mention three considerably less sinister though traditional minor processes which cater to the jealous witch.

Three Simple Spells for the Jilted Witch

Rise before sunrise on a Saturday or Tuesday when the moon is waning. Select a branch (traditionally of hazel, but any tree will do) of *one year's growth* and lop it off with your Athamé, chanting these words as you do:

> I sever thee, thou virgin branch, in the name of [victim's name] for the purposes of his downfall!

Return home with this switch, and that night, when you feel sure your enemy is sleeping, cast a circle using an incense of wrath and chastisement. Then visualizing the face of your victim in the altar triangle, and beginning at the east, begin circling the altar and rotating on your own axis *counterclockwise.*

As you do, chant these words with each personal revolution; make as many of these pirouettes as you can fit in.

>Droch! Mirroch! Esenaroth!
>Betu! Baroch! Maaroth!

Whenever you find yourself facing the altar, strike it hard with the switch held in your *left* hand. Make three complete revolutions of the circle. When you finally reach the east after your last circuit, drop to the floor, completely "letting go" and chanting the words "So mote it be!"

Traditionally, the person who has offended you will feel the blows, if not actually on his face, then at least dealt out by fate. However, as this spell uses no power object or object link, it relies solely on the witch power of the operator, and as such must be classified as an elementary, less complicated process than most.

Another uncomplicated bit of sorcery, which uses a power object in the form of a philter to be made into cakes or cookies; these must be sent to the unsuspecting victim and his newlywed wife, hopefully as a wedding gift, shall we say.

Lovers' Dissension Spell

When the moon is waning, cast your circle; in the altar triangle place your chalice. Wreathe the triangle as for your Hecate-Nocticula spells. Within it, place the following items:

A pinch of grated orange peel, a pinch of salt, and a few grains of pepper, cumin seed, and powdered rue. On top of this, pour a small amount, say a quarter cup, of boiling, distilled water, which should also be on hand. As you pour the water onto the mixture, chant the following charm, and visualize strongly those persons caught in the hostile predicament it is designed to effect.

>I [witch name] make this philter.
>May it bear
>malediction, deep affliction,
>here upon this married pair,
>[X] and [Y] [their names].
>May they never be united,

> may they quarrel every day,
> may their marriage-bond be blighted
> ere a year has passed away!
> This shall be the life between them,
> let that life be as it may!

Seal the spell with "So mote it be!" and three crosses made with the left hand. Finally, introduce the philter as you would any other, in chocolates, cookies, a bottle of homemade wine or in whatever way you can best accomplish it.

You may also wish to reinforce the potency of the philter by backing it up with this third process, which may be put into operation on the same evening, within the same circle.

The Sending of Eight

This spell, dating back to medieval times, makes use of the device of sending out "devils," or small magical servitors. Though called upon by such dog-Latin appellations as devorator ("devourer") and seductor ("seducer"), they should not be thought of as constituting independently existing entities, but rather as the witch's objectified desires, small scintillations of magical fire formulated by the imagination and sent out to accomplish a specific goal. In this case one of amatory disenchantment!

Here is the method:

Obtain photographs of each of the erstwhile lovers, on which within a properly cast circle in the waning moon should be written their respective names with pen and ink of art. Name them with fire and water, as you did in the spell of the reversed pentagram, exhibiting them likewise to the four quarters, thus identifying the photographs firmly with their owners in your magical imagination.

Having done this, proceed to glue the photographs together, firmly, *back to back*. Now, move to the south side of your altar table, facing north across it, and place a small amount of sulphur powder or asafetida gum on the hot coals in your thurible. Hold the photographs in the fetid smoke with your right hand, and press the Athamé blade point, held in your left, against them. Chant the conjuration. As you speak each of the eight names, imagine a bolt of witch power flashing down your magical weapon into the photographs!

> Soignator! Usor! Dilapidator!
> Dentor! Concisor! Devorator!
> Seductor et Seminator!
> > You who sow discord, where are you?
> > You who infuse hate and propagate enmities,
> > I direct, conjure, and constrain you
> By the Dark One and her Horned Consort,
> > As the face of one image be set
> > contrary to the other,
> > So let the face of [X] be set contrary
> > to the face of [Y] [victims' names]!

Similarly, when you arrive at the section about setting the face of the one contrary to the other, actually *see* the quarrels and upsets in your fortified witchly imagination! "It could not be otherwise" must be your attitude here, of course.

Finally, bury the photographs in the earth for twenty-four hours and dig them up the following night, chanting these words softly as you do:

> Soignator! Usor! Dilapidator!
> Dentor! Concisor! Devorator!
> Seductor et Seminator!
> > You who sow discord, where are you?
> > You who infuse hate and propagate enmities,
> > I direct, conjure, and constrain you
> By the Dark One and her Horned Consort,
> > Go!
> > Accomplish that which is commanded of you!

Seal with "So mote it be" and the left-handed triple cross; to complete the spell, you must now somehow contrive that the photographs pass into the victims' possession. Concealing them in the binding of a gift book is one of the best methods here. Or possibly hidden under a false bottom in the box in which you send your "philtered" chocolates. As a last resort, you can bury the symbol under their threshold or on their property. This is the traditional method.

The operation of grand bewitchment

One of the darkest, most potent operations of adverse witchcraft is that of grand envoûtement, or to give it its English title, *"The Operation of Grand Bewitchment."*

To effect its aim, this spell makes use of all the magical tricks it can muster; repetition, evocation, object link, power object, the power of iron, incense of wrath and chastisement, the square of Mars, baneful herbs, and the candle of bewitchment! It is rather complex, as you will see, and should be performed only as a last resort when all else fails.

Vengeance and Attack

On a Tuesday at midnight just before the new moon (ideally speaking, the nearer the winter solstice the better), tape a triangle around your altar pointing *north*. Similarly, line the table of practice itself up so that the altar triangle also points north. Within it should be placed your paten pentacle bearing your chosen modeling material, clay or wax, while wreathed about it should be your usual Cernunnos paraphernalia—horns, evergreens, etc. *Outside* the altar triangle, place:

> Your thurible burning an incense of wrath and chastisement
> Your chalice of bitter wine (rue or myrrh)
> The wand
> The cord
> The Athamé
> An unlit candle of bewitchment (red)
> Lamps of art
> Phial of Sabbat oil
> Your square of Mars
> Object links
> Baneful herbs and graveyard dust (see end of chapter)
> Your Dagydes, or exorcised needles of art

In this type of complicated ritual there is generally no room for the workbook on the altar, so you will probably have to either learn the process by heart or do what many witches do, namely, place the book on an exorcised book or music-stand beside the table.

Begin your operation by performing a meditative numerical progression on the square of Mars to attune your deep mind, using the same form of words you spoke in its consecration. (In order to preserve them exactly, these may be recorded with pen and ink of art on the back of the square.) Having alerted your deep mind to the right Martial level, return your square to the altar, and proceed to consecrate the floor triangle with your wine and Cernunnos invocation, "Eko, Eko, Azarak, etc." When you have brought the Horned One's presence to your proceedings, you may turn your attention to the pestle and mortar.

Place therein the herbs of bane and graveyard dust, grind

them to a powder, and softly chant your intention to yourself over and over rhythmically.

> I work to the destruction of [victim's name]!
> I work to the destruction of [victim's name]! etc. . . .

Mix the resultant powder with the clay or beeswax in the Paten Pentacle, kneading it in well, continuing your chanted intention.

Then begin to model your puppet (making it anywhere from five to eight inches long), this time slowly chanting the name of your victim over and over to yourself. Again, as in the case of your amatory puppet, model the figure to the best of your capability. Some witches incorporate a photograph of the victim's face into the puppet's quite effectively. This is not essential, however; the main thing to remember is that the image must be recognizable as the victim by *you*. Make sure the puppet has the correct sex; it also helps if you concentrate on accenting the detail of those parts of the body where you intend to focus the attack. If it is in the head, make sure the face has eyes, nose, mouth, and ears. If it is in the feet, make sure there are some, even if they are only blobs at the end of the legs.

When you feel the puppet is completed to your satisfaction, insert the hair or nail clippings at the appropriate places. (If the object link is liquid, like blood or saliva, incorporate it into the base material before you begin modeling.) This done, engrave on the puppet with the point of your Athamé, the victim's name, and underneath it, these words of power: Cabye. Aaaze. Hit. Fel. Meltat.

Then consecrate the puppet with a dab of wine, chanting your intention and projecting the victim's image onto it in your mind's eye:

> "In the name of Cernunnos, the Horned One
> Creature of wax (or earth) I name thee [N]!
> Thou art [N]!"

Transferring the puppet to the *right* hand, and taking the wand in your *left*, infuse "life" into the image by tracing over it with the victim's name written in witch fire. Complete the

Vengeance and Attack

identification by exhibiting the puppet at the north, west, south, and east, chanting the victim's name at each quarter. Then place the figurine in the altar triangle with its head pointing to the north.

This completes the first section of the ritual.

Now take up your scarlet candle of bewitchment, and begin rhythmically anointing it in the correct manner with Sabbat oil, softly chanting a litany of hate and destruction directed at the victim as you do; specify the exact torment you wish to inflict upon him, and let yourself wallow in the fantasy evoked. Keep this up for a previously decided upon number of times, until the message has well and truly sunk into your deep mind. Eighty-one is a good number, but some practitioners would advocate more.

When you have completed the anointing, place the candle at the northernmost tip of the altar triangle, beyond the puppet's head, and light it. Then move to the north of the triangle yourself and, facing south across the altar, cross your arms upon your breast in the traditional gesture of the God of death. Chant the words of identification:

"It is not my hand which does this deed,
but that of Cernunnos, the Horned One!"

As in your Amatory Puppet Spell, feel the Horned God standing behind you. Feel him guide your left hand to the enchanted needles of art, the Dagydes! Feel him burn within you, with rage and passion and intensity! Again forcibly mentally project your victim's face onto the image before you. Accelerate your pulse by swift, sharp breathing at this point. Let the Horned One grasp a Dagyde with your left hand! Hear him chant the dog-Latin words of the medieval grand envoûtement through your lips. See the "devil" sparks flit about the needlepoint like moths around a lamp!

Arator, Lapidator, Omtator!
Somniator, Subaerfor, Iquator!
Signator, Sudator, Combustor!
Pugnator, Ductor, Seductor!
Comostor, Onerator!

> Vos omnes ministri odey et destructiones,
> et Seratore discorde,
> et qui libiter opera facitis et tractibus.
> Quod eat noce!
> Vos conjurase idec nos conjuro et deprecur
> quod ministrare et consecrare ista imaginem
> et odid fiat mier alve [victim's name]!

Let the God of Wrath now vengefully stab the Dagyde into the part of the puppet designated for torment with the words "So mote it be!" If the torment be one of head pains or loss of hair, stab it into the crown of the head; stomach or heart pains, into the central body; rheumatism in the limbs, a Dagyde to each extremity; and so on.

Should general wasting away be required, the traditional method of accomplishing this is by transfixing with a single Dagyde through the heart, and then dissolving the image slowly in fire if it is made of wax, water if of clay.

After the immolation has been accomplished the candle of bewitchment should be left to burn itself out.

Needless to say at this stage, for best effect a ritual such as this should be repeated on several occasions, thus ensuring the formation of an irresistible vortex, cone, or pyramid of power. It is, or rather, should be extremely taxing for the individual witch, involving considerable strain and sometimes risk, and for this reason is often left, like the operation of necromancy, for full coven performance. The actions here are still performed by a single operator, though the words and visualization are joined in by all, in the manner of responses. In this instance a circle surrounding the floor triangle should be used as well.

There exist, of course, many variants of this process, some of them remaining in extremely rudimentary form. One such primitive example involves the hammering of three iron nails in triangular formation into the north side of a tree, naming the victim's name at each blow; I believe this is still practiced in the Ozarks to this day. On the other hand, some ultra-modern practitioners on the European continent have embroidered upon the theme and, instead of using the traditional Dagyde as an instrument of immolation, mix a small quantity of iron filings into the modeling matter of the puppet, and then proceed to connect the head and feet of the image to the input and output leads of an electric generator. At the appropriate moment, the switch is thrown, and the doll is either dissolved by the heat if it is a waxen one or, if it is made of dried clay, shattered to small pieces! Those practitioners who would rather not rely merely upon their own witch power, fortified though it be with the magical images of Cernunnos or other witch entities, may also supplement their bewitchment by a separate conjuration of that demonic being of fire and destruction, the giant Flauros, of whom it is said in the *Lemegeton*:

> ... A strong and mighty duke, appearing primarily as a terrible leopard, but assuming the body of a man with burning eyes and dreadful aspect at the command of the Operator ... He will destroy and incinerate those who be enemies of the Operator, should he so desire it ...

Needless to say, there is the greatest peril attendant upon performing this conjuration. It should, moreover, be performed within a grand circle of protection, fully fortified by the four watchtowers. A triangle of manifestation should also be drawn at the north, wherein should be placed the sigil of Flauros drawn on exorcised paper with pen and ink of art. The date of its performance should be when the moon is two, four, six, eight, ten, twelve, or fourteen days old, between sunrise and noon when the weather is clear.

Again a Martial incense or pure asafetida gum should be burned in your thurible, and the sigil of Flauros worn, with your pentacle of protection on your breast. (It can be tucked into the same chamois or silk sachet.) The words of power in this process are: "Themesho—Masanin!"

Conjuring to visible appearance is most inadvisable. It is unnecessary in most cases and quite undesirable in this one. If ever a demonic manifestation could be classified as satanic, that of Flauros can.

In order to further enforce the obedience of the demon, after performing the initial identification ritual with fire, water, and wand, many practitioners incorporate into the spell part of the initiation ritual to be found in the last chapter. The sigil is taken from the operator's breast, bound with the cingulum and "hooded" with a black cloth, and then carried around to the various quarters of the circle to the "challenged" with the sword, or Athamé, at each quarter. It receives further consecration of fire and water and is finally unveiled and placed within the altar triangle, at which point Flauros himself is constrained to concentrate his presence within the triangle of manifestation.

After charging the demon with his mission of destruction, the operator should not only "license him to depart," but fol-

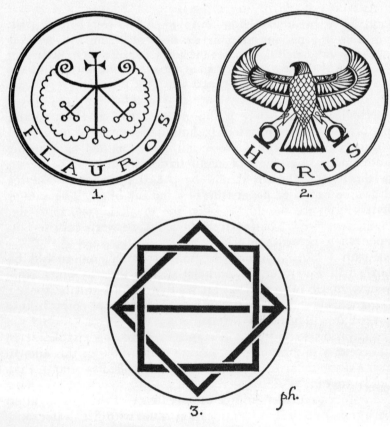

1. *Sigil of Flauros*
2. *Its original derivation*
3. *Symbol for top of witches' drum*

low this up with a thorough purification of the room with fire and water, burning in his thurible one of the exorcism incenses mentioned in Chapter 5.

I treat this conjuration sketchily, as it pertains to the field of study of an advanced practitioner, who should be more equipped by dint of experience to handle demonic manifestations of a violent nature, if needs be.

Storm Raising

As a process which can obviously be put to mischievous uses (and in the medieval Christian mind always was), I deal with storm raising and its more far-reaching concomitant, weather working, under this particular chapter heading as a matter of convenience rather than one of hard definition. Far back into recorded history, powerful practitioners of the occult have generally been credited with powers of weather working. From Kublai Khan's eastern shamans, to the Druids of the British Isles, they have all possessed one skill in common, the mysterious power of controlling wind, rain, mist, and thunderbolt. During the Middle Ages, however, in Christian lands, at any rate, this skill, where demonstrated, was seen simply as another manifestation of ever-present Satan's power. The orthodox Christian doctrine ran thus:

Almighty God in the depths of his wisdom and for reasons best known to himself had temporarily delegated the power of control over the elements to Satan, under whose regency the world had been placed until such a time as the Second Coming took place. Hence, Satan's title, "Lord of this World." This power Satan in turn conferred on witches, wizards, and other practitioners of the Black Arts, all seen as being if not subservient to, then at least in league with him. The delegated power of weather working was then used either for the ignoble purpose of blighting the crops of God's faithful or, should the effect produced be a benevolent one leading to increase of crops, as a means of leading the unwary astray from the path of righteousness by dint of heretical reliance on devilish practices. Whatever the ecclesiastical dogma, however, witches had their own beliefs and apparently managed to maintain them fairly consistently throughout the various periods of persecution in

Europe and England, although the years of total secrecy contributed much to the almost total fragmentation and hybrid diversification of the knowledge such as it exists today.

Apart from the direct application of witch power, whether inherited as an inborn talent or learned in a coven, the actual methods of accomplishing the feat of weather working are about as varied an assortment as you are ever likely to encounter. To one familiar with the weather-working practices over the centuries, at least nine different processes of rain making, for instance, will come to mind. There is the one involving the burning of the desiccated liver of a chameleon on the rooftop; another specifying the casting of flints behind one's back; the flinging of sand into the air; beating up a spray of water from a river with a besom. Boiling hogs' bristles in a cauldron; vigorously stirring the water in a hole in the earth with your finger; sprinkling cold water over a naked virgin; and, finally, sacrificing a coal-black cockerel. Most all of these are what Frazer would have categorized as "sympathetic" magical gestures, processes designed to effect their aim by reason of the magical axiom that if you perform an action symbolically, that which it represents may in fact occur, due to the oneness of the universe, the interaction of the microcosm with the macrocosm. This, of course, is the basic working thesis of witchcraft. What Frazer leaves out, however, and it is the thing which differentiates a child's game of make-believe from a genuine witch's magical operation, is that vital occult factor of the deep mind's part in the work. Unless that underlying stratum of psychical coexistence here designated as the deep mind is penetrated, the "magic" remains totally within the personal sphere of the operator, at best remaining purely an exercise of surface autosuggestion; at worst, a fantasy game to be taken to in refuge from a hostile outside world. Only when the "deeps" are contacted, only at that point does any real witchcraft take place.

This principle applies as much to the process of weather working as to any other magical field. Most of the work being done in this direction by present-day covens is concerned mainly with the direct use of personal or collective witch power used to "split" or dematerialize cloud formations while under personal scrutiny, and is often performed in an impromptu manner rather than as an elaborately thought-out ritual. The "splitting" process consists of simply a bending of your pyramid powers toward the event which you wish to take place, namely, the dissolution of the cloud mass, an operation taken thus far and no farther. In fact, it is a simple process of binding, in this instance performed on a natural phenomenon rather than on another living person. You "see" the clouds as splitting and parting, harrying them with your fortified will and imagination.

However, for those witches who would prefer a more deliberate approach, the seeds of the process will lie in the use of the archetypal symbolism of the four elements of the wise. In order to raise a tempest or wind, whether it be used to split clouds or tear up trees, contact has to be made with the powers of the air, using as many magical images congruent with the airy principle as appeal to you. The square of Mercury may be of use and Herne invoked. The Kerubic Eagle, or Great Bird, from the watchtower of the east should be called upon. The wand should be used as the emblem of power in your ritual, and you should seek to call up all the stormy, howling, blustering, wind-swept memories of gale and hurricane within your experience, and augment them by rhyming spell within a circle properly cast with Mercurial incense. For a benevolent zephyr, invoke on a Wednesday with the moon waxing at 8 A.M., 3 P.M., or 10 P.M.; for a destructive storm, conjure at one of the same hours on a *Thursday* with the moon waning. For an *electrical* storm, call upon Cernunnos and all the powers of fire on a Tuesday with the moon waning. The Great Lion from the watchtower of the south must be invoked, and your fiery Athamé or sword must be brandished as a magical emblem; burn an incense of wrath and chastisement. Thunor and all the storm gods must attend on you! Finally, for mist, cloud, or rain, invoke the Lady Habondia as Ruler of the Great Waters, and that Serpent of Old, Mighty Tiamat, from the watchtower of the west. Burn your lunar incense from Chapter 3, and use your chalice of salt water as the magical weapon of invocation, performing the operation on a Monday at 8 A.M., 3 P.M., or 10 P.M.

Should you wish to "pre-set" the storm for a future unspecified time, an old witch device is to bind the invoked force into a talisman which is then "discharged" at the appropriate moment. About the best device for this purpose is the knotted cord.

Construct your elemental ritual *around* the action of braiding a cord of red ribbon or yarn, as in the creation of your original cingulum, binding in the invoked forces by means of a repeated jingle of your own composition.

Complete the operation by tying three deliberate knots in the cord, two on the outside, one last in the center, with words to the effect of:

"As these knots are loosed, so mote the weather be!"

At the time the effect is desired, the operator should take the cord in hand and turn to the correct direction, east for gales, south for thunderstorms, west for rain. He must then summon up all the powers of the required element from the depths of his being with all the force of his will, faith, and imagination. Traditionally, he should at this point whistle thrice for a wind, clap thrice for thunder, or spit thrice for rain. A metrical incantation of intent devised by the operator should then be thundered forth, punctuated by the untying of the three knots *in reverse order* to that in which they were tied.

Should you be disposed to combine the powers of all *three* elements and raise a hurricane, then you must perform your three operations on separate occasions, tying the knots *on top of* the previous knots in the same cord, making three large triple knots in fact. When you release them, again make sure you work in the *reverse* order, chanting an all-embracing spell which effectively enumerates *all* the elemental images concerned.

The important thing to observe throughout is that the operator be "possessed by a wave of godhead," using as a triggering device all the *previously activated* archetypal element images within him. This is where the knack lies.

Weather working is a thing that has to be worked at. The all-important factor is contact with the archetypal elemental powers in their most fundamental form. As a beginner, you would be wise to begin experimenting with this type of magic at a season when the type of elemental activity you are trying to induce would not prove too uncommon. As I have said elsewhere, don't strive for the "impossible." Not yet, anyway. Stick to the "improbable" for the time being. You must take great care not to impair your newly established magical faith in yourself at this early stage of your career.

Herbs and Incenses

Finally, to conclude this chapter of magical methods of aggression, here are some leads to the baneful herbs traditionally in accord with such matters. However, I would strongly advise the avoidance of the poisonous varieties in your sachets and incenses; keep to the more chemically harmless ones. Remember, you are seeking to use *magical,* not *physical,* power. To pin a case of magical assault on anyone and make it stick is very difficult, whereas the use of very real botanical poisons could easily be construed as a highly antisocial activity, regardless of how the herbs happened to be administered.

The herbal compositions, like the other subject matter of this chapter, fall into two distinct categories; those of a Saturnian or inertia-inducing nature, and those of a Martial one, the herbs of torment. I shall deal with the latter first.

Martial Incenses

The traditional magical Martial Incense of Wrath and Chastisement was composed of the following ingredients:

Gum ammoniac, euphorbium, bdellium, black and white Hellebore roots, powdered lodestone or magnetized iron filings and sulphur, mingled with a few drops of blood of a man, a black cat, and the brain of a hart.

Many of these ingredients are, not surprisingly, poisonous, and two at least of the last difficult, if not objectionable, to get hold of.

In view of that, an alternative more modern Martial incense may be composed more readily of the following:

- 4 parts powdered dragon's blood resin
- 4 parts dried powdered rue
- 1 part dried ground peppercorns
- 1 part dried ground ginger
- 1 pinch sulphur
- 1 pinch magnetized iron filings or powdered lodestone

Alternatively, you may burn pure dragon's blood, sulphur, or asafetida in your thurible. The last two are of an extremely offensive and pungent odor and should not be used in large quantities. Sulphur especially should be used very sparingly owing to its choking fumes.

Martial Sachet Powders

"Fell," or "baneful," amuletic herbal sachets, better known in the United States as hex powders, can be composed from the following herbs and woods used simply or in combination. If required in sachet form, they should be bound with red ribbon or yarn in the waning moon, preferably in the day and hour of Mars (8 A.M., 3 P.M., or 10 P.M.). Most of them should *never* be administered for consumption in philter form, being extremely poisonous. They are traditional witch herbs, however, and deserve to be mentioned for that reason, though maybe best left well alone.

The first listed are not poisonous and, as such, are those you should find a place for in your witch's cabinet.

"Strafe"—blackthorn leaves (*Prunus spinosa*)
Pepper—black, white, and cayenne
Ground ginger root
Dried chilis
Dragon's-blood resin (used as stain by violin makers)
Powdered sulphur (flowers of sulphur)
Pulverized holly chips—*Ilex aquifolium* (do not eat)
Pulverized ash chips—*Fraxinus excelsior* (do not eat)
Pulverized hickory chips—*Carya alba*
Dried stinging nettles—*Urtica dioica* (and any other herbs or spice of an astringent nature)
Euphorbium—*Euphorbia corollata* (in the United States, "Snow on the Mountain"—poisonous)
Gum bdellium—balsamodendrum
Wolfsbane—monkshood, *Aconitum anglicum* (of the same family as the field buttercup, *Ranunculaceae*—poisonous)
Gum ammoniac—(formerly used as a cement—poisonous)
Death cup mushroom—*Amanita phalloides* (*deadly*)

The remaining complement of baneful herbs are those of a Saturnian nature.

The traditional Saturnian incense of wrath and chastisement is composed of black poppy seed, henbane, mandrake root, powdered lodestone, and myrrh. This should be well mingled together and incorporated with the brain of a cat and the blood of a bat.

However, for your purposes, the following recipe can be used quite satisfactorily:

- 4 parts gum myrrh
- 1 part dried, powdered yew or juniper
- 1 part dried elderberry leaves or twigs, powdered
- 1 part dried, powdered cyprus twigs
- 1 part patchouli leaves (or a few drops of patchouli oil)
- 1 pinch of magnetized iron filings or lodestone dust

Failing this, pure gum myrrh may be burned alone in the thurible.

Graveyard Dust

To the experienced practitioner of witchcraft, this may mean one of three things:
1. Either purely dust or earth taken from a churchyard.
2. Dried, powdered mullein herb (*Verbascum thapsus*).
3. Bone ash and asphaltum, also known as mummy dust, originally obtained by grinding up Egyptian mummies. This is a great rarity nowadays for obvious reasons.

Any or all of these graveyard dusts may be used singly or in combination in Saturnian hex powders or sachets, designed to bring inertia or restriction of some sort. Similarly the following "simples" may also be used:

- Pulverized myrrh wood
- Black poppy seeds
- "Holda" berries, leaves, and flowers (elderberry or *Sambucus nigra*)
- Rue (*Ruta graveolens*)—edible but bitter
- Bitter aloes
- Sourgrass (sorrel)—*Rumex acetosa* (edible but sour)

Hawthorn blossoms (*Crataegus oxyacanthus*)
Periwinkle blossoms (*Vinca major* or *minor*)
Pulverized juniper wood and berries (*Juniperus communis*)
Pulverized yew wood and berries (*Taxus baccata*)
Felonwort (bittersweet or woody nightshade—*Solanum dulcamara*—poisonous)
Dwale (deadly nightshade, devil's herb—*Atropa belladonna*—poisonous)
Enchanter's nightshade (*circaea lutetiana*—poisonous)
Twilight sleep (henbane—*Hyoscyamus niger*—poisonous)
Devil's apple (Jimson weed, Thornapple, devil's-trumpet—*Datura stramonium*—poisonous)
Mark of Cain (Hemlock—*Conium maculatum*—poisonous)

The last seven may be traditionally magical herbs, but they also happen to partake of the nature of powerful vegetable drugs. Again, as in the instance of the Mars variety, *be careful.*

CHAPTER 7

The Coven and How to Form One

As regards environment, whenever you wish to perform an operation of witchcraft solo, all you basically need is a corner of your own home, the only prerequisite being privacy and a modicum of soundproofing. The latter is required not so much as a precaution against the neighbors' objecting to your noise, but rather as a further aid to the discarding of inhibitions, which is of such primary importance in all magic.

However, should you wish to gather a group of likeminded friends around you for regular witchcraft sessions, then of course you will need a larger space to operate in than the one required for solo work. Apart from the more obvious aspect of companionship and mutual enjoyment of the practices, the formation of a group, or coven as it is called, brings with it certain advantages not present in the solo approach.

It is well known among practitioners of the occult arts that a magical operation performed by a group will often succeed spectacularly, whereas a solo effort may achieve only moderate success. The old adage about strength in numbers is particularly true in the case of magic. This is the occult rationale behind the witches' coven. The proviso exists, however, that the group, first, be *like-minded,* that is, sympathetic to one another in basic belief and emotional rapport, and, second, that there be present a certain amount of magical dedication and intensity of purpose. This does not necessarily imply a rigid fanaticism among the members but rather abilities first to bring the mind to bear upon a problem, and second to let the imagination loose within certain limits. In fact, the members must all be fully, and practically, conversant with the four powers of the witches' pyramid. The more magically powerful are the individuals belonging to a coven, the more potent does the coven become as an entity. And it does become an entity. If enough pyramid power is brought to it and tied in place by sufficient emotional rapport among the members, witches believe that a pool or vortex of magical energy begins to form, which, if sustained by regular performance of a ritual, not only becomes an "energy bank" upon which the comprising members can draw to supplement their personal resources, but also an artificially constructed collective deep mind, independent in its own right. This is the magical rationale behind the formation of most occult groups that require secrecy from their members.

The rituals and symbols special to a group such as this are kept from the eyes of "cowans," or the uninitiated, not so much for fear of the powers supposedly conferred being abused, but because, by meddling with the "triggering devices" involved in the symbolism, such outsiders set to naught all the careful work involved in building the coven entity. This is particularly the case should the intruder be of a hostile or skeptical turn of mind.

The total number of members to a coven is traditionally limited to anywhere up to thirteen, inclusive of the leaders. Should the full complement of three leaders be present, that makes ten other members possible. Whenever the number of members grows to exceed that, a new coven is formed, which splits away from the original one. In goddess-oriented covens, with their concentration on the sexual aspects of witchcraft, the group is ideally made up of six male-female couples and a leader. Similarly, these covens also require that initiations only be conferred from sex to sex, by man upon woman or vice versa, the only exceptions made being those of parent and child. In other branches of the craft, however, this ruling does not apply in any way.

Traditionally, covens are supposed to have at least three miles between their physical meeting points. This seems to stem partly from an old custom dealing with "territorial rights," in some circles referred to as the covendom, and partly from the days of the persecutions, when smallness of number was considered a wise precaution. Similarly, the unusual number of thirteen members may also have this foundation, although there are many magical reasons behind the number, not least of them being the thirteen full moons to a lunar year. Some modern witches claim, however, that thirteen has a more pragmatic import, inasmuch as it is the largest number of folk that can comfortably be squeezed into a nine-foot circle.

The word "coven" itself is derived from the Latin noun *conventus*, meaning "a gathering or assembly." It is the same root which gives us our words "convent," "convention," "covenant," and "convene."

The occasions at which a witches' coven meets informally are known by the name "Esbats." The word itself, derived from the French word meaning "to frolic," hints at how unponderous and nonreligious in the generally accepted meaning of the word the medieval concept of a witches' meeting was!

Similarly, the eight annual Sabbats, in addition to their magical import, have always been considered as great occasions of festivity, celebrating the beginning, midpoint, and end of the seasons, the ebb and flow of the elemental tides. So if and when you form your own coven, always bear in mind that, first, Sabbats are a time of renewal of friendship and elemental power; and, second, Sabbats are a time of enjoyment.

The actual details of establishing your own coven can be considered under the following seven headings:

1. *The Nature of Your Coven*—the coven "logo," totems, and general symbolism.

2. *Your Coven Hierarchy,* if any.

3. *Your Initiation Ritual* (or rituals if you establish a coven hierarchy) making use of coven symbolism.

4. *A Binding Oath of Secrecy* imposed upon all members on admission to the coven, fortified with the additional threat of magical reprisals. This is usually facilitated by the candidate surrendering certain object links, such as a drop of blood or a lock of hair, et cetera.

5. *The Taking of a Magical Coven Name.* This may be the same or in addition to the witch name initially assumed for solo practice.

6. *The Actual Witch Insignia* to be worn, such as pendant, ring, bracelet, necklace, or garter.

7. *A Ritual or Rituals* to be performed on any of the eight Sabbats you care to celebrate, again involving considerable use of coven symbolism.

What you do with the coven after you have established the preceding seven points is entirely up to you and the other members. Some covens concentrate on attempting to heal the sick, others specialize in necromancy, but the general goal is one of knowledge and power. In further pursuit of the latter, a few groups try to bring their powers to bear on political matters, singling out individuals who stand high in public office on whom to cast their spells. Then there exist those groups who devote their energies solely to invoking the witch entities as deities, worshiping them not so much for practical and magical reasons, but rather as an expression of that simpler and maybe purer life of the spirit which takes its inspiration from pre-Christian, European sources. It is these "witch cultists" who have largely held the public gaze over the past fifteen years, despite the fact that the word "witch" embraces a far wider circle of people than merely the followers of Gerald Brosseau Gardner.

The Nature of Your Coven

In the same manner that you sounded out suitable symbolism in your attempt to find an appropriate witch name for yourself, so you should evolve the basic idea on which to found your coven. However, most tradition-minded witches would insist here that, instead of throwing your limits wide enough to include all areas of magical and mythological legend, you should restrict yourself to those of a European basis, seeing that it is with the Western magical tradition that you seek to put your group in contact. With this thought, you may disagree, citing maybe with good reason the magical maxim popularized by the Cabalistic writer Dion Fortune that "All Gods are one God, all Goddesses are one Goddess, and there is one Initiator." Dion Fortune began her magical career as a theosophist, and throughout all her works, there is much of a theosophical nonsectarian approach. Such an approach to witchcraft would seem to be objectionable only to the most sectarian-minded of witches; but they do exist, and the paradox is apparent.

Quite obviously, the strong point about occult paths such as that of witchcraft is that, unlike organized religion, they leave the "way to salvation" solely up to the individual. There is no attempt at proselytizing. Indeed, the frantic need to convert the unbelievers whether by verbal persuasion or violence is totally lacking. It is solely a matter of *chacun a son goût*. Further than this, in fact; it does not remain a matter of take it or leave it, but rather one of take it and do something with it! Witchcraft remains, in its broadest sense, the shamanism of the West, the underlying, barely organized bedrock of magical practice, on which all later religions and metaphysical schools of thought rest; any substantial attempt to deal with it as a semi-"established" faith is doing it the utmost disservice and is entirely at odds with the idea behind the practices. The nearest a witch can get to the term "orthodox" is only "the most traditional." Witchcraft is basically performed by and for the individual. Covens are, or should be, made up of individuals, held together by a common interest, whether it be a desire for knowledge, power, or a love of the elder gods.

When you set about forming your coven, choose symbols to represent its general orientation. If it is one of knowledge, those symbols consonant with Herne and the Sky Power, in all its manifestations, would perhaps be appropriate. On the other hand, a power orientation should perhaps suggest the development of a set of symbols appropriate to the Horned One, Lord of Fire and Energy. A preoccupation with healing would suggest contact with Mother Hertha; a simple desire to worship the powers of love maybe indicates a bias toward the Lady Habondia.

All of these witch beings, whether they are seen as independent entities or aspects of two single deities, possess animals and symbols special to themselves, and it is from these appropriate images that you should draw your coven "totems" and "logo," or composite symbol.

Books of mythology can be very helpful here—for those of European inclination, the Norse myths; the Welsh-Celtic tradition as presented in the *Mabinogion*, the Irish-Celtic in *The Book of the Dun Cow, The Yellow Book of Lecan,* and *The Book of Leinster;* and, finally, the *Matter of Britain* as presented in such works of the Arthurian Cycle as the *High History of the Holy Grail*, and the like. (See the bibliography at the end of the book for more suggestions on this point.) For those that would follow a more Cabalistic path, works dealing with "magical correspondences," such as Aleister Crowley's 777 and Dion Fortune's *Mystical Qabalah,* are very handy. Classics-minded witches would do well to consult such books as Robert Graves's works on the classical myths, those of C. Kerenyi; and of course Godfrey Leland's *Aradia* and *Etruscan Magic and Occult Remedies,* among others.

Should you, on the other hand, wish to give your coven a more African flavor, then the myths of ancient Egypt and maybe the magical elements inherent within the West Indian voodoo cult should be incorporated. The entities involved are exactly the same. They differ only in their outer cultural manifestations. The powers are identical.

Only when we encounter Far Eastern *thought* do we find any radical change. The difficulty of mixing Oriental and occidental magical philosophies has been recognized by many, so I will not enlarge upon the subject. The basic magical practices of both East and West, however, appear to derive from a common prehistoric shamanic stock, and remain in many cases similar, if not identical.

Finally, whatever your coven's inclination, Frazer's *Golden Bough* and Robert Graves's *White Goddess* will be invaluable source books.

The "logo," or coven emblem itself, should be designed in the same manner as a heraldic crest, incorporating the symbolism you have elected to use into a single composite design; the design should be simple enough to engrave or embroider upon your witch jewels and to be visualized easily in meditations.

Your Coven Hierarchy

Similar to the priesthood, from very primitive times down to the present day, secret magical societies, including witch covens, have organized themselves into hierarchies, the policy of the group being dictated by the leader or leaders at the head. These people were usually held to be stronger, wiser, or merely older than the rest of the group, and maintained a position of authority until such a time as either they had it challenged from

The witch god and witch goddess

below or they themselves handed it on to a successor in due course. Some witches believe, mistakenly, I feel, that at one time the periodical death of the coven leader was demanded, thus forcibly ending his term of office. This was considered a magical sacrifice, a renewal of power for the rest of the coven; a recharging of the coven entity, in fact. Whether this form of sacrifice was, in fact, ever indulged in by witches is a moot point. It is certainly a practice common to many primitive societies. It seems, however, to be more connected with the beliefs fostered by established priesthoods, such as that of the Druids as recorded by Caesar, rather than of secret witch covens. The whole concept of guilt, scapegoats, and atonement is totally absent from witchcraft. The only rituals nowadays containing elements of sacrifice are those of cakes and wine, and various libations thereof. The occasional use of minute amounts of blood in certain operations is by no means seen as a method of deity appeasement or atonement for a sin, but solely as a means for conveying a certain type of magical energy held to be resident in the blood. (Many present-day witches who are often of an extremely nonviolent nature even draw the line at using a few drops of blood, preferring to use that old magical substitute, the white of an egg!)

Traditionally, there may be as many as three leaders to a coven, again recalling Dion Fortune's dictum about one god, one goddess, and an initiator. The male leader representing the "masculine" power generally takes first place; the female, the "feminine," second; and the second male "executor," or "officer" third. Different covens have different titles for their leaders, all equally traditional. In covens which stress the love and fertility aspects of witchcraft and perform their rituals naked, the male leader is known as the high priest, the female as high priestess. On the other hand, in those which stress the knowledge and power aspect, the male is known as the magister, grand master, or "devil" (meaning "little god") and the female as the lady or queen of the Sabbat. The second male, known as the "officer," "executor," or "summoner," is he who relays the requests of the magister or lady to the rest of the coven membership. He is the go-between and lieutenant of the leader or leaders, and traditionally he wore black from head to foot to designate his rank. Hence his old title, "the Man in Black."

Occasionally, in medieval France, he was dressed in green and named "Verdelet." His badge of office was a pilgrim's crutch or blackthorn staff, whence derived another of his titles, "Black Rod." It was the summoner's job to attend to the mundane functioning of the coven, the membership dues if any, and the passing out of information to the members about time and place of the next Sabbat, what to wear, what food to bring and so on. In the absence of the magister, the summoner could and would frequently lead the coven.

In those covens which concentrate on knowledge and power, the lady or high priestess holds little or no executive power. She sits at the magister's right hand during the feasts, leads some of the dances and ceremonies, and on occasion performs the task of a seer or spiritistic medium under the magister's control.

On the other hand, in the goddess-oriented covens, the high priestess is definitely leader, the high priest being merely her consort.

The magister may wear furs or pelts, a robe, or nothing at all, depending on the variety of coven he leads. Upon his head he may wear the traditional shamanic horned helmet, rather like that of a Viking warrior, or a mask covering his whole head and representing one of the coven's totem animals, be it goat, ram, horse, cat, or whatever. Or he may don a metal helmet which covers his entire head. (Hence the old comic epithet for the magister, "Old Brazen Nose!") He will naturally wear any witch jewels he possesses, also.

The lady or high priestess, on the other hand, may likewise wear a robe or nothing at all, depending on the type of coven she belongs to. The robes can vary in color, the usual color preferred being white, although black, green, red, or blue ones have been used. Upon her forehead she may bind a silver lunar crescent, horns upwards, or alternatively have her hair flowing and free. She will wear all her witch jewels as well, including of course the mandatory necklace.

During the Sabbats, the magister's headpiece will be adorned with a simple short candle rising from the center, which is lit during the proceedings. This symbolizes his role as the Lord of the Sun, Lucifer, the light bearer. In some covens, the high priestess will likewise wear an illuminated headpiece to lead the Sabbat dance, this time, however, a whole coronet of candles.

Members may bring their own robes or work nude, as the case may be. As I mentioned before, a certain uniformity of dress is desirable, and the black, cowled robe, or tabard, is ideal for this purpose. Witch jewels should be worn, and members should bring their Athamés and wands for participation in the group rituals. In the old days swords would be brought if the participants were gentry or nobility, or pitchforks if they were peasants. The wands or riding poles were, however, generally disguised as broomsticks. The Athamés and wands are the modern substitutes.

During the coven meeting itself, whether it be formal Sabbat or informal Esbat, the magister and lady may be known by any of the following titles, apart from their own coven names. These are some of the traditional names for the various witch spirits you already know about, whether they be held to be independent entities or aspects of a single divine pair, a god and goddess. The coven leaders are seen as direct representatives of these witch spirits during the Sabbat.

The magister's titles are, among others:

Cernunnos. The title is derived from the ancient European Celtic horned deity of the same name.

Dumus. Derived from "Dumuzi" or "Tammuz," the young consort of the Mesopotamian Mother Goddess.

Puck. Also known as "Pookah" or "Bok," the horned, satyr-like mischievous spirit said to be a Reformation folklore version of the Horned God. He was also known as Robin Artisson and Robin Goodfellow.

Hu. Channel Island version of the Horned One, possibly derived from the Welsh-Celtic deity, Hu Gadarn.

Barabbas. Hebrew *Bar Abba* meaning Son of the Father or Divine Son—reference to the incarnate god.

Mamilion. Derivation unknown.

Dianus or *Janus.* A twin-faced god of the Romans, who guarded the threshold of the house and supervised all beginnings and endings. He is referred to by some witches as Alpha and Omega, the first and the last. Another version of the Horned One.

Janicot. A Southern French diminutive of Janus or Dianus.

The Devil. Literally, "little god." Derived from early Aryan stem *div* or *dev,* meaning "holy" or "shining."

Lucifer. "The light bearer." The god seen as the spirit of light and, hence, the sun.

Simon. Possibly a reference to the Gnostic magician, Simon Magus.

Herne. Witch name derived from early English version of the Anglo-Saxon god, Odin or Woden. A god of wisdom and storm, and also a guide of the dead, he leads his wild rout across the winter skies accompanied by the baying of his death hounds!

Gogmagog. Prehistoric version of the god and goddess in giant form.

Andras. The god as worshiped in the Weald.

Adonai or Adonis. Hebrew for "the lord." Dying god, consort of Astarte.

Sabaoth. Another Hebrew name for God.

Baphomet. Horned deity allegedly worshiped by the Templars, a Christian order of fighting monks of the twelfth century. The name has been variously construed to mean "The Father of the Temple of Universal Peace among Men," the initials of which phrase in Latin spell the name backwards: *Templi Omnium Hominum Pacis Abbas;* or by others as a corruption of *Bathos Metis,* "purification by wisdom." However, many witches take it to refer to "the Stone of Buffo," Buffo being an ancient name for the island of Cyprus where legend has it the Greek Love goddess Aphrodite was born; from whence also certain of the feminine witch mysteries were said to have emanated. Which brings me to my second consideration, namely, the titles bestowed upon a female witch leader whether she be designated high priestess or queen of the Sabbat.

Among the Lady's titles are:

Andred. Witch goddess name coming from the Forest of Weald in England.

Bensozia. Twelfth-century French name for the goddess, meaning doubtful.

Nocticula. Similar twelfth-century appellation meaning "little night."

Rhiannon. Welsh-Celtic mother goddess.

Arrianrhod. Similar Welsh Goddess, mother of Llew.

Herodias or *Aradia.* Italian name for the witch goddess, being the daughter of the Great Mother, "Diana," "Dione," "Dana," or "Jana." Referred to in Leland's *Aradia, the Gospel of the Witches.*

Habondia or *Dame Habonde.* Goddess seen as Lady of Love and Plenty.

Holda or *Hulda.* German version of the same.

Morgan or *Morrigan.* Celtic names for goddess seen as Lady of Death, variant of classical Hecate. Also King Arthur's half-elven sister.

Brigid or *Bride.* A Celtic mother goddess.

Astarte or *Ishtar.* Mesopotamian goddess of love. Bride of Adonis-Tammuz.

The Virgin or *Maiden.* Referring to Persephone, the Greek underworld goddess. Should the lady or high priestess have a daughter present within the coven, the latter title of "maiden" is sometimes conferred on her.

Let me reiterate: the titles bestowed upon the leaders vary considerably from coven to coven, depending on the approach adopted, Dianic or Druidic, Celtic or Cabalistic, Robed or Sky Clad. In one you may find it is the magister or Lord of Misrule who holds sway, in another the high priestess or Queen of Elfhame. And likewise, when you wish to consider forming your own coven, the choice of leadership, who, how, and in what manner, remains, as it always has done in the past, entirely your own.

Your Initiation Ritual

Your initiation ritual will mark the ceremonial request for admission and consequent acceptance of a prospective member into the coven. As such, it is a type of ritual common to all secret societies, and indeed most of them generally have many elements in common. The magical reasons behind such a ritual are those of acceptance of the individual into the coven group mind. Inasmuch as the candidate's individual interests fit into harmonious rapport with the aims and ideals inherent in the coven, so in the same measure will he be able to draw from the coven "energy pool."

The Coven and How to Form One 219

Most coven initiations are performed at one of the eight Sabbats if possible, preferably one of the grand Sabbats of Beltane or Hallows, when the whole coven, such as it exists, is present.

Those ceremonies performed at Esbats are just as valid, however, though usually of a less spectacular nature.

In accord with the magical orientation of the coven, so will the initiation ritual, and indeed all the other rites, differ. Because of this factor, coven initiation ceremonies such as they exist today contain many divergencies from one another. In fact, it would be almost true to say that there are as many different witch cults as there are covens!

Some covens follow formal Cabalistic and Hermetic patterns of ceremonial, while others advocate the more exuberant "'cult-of-freedom-and-love" approach of G. B. Gardner and his followers, concentrating on naked worship of the goddess seen as the Great Mother. Still others return to the medieval preoccupation with the Horned One and all his attributes, while yet another group will return to Celtic fundamentals, concerning themselves with ancient Druidic lore. (Druidic in the sense that W. B. Yeats understood the word, as a shaman or wizard rather than priest of a solar cult.)

Here are the rudiments of two types of initiation ceremony. The first is of the sort used by those covens who work "robed" and concentrate more on matters of knowledge and power directing their energies toward the more "male" aspect of the godhead. The second represents the type used by those covens who work naked, directing their energies to the healing and love aspects of the cult, concentrating more upon the goddess. You may use which you wish and incorporate those elements you feel to be most in accord with the basic attitude of your coven entity.

The first initiation process is one which holds more in common with the witch cult as it existed in medieval Europe. It should take place at one of the eight Sabbats, ideally one of the grand Sabbats, Beltane or Hallows. The idea behind both this and the following process is one of purification and release of the candidate from mundane ties, in much the same way as you would exorcise an object before making magic with it. This first process, which is performed robed, uses the device of ceremonial purifications of fire, air, earth, and water. However, the second, performed naked, makes use of that of scourging, or flagellation, likewise as a symbol of purification. I am bound to add, however, many tradition-minded witches feel that this second method, though peculiar to certain aspects of later Roman versions of the Greek mysteries, seems to be more bound up with English "public school" and "spankers' club" traditions than any inherent in the craft itself. To be beaten, whether symbolically or in actuality, does not by any means arouse in everyone the same feelings of glowing inner cleanliness or spiritual tone-up that it apparently did for a Nordic warrior, cloistered medieval monk, English public school boy, or sky-clad witch.

The Robed Initiation

Since the ceremony takes place during the Sabbat, the circle itself will already have been erected and consecrated by watchtower, with a small ceramic chafing dish glowing on top of the altar should it be indoors, or a balefire blazing in the center should it be outdoors. All the magical witch implements should be present. Both masculine and feminine aspects of power will have been invoked, perhaps by the Eko Azarak formula and the Hertha chant. The grand master will be wearing his horned helmet or animal mask, with the torch or candle blazing at its crown. He and the rest of the coven should be standing within the circle. The candidate should be led by the officer, or summoner, to the northern perimeter, already robed and fully blindfolded or "hoodwinked" and *divested of all metal artifacts*. At that point, one of the coven, previously selected, should with the point of his or her Athamé or coven sword touch the candidate upon the breast and challenge him with appropriate words. The challenge is issued from the point of view of the guardian of the watchtower of the north, the realm of the element earth.

The words may take the following form:

CHALLENGER. Whence come you?
CANDIDATE. From the north, the place of greatest darkness.
CHALLENGER. Whither goest thou?

CANDIDATE. I travel east in search of light.
CHALLENGER. What passwords dost thou bring?
CANDIDATE. Perfect love and perfect trust.
CHALLENGER. I, the guardian of the watchtower of the north, forbid thee entrance. Thou canst not enter this holy place from the north, save thou first be purified and consecrated. Who vouches for you?
SUMMONER. I, Guide of Souls, so do.
CHALLENGER. Child of Darkness, approach thou the watchtower of the north and receive of me the bonds of death and blessing of earth!

The candidate now has his hands tied behind his back with a witches' cingulum, which is drawn up and tied around his neck, with the free end hanging down in front of him as a lead or "cable-tow." Similarly, a short piece of red cord is also bound around his right and left ankles, loose enough to allow him to walk and leaving his feet "neither bond nor free." Finally, a few grains of consecrated salt are sprinkled on his forehead, and a coin symbolic of the earth pentacle placed between his lips. He is then led by the summoner deosil an entire circuit around the outside perimeter of the circle and brought to a halt at the west, where, after the coin is removed from his lips, a similar challenge is issued by the watchtower representative of that quarter. In answer to the first query, however, the candidate should now respond, "From the north, the gate of death." Likewise, in the challenger's reply, in place of the word, "north," "west" is now used, and the guardian of the west subsequently administers the "cup of memory," a draught of pure water from the chalice, and the "purification of water," a few drops upon the forehead.

The candidate is then led on another clockwise circuit of the periphery, and ends up in the south, where he is again challenged, this time by the representative of fire, who, by laying the flat of his sword, or Athamé, on the candidate's right shoulder and censing him thrice with Cernunnos Incense, bestows upon him the sword of power and the consecration of fire.

Finally, on being led circuitously to the east of the circle, the candidate is challenged by the representative of air, who, by breathing on his head thrice, bestows on him the breath of life, and the gift of light by subsequent removal of the blindfold. The first sight which should greet the candidate's eyes must be the grand master in his blazing mask: Lucifer, the Sun at Midnight.

Having been purified and consecrated by the four elements of the wise, the candidate is now actually conducted *into* the circle at the north. His hands are then unbound; the grand master extends the blade of his sword, or Athamé, to the candidate, who, kneeling before him and placing his right hand upon the blade, repeats the words of the ceremonial oath:

> I [Witch name] in the presence of all here assembled, man or god, living or dead, do of my own free will most solemnly swear that I shall ever keep secret those things entrusted to my ears alone by this coven, except it be to a proper person, properly prepared, within such a circle as I am now in; And that I shall never deny the secrets to such a person should he be properly vouched for by a fellow member of this coven. All this I swear upon my life, now and hereafter, and may those powers I possess, now or hereafter, turn against me should I break this most solemn oath! So mote it be!

At this point, the coven workbook, Book of Ceremonies (or Book of Shadows, as it is called in some covens) is produced, and the candidate signs his witch name in the register section and dates it. Some covens also measure the height of the candidate and record it by the name, the traditional process of "taking the measure." Likewise a drop of the candidate's blood taken with a sterilized needle or, alternatively, a few hairs of the candidate's head, are requested, and either placed in the register by the name or filed away separately. These are both tokens of the bond now existing between coven entity and candidate, but also underlying it is the threat of magical reprisals in the event of his breaking his oath.

The grand master should now lay his hands upon the kneeling candidate's head, and call down the blessing and acceptance of the coven on the new initiate. He then invests him with his "charged" coven witch jewel—pendant, garter, bracelet, necklace, or ring—and salutes him as a new member. Some covens also include a consecration by Sabbat oil and wine at this point.

The new initiate now rises and is presented to all the other members in turn by witch name. Finally, the coven's working tools, sword, chalice, lamps, *et al.*, are presented in turn to the candidate.

The Sabbat festivities and ceremonies such as the feast of cakes and wine then continue as usual.

The Sky-clad, or Naked, Initiation

In this type of ritual common to covens which practice the goddess-oriented variety of witchcraft, the ceremony is performed by the high priest if the candidate is a woman, the high priestess if it is a man. As in the previous ritual, the circle should be cast by watchtower, and the candidate blindfolded at the perimeter, challenged by the initiator at sword or Athamé point, and the passwords of "perfect love and perfect trust" given. The candidate is then pulled into the circle backwards by his initiator, who has her left arm around his waist, her right arm around the neck, and given the third password, a kiss. The breach created in the circle is then repaired with the Athamé, and the candidate bound with a cingulum and ankle cord as previously. He is then led round the circle and proclaimed to the east, south, west, and north watchtowers as a prospective candidate for admission. At this point the charge of the goddess is made to the candidate by the high priestess. It is claimed to be traditional, and because of that, I shall quote it in full:

> Listen to the words of the Great Mother, who was of old called among men Artemis, Astarte, Dione, Melusine, Aphrodite, and many other names. At mine altars the youth of Lacedaemon made due sacrifice. Once in a month and better it be when the moon is full, meet in some secret place and adore me, who am the queen of all magics.
>
> There assemble, and to those who would learn sorcery, I will teach things yet unknown. And you shall be free, and as a sign that you be really so, be naked in your rites, dance, sing, feast, make music and love. All in my praise, for I am a

gracious goddess, who gives joy upon earth, certainty, not faith, while in life; and upon death peace unutterable, rest and the ecstasy of the goddess. Nor do I demand aught in sacrifice, for behold, I am the mother of all living, and my love is poured out upon the earth!

The candidate, still clasped by the waist, is then led around the circle with a skipping step and, south of the altar after eleven knells on a small bell have been rung, has the fivefold kiss bestowed upon him or her by the initiator.

Kissing the feet: "Blessed be thy feet that have brought thee in these ways."

Kissing the knees: "Blessed be thy knees that shall kneel at the holy altar."

Kissing the phallus or vagina: "Blessed be thy organ of generation without which we would not be."

Kissing the breasts: "Blessed be thy breasts, formed in beauty and in strength."

Kissing the lips: "Blessed be thy lips that shall utter the sacred names."

The candidate then kneels at the altar, and the cable tow is tied closely to a ring set therein, thus forcing him or her over into a crouching position. The feet are also bound together at this point, and he is asked whether he will always be "true to the art." If he answers affirmatively, a knell of three, seven, nine, and twenty-one strokes is rung, and the candidate is then "purified," or flagellated with forty strokes of a whip made of cords, the scourge of art. After he makes an earnest promise to always help and defend his brothers and sisters of the art, the oath is then administered; this oath does not differ substantially from the one outlined in the first ritual.

The candidate's feet and eyes are then unbound, and the triangle consecration is performed, anointing the phallus or vagina, right breast, left breast, and genital organ again, first with Sabbat oil, then with consecrated wine, and finally with a kiss, naming the candidate priest or priestess and witch in the process.

Finally, the new initiate's hands are unbound, the working tools are presented in turn, with a kiss for each, and he is presented to the four quarters, saluted at each in the name of the gods as newly made priest or priestess and witch.

A second degree or grade is sometimes bestowed to elevate the witch in the coven hierarchy and enable him or her to form his own coven, which differs only from the first in that the candidate, though bound, remains unhoodwinked, gives no passwords, and joins in the initial ceremonies and chants. After an oath on "his mother's womb," he or she is consecrated by the pentacle as opposed to triangle; this involves anointing with oil, wine, and lips the genital organ, right breast, left hip, right hip, left breast, and genital organ again, in that order; an inverted pentacle, in fact. The new initiate, after being empowered by the laying on of the initiator's hands, is then instructed in the use of the magical implements and also in the mysteries of the return-in-threefold witch law, whether it be used for good or evil, blessing or cursing. By dint of this, the ceremony concludes with the new initiate scourging his initiator with thrice as many blows as he himself received, namely, one hundred and twenty in all. He is then presented to the powers at the four quarters as a duly consecrated high priest and wizard, or high priestess and queen of the Sabbat, whichever the case may be.

In the second ritual, instead of the progress of the aspirant through the four elements, the myth of the goddess is implied, where the witch goddess Andred, Aradia, Habondia, or whatever other name you may care to know her by, descends into the world of the dead somewhat like Persephone in Hades or Ishtar in the realm of Ereshkigal, and receives the scourge and fivefold kiss of the Horned God of Death and subsequent conferment of power. Sometimes this myth itself is enacted during the initiation rite, in the manner of a mystery, but this is a supernumerary addition, the myth itself being implicit in the entire initiation ceremony.

As you can see, both rituals have many things in common, as well as their considerable differences, all or any of which can be incorporated into an initiation ceremony by the resourceful practitioner; he should also include any additional coven symbolism required. As always, it remains a matter of personal choice and intuition as to what is included and what left out, what bias the ritual should have—knowledge and power with its Hermetic overtones or love and joy with its Dionysian ones.

Evolve your coven emblems first, and the rest will follow naturally. The central idea to adhere to is one of the purification and regeneration of the candidate, symbolized by the impositions and removal of the blindfold and ligature, leading to his enlightenment and acceptance by the leaders by and for the entire coven.

The Sabbat Rituals

Items 4, 5, and 6 have already been dealt with; all that remains to be discussed are your regular coven rituals, which will form the main bulk of your Book of Shadows.

The witches' year, like the regular variety, is divided into four seasons—winter, spring, summer, and autumn. Each season was characterized originally by a Sabbat, nowadays two Sabbats. They are more of an either/or nature, however, the first representing the beginning of the season, and the second, the height. In the past, their observance differed with location. For instance, in some parts of Europe, Beltane was celebrated as the summer festival, while in others, midsummer was accorded the same honor instead, with identical symbolism. Of the two varieties, however, the so-called great Sabbats of Candlemas, Beltane, Lammas, and Hallows appear to be the older, antedating the solstices and equinoxes which sprang directly from the advent of a more sophisticated astronomical science, characteristic of the Druids.

But nowadays all eight appear on the witches' calendar, and you can take your choice which you will celebrate. Of course, most witches celebrate the grand Sabbats of Hallows and Beltane, if not all four. Some ardent practitioners even fit all eight in, but they are generally performed more on the scale of Esbats than Sabbats.

Ideally, a Sabbat should be held in a place hallowed by tradition; a spot sacred to the old gods, many of which exist still in Britain, the name usually being well-disguised under that of a Christian saint or the like. Often you will find a church has been deliberately built on the spot. This is one of the reasons for the traditional practice of witches' Sabbats being conducted in a churchyard, possibly even in the church itself, as in the instance of the North Berwick witches in sixteenth-century Scotland.

A "Druidic" dolmen, barrow, or stone circle, which have always been thought of as gates to the other world, places still frequented by elvenfolk and the old gods, are also held to be ideal.

However, as a modern witch, maybe living in a land like the United States where traditional holy places, Amerindian in this case, are few and far between, you will probably have to content yourself, as most others do, with following the more general advice outlined in Scots 1665 edition of *The Discouverie of Witchcraft,* namely, that the place chosen be "dark and lonely; either in Woods or Deserts, or in a place where three wayes meets, or amongst ruines of Castles, Abbies, Monasteries, etc. or upon the Seashore when the Moon shines clear, or else in some large Parlour. . . ."

Any unfrequented crossroad, hilltop, or woody grove can, in fact, be used, the first locale being traditionally sacred to both Hermes and Hecate, the second and third to all ancient rural deities; the farther away from man and all his works, the better. However, as a last resort, your living room or den will suffice.

The general outline for your Sabbat will be presented in the following pages, with any innovation germane to your chosen coven orientation being woven into the traditional framework.

Sabbat Oil

Prior to attending Sabbat, preferably even before leaving home, anoint yourself with Sabbat oil. A traditional recipe for this is as follows:

   Wild parsley root
   Celery root
   Poplar leaves (balm of Gilead)
   Cinquefoil
   Saffron

Or a more complicated, post-Columbian variety:

Smallage
Wolfbane
Cinquefoil
Henbane
Hemlock
Mandrake
Moonwort (*Botrychium lunaria*)
Tobacco
Poppy
Poplar leaves
Saffron

Ideally, the herbs should be freshly cut with the Athamé while the moon is waxing, but this is not always possible. At least they should be crushed and steeped in purified vegetable oil during the waxing moon. The oil should subsequently be strained through a thin muslin cloth to remove all the impurities and solid matter.

Or, alternatively, the crushed leaves can be steeped in pure alcohol, which is then mixed in later with the oil.

Most modern witches tend to bypass these two recipes, however, in view of the baneful herbs involved, and employ a more popular variety which is composed by the same maceration procedure but uses the following herbs instead:

Balm of Gilead (poplar leaves)
Cinquefoil
Saffron
Lemon verbena or vervain

Many witches will also use vervain by itself, or even garden mint as a standby, although as far as I have been able to find out, this latter is quite untraditional.

To all of these may be added the following essences for increased effect:

Musk
Civet
a suspicion of ambergris
patchouli or cassia

A few drops of your Cernunnos perfume, in fact. It is quite a heady mixture as you will find out, and you only need the smallest drop. Should you wish to increase the texture of the oil and compose a cream or ointment, mix it with a little finely ground oatmeal or orris powder. An oil should be kept in a small, well-stoppered phial, while the traditional receptacle for an ointment is one made out of an animal's horn. When you anoint, place a dab of the oil on the soles of your feet, the perineum, wrists, and temples, chanting these quaint witch words as you do:

> Emen Hetan! Emen Hetan!
> I am of thee and thou art mine,
> I have nothing which is not thine.
> In thy name [god's name if you are male; goddess, if female]
> Behold thy servant [Witch name] anointing herself/
> himself; I should some day be great like thee!
> Thout a thout, thout, throughout and about!

This is, in fact, a simple form of identification with a witch deity, and an affirmation of your aspiration to power, wisdom, or love, whatever your chosen path.

You must organize your Sabbat so that the lighting of the balefire occurs at the hour of midnight. This you should determine precisely beforehand, halving the hours between the time the sun actually sets on the eve and when it rises the following day. Midnight, in fact, will not always occur at 12 P.M., depending on the time of the year.

Having exchanged the customary witch greetings of "Merry meet," the Sabbat begins with the casting of the circle. This should be the nine-foot inner diameter variety, using the largest measurements on your cingulum as a compass cord. Or, if you have the space, a special eighteen-foot one can be constructed, as is done when several covens meet. If you are working indoors, it will take the form of your regular taped circle with the four lamps of art, *unlit*, placed outside at the four quarters. On the other hand, the traditional form of circle for an outside meeting is a narrow, shallow furrow, or trench, dug deosil with the sword, or Athamé; however, to do this, you must stand *outside* the perimeter as you dig. The reason for this will be apparent shortly.

The triple tracings and fire and water exorcisms remain the same in form, but again they must be performed from *outside* the circle. The thurible fumigation should be Sabbat Incense (see the end of chapter for this). The northern segment of the circle is now regarded as the entrance and exit for the Sabbat participants, and is referred to simply as the "gateway" or more explicitly as the "way between the worlds."

All the coven members should pass into the circle through this gateway, *but not, however, before divesting themselves of all metal implements, witch jewels, or insignia.* Even the magister's or high priestess' metal headpieces must remain outside; the cup, the sword, Athamés, everything and anything of a metal nature must do likewise. This is most important. Only after the balefire is well and truly alight, when the circle can be crossed and recrossed time and again without impairing its magical efficacy, can the metallic implements be brought in again, and your witch jewels reassumed.

The reasons for this step are threefold. The magical one is that which you are already acquainted with, namely, the jamming effect of metals on certain delicate vibrations which are going to be initiated during the ritual. The second, more traditional one, having to do with ideas of ritual purity and poverty, is that on coming into the presence of the gods, you divest yourself of all worldly valuables, and any metals, of course, were recognized as the earliest form of currency. Third, it refers back to ancient Prytanic "elvish" custom.

Thus, having cast the circle, purified it by fire and water, and removed all metals, the time will have come to prepare the balefire itself. This is the ritual Sabbat fire which is lit in the center of the circle. It is the unmoving pivot of the eight-spoked witches' wheel, the Wheel of Fortune, or Solar Wheel of Life. It represents, among other things, the constant rotation of the elemental tides, the ebb and flow of life itself.

The balefire itself must be composed of nine different varieties of wood. The choice of which species you select is up to you. But they must be nine distinct genera. It is best to choose from those which burn well. Good indications of these are given in the old Dartmoor verse:

Oak logs will warm you well,
That are old and dry.
Logs of pine will sweetly smell
But the sparks will fly.

Birch logs will burn too fast,
Chestnut scarce at all;
Hawthorn logs are good to last—
Cut them in the fall.

Holly logs will burn like wax,
You may burn them green;
Elm logs like smoldering flax,
No flame to be seen.

Beech logs for winter time,
Yew logs as well;
Green elder logs it is a crime
For any man to sell.

Pear logs and apple logs,
They will scent your room;
Cherry logs across the dogs
Smell like flower of broom.

Ash logs, smooth and grey,
Burn them green or old,
Buy up all that come your way—
Worth their weight in gold.

Poplar, cornel (dogwood), sandalwood, cedar, and juniper are also worth considering, the first two being highly traditional.

The sticks themselves should be set crossways on top of one another: "cross them, cross them, cross them," the old rune says. In order to facilitate lighting, a spirit such as alcohol may be sprinkled on them, or a bed of quick-lighting charcoal laid underneath. In order to light the balefire, you are going to employ what is variously known as need fire, wildfire, elf fire or living fire. This is flame produced either by the friction of wood on wood or from the flame of a taper lit by the rays of the sun, concentrated by a burning glass or concave mirror. However, many witches nowadays simply use matches, going on the assumption that the main thing to avoid is the use of metal, as would have been the case in the old days of tinder-boxes and flints. The fire seen to be resident in nonmetallic substances or the sun is what is required.

So now you have your coven assembled, the circle drawn, the balefire laid out but not lit, and finally all metals including your witch jewels removed from the area. Now, exactly at midnight, the hour of greatest darkness, extinguish all lamps or lights in the vicinity. If the Sabbat is performed indoors, turn out all the lights in the rest of the house.

You stand at the end of the old season; the elemental tides are about to change, the old quarter gives place to the new and the Wheel of Life is turning another quadrant. You are about to invoke the descent of a new influx of power to renew and regenerate the life of your body corporate, the coven entity.

The coven members should remain silently standing, kneeling, or sitting in a circle facing inwards, clasping hands. The magister must pass to the east of the circle and bow down nine times eastward. An unlit taper should now be placed in his right hand by the summoner, and he must slowly and powerfully chant a solar invocation such as the following:

> Eastward stand I!
> For favors I pray!
> I pray thee, Mighty Prince of Light!
> I pray thee, Holy Keeper of the Sky!
> Up to Heaven I pray
> and down to Earth I call thee!

The assembled coven should now reiterate the chant in unison:

> Eastward he stands,
> for favors we pray.
> We pray thee, Great One!
> We pray thee, Mighty Prince of Light!
> We pray thee, Holy Keeper of the Sky!
> Up to heaven we pray
> and down to Earth we call thee!

The assembled coven must now exert all its witch power in visualizing elemental power descending upon the taper as the summoner lights it, a great flake of fire or triple tongue of light floating down from the dark sky! The leader should apply the flame to the balefire. As it blazes up, the coven should chant the following words, visualizing the coven symbol as a corruscating, living form burning in its center!

IO EVOHE! [pronounced "EEE-OOO, AAH VOH AIEE"]
Blessed be!

The leader must then circle the balefire three times southways, halting again in the east. At this point, the high priestess should prostrate herself to the west upon the ground. She must pound with her flat hand thrice three times upon the earth (thrice for each utterance of the goddess' name) as she chants the invocation of the earth:

> Hertha!   (three blows)
> Hertha!   (three blows)
> Hertha!   (three blows)
> Mother of Mankind,
> hail to thee, Great Mother!
> Be fruitful in the gods' embrace!
> Be filled with food for the use of men!

The coven should likewise repeat this chant, feeling the answering earth tremble beneath them as they beat upon it. While they do this, the high priestess should crumble a Sabbat cake in her hand, and cast it in the circle furrow at the west, or upon the circle boundary line if it be an indoor Sabbat.

Now, having consecrated the Sabbat ground and balefire, all the ritual metal implements, including personal witch insignia, may be brought into the circle from the north. The leaders assume their headdresses, and the taper upon the master's headdress is lit from the balefire. He is the direct representative of the solar force within the coven. The coven members should also now assume their individual witch jewels. The magister, who should be standing in the east facing west with his arms crossed upon his breast, is then saluted as the

"Sun at Midnight" by the assembled coven. The traditional gesture for this is the horned hand, right hand raised, fingers clenched, thumbs and little finger extended.

Likewise, on the other side of the circle in the west the high priestess stands, with her feet apart and her arms raised in a wide crescent, representing the goddess, Our Lady of the Moon.

As both sun and moon are now "standing in their signs of power," both magister and high priestess should be seeking at this moment to place their personalities in abeyance, and "bring through" the god-personae. This act of dissociation will have taken considerable previous practice on their parts, by way of meditation and visualization exercises, the constant building up of the traditional god-forms within an imagined "temple" or appropriate landscape, and the subsequent fantasy identification with them. The sun and moon have to be effectively magically "drawn down."

The high priestess is likewise saluted by the coven with the horned hand, but as Our Lady of the Moon.

The gesture of the magister, arms crossed upon the breast, is of course none other than the sign of death and rebirth used in your necromancy ritual. It signifies many things. Primarily it is the sign of Osiris, seen as synonymous with Hades, Dis, and the Horned One as God of Death. It also represents the skull and crossbones itself, and finally the erect phallus flanked by twin testes below.

The gesture of the high priestess is the mirror image of the magister's. It represents both the lunar crescent, the womb of space, and the horns of Hathor, all of which are symbols pertaining to Isis, the great Egyptian Mother Goddess and consort of Osiris. As such, the magister and high priestess are the human representatives of the two great archetypal poles of life, whether you conceive of them as Isis and Osiris, summer and winter, life and death, or *yin* and *yang*.

Having called down the two powers, such magical operations as required by the coven, if any, are now performed. The initiation of new members follows this, in order that the new initiates may be able to join in the ceremonial dances afterwards.

The Witch Dances

These dances are many and varied, differing from coven to coven and allowing for considerable invention and renovation.

The two main witch dances are the Spiral Dance, known otherwise as the Maze, Meeting Dance, Wheel, or Round Dance; and the Chain Dance.

The first, or Meeting Dance, is related to the concept of death as symbolized by a northways movement, widdershins, leading to the still center, and then returning on its tracks southways. The magister stands at the center of the circle, beside the balefire, facing north. His arms are crossed and he represents death. The coven, beginning at the northern periphery of the circle, makes a widdershins spiral chain to the center, consisting of three circuits, each member similarly turning widdershins on his individual axis, and on reaching the still figure of the magister at the center, one by one light the tapers they carry in their hands. They then double back on their tracks and, spiraling clockwise, return the way they came, again on a triple circuit. The Spiral, as well as signifying the interaction of the dark and bright tides, is also said to represent the labyrinth, dolman, or House of Death and Initiation. Witch symbolism refers it to the Glass Castle of the North, Caer Arrianrhod, and the Corona Borealis.

Accompanying the music of the Meeting Dance, which may be recorded or played on a variety of instruments to be discussed later, wild cries of "EEE-OOO AAH VOH AIEE" are often given by the members of the coven as they whirl ecstatically, usually after the words of a chant such as one adapted from the Invocation of Hertha from Chapter 5, or if the coven be a solely goddess-oriented variety, the following traditional one:

> Queen of the Moon, Queen of the Sun,
> Queen of the Heavens, Queen of the Stars,
> Queen of the Waters, Queen of the Earth,
> bring to us the Child of Promise!

> It is the Great Mother who giveth birth to him;
> it is the Lord of Life who is born again.

> Darkness and tears are set aside
> when the sun shall come up early!
>
> Golden Sun of the mountains,
> illumine the land, light up the world.
> Illumine the seas and the rivers,
> Sorrows be laid, joy to the world!
>
> Blessed be the Great Goddess,
> without beginning, without end,
> everlasting in eternity!
> IO EVOHE, blessed be!

However, the latter chant is used only at Halloween or Yule, as it refers specifically to the coming of winter and the rebirth of the sun at Shamain (Hallows) or midwinter.

The Meeting Dance often leads directly into the Chain Dance. This is traditionally led by a female member or the high priestess herself, the magister bringing up the rear. Hence the old saying, "May the Devil take the hindmost!" The dance is performed with the rod used as a riding-stick or hobby-horse placed between the legs, and the lighted taper born aloft. On stormy Sabbats the tapers were and are still sometimes replaced by oil lamps or lanterns.

The Chain Dance itself probably celebrates the transformation of the seasons, and its device is that of the pursuit of an animal by a predator. The season, represented by either the god or goddess, changes shape repeatedly in an attempt to avoid capture. This magical shape-shifting theme is a very ancient one, and it turns up in innumerable traditions—Celtic, Norse, Greek, and even creeps into the Arabian Nights. Sometimes the male is the pursuer, other times the female.

The coven god or goddess orientation generally indicates whether the magister or the high priestess leads the dance. The traditional style seems to be the high priestess in the lead, with the summoner next followed by the coven and the magister bringing up the rear. The dance itself begins with a southways circuit of the circle before leaving it through the gateway at the north. In the old days the dance would wind all over the surrounding territory, through churchyard and barnyard, over hill and dale.

The leader must imitate the movements of the animal he or she represents. The rest of the coven must in turn imitate those of the predator that they are identifying with in their verse. All the powers of the witchly imagination must be brought to bear here. You must feel yourself actually becoming the animal!

The animals themselves differ from coven to coven, largely depending on which totems the group possesses. The rhyme also changes accordingly, but the sense always remains the same. Here is the Chain Dance verse designed for one set of totem animals, each pair representing one of the four seasons:

LEADER. I shall go as a wren in spring
with sorrow and sighing on silent wing,
and I shall go in Our Lady's name,
Aye, till I come home again!

COVEN. We shall follow as falcons gray,
and hunt thee cruelly as our prey,
but we shall go in Our Master's name,
Aye, to fetch thee home again!

LEADER. Then I shall go as a mouse in May,
in fields by night, in cellars by day,
and I shall go in Our Lady's name,
Aye, till I come home again!

COVEN. And we shall follow as black tom cats,
and chase thee through the corn and vats,
but we shall go in Our Master's name,
Aye, to fetch thee home again!

LEADER. Then I shall go as an autumn hare,
with sorrow and sighing and mickle care,
and I shall go in Our Lady's name,
Aye, till I come home again!

COVEN. But we shall follow as swift grey hounds,
and dog thy tracks by leaps and bounds,

>   and we shall go in Our Master's name,
>   Aye, to fetch thee home again!
>
> LEADER. Then I shall go as a winter trout
>   with sorrow and sighing and mickle doubt,
>   and I shall go in Our Lady's name,
>   Aye, till I come home again!
>
> COVEN. But we shall follow as otters swift,
>   and snare thee fast ere thou canst shift,
>   and we shall go in Our Master's name,
>   Aye, to fetch thee home again!

The chant is repeated as long as necessary, and by the end of the final repetition of the last verse, the entire coven should have reentered the circle at the north and be back at their places, with the magister in the east, the high priestess in the west.

In medieval days, the finale of the Chain Dance usually culminated in the "marriage of heaven and Earth," as symbolized by the ceremonial coupling of the magister and the high priestess. The entire female membership of the coven was sometimes also mounted, sometimes being penetrated by means of an artificial phallus wielded by the magister, or simply by the other male participants. However, in most modern covens, the actual marriage rite seems to have been replaced generally by the cakes and wine ceremony which then leads into the feast. The chalice held by the high priestess is raised high over the balefire, and Sabbat wine poured in. The magister then lowers his ceremonial rod, wand, or Athamé into the cup briefly, and then removes it. Both he and the priestess then hand it on to the coven, who drink from it. Similarly, the Sabbat cake is presented on the paten-pentacle by the priestess, divided up by the magister with his Athamé, and then distributed likewise. On handing the chalice or pentacle to one's neighbor, the words "Blessed be" are often uttered.

The initial ceremony of the cakes and wine leads on to the actual feast, which is usually contributed to by all the coven members, each bringing some particular delicacy. The food, far from being the eye of newt and toe of frog variety, is the type you would expect to find at any buffet supper.

The meal itself does not have to be eaten within the circle, the only ritual proviso being that if the company actually sit down at table, the magister be seated at the head. After the meal is concluded, the Sabbat may continue as a regular party with dancing and singing usually of the folk rock variety being performed by more exuberant members within the circle, often jumping hand in hand over the flames of the balefire.

At last, when all is said and done and the party draws to a close, often approaching dawn, traditional farewells of "Merry part" and "Blessed be" are exchanged between departing members, who after exchanging their ritual garments for everyday clothes, hurry off into the chill morning air. The Sabbat is over, the old gods have been reinvoked, and a new season begun.

The basic Sabbat rites should remain the same throughout the year, differing only in small details appropriate to the season. For instance, many covens will divide the year in two and give the magister presidency of the circle during the winter months, the Lady in those of summer.

The Midwinter Festival of Yule, Christmastide, celebrates the sun's rebirth with all the customary decorations and festivity later borrowed by the Church Fathers, the indoor balefire or yule log, evergreen decorations, holly and ivy tied with scarlet ribbon, and of course the Christmas Tree. Father Christmas and Mother Holly are but two Christianized images of the Lord and Lady; the Christ child legend is built upon that of the rebirth of the sun, the light of the world.

Candlemas (February 2) is the Feast of St. Bride or Brigid, a Celtic name for the goddess, and corresponds to the Roman yearly inauguration of the vestal fire. It is a celebration of the waxing light, and the high priestess, or indeed, all the coven, may each don a candle-crown for the ritual dances.

The vernal equinox, or Lady Day, again a reference to the goddess, has all the trappings of traditional Easter. (The word "Easter" in fact is but a modernization of Eostra, the name of an Anglo-Saxon dawn goddess cognate with the classical Eos.)

Beltane, Cétshamain, or Roodmas, as it was Christianized,

has as its theme the May day ceremonials still practiced throughout rural England and Europe with stave dancing and flower garlands tied with white ribbons.

Midsummer, or St. John's Eve, marks the nearest point of the sun's approach to Earth. The Catherine Wheel, or blazing cartwheel rolled from the summit of a hill to plunge into the cold waters of a lake or river below, is yet another expression of the wedding of heaven and Earth.

Lugnassad, or Lammas, celebrates the coming of the harvest-tide, the decorations of corn sheaves, berries, and fruits, while the autumnal equinox, or Michaelmas, marks its zenith with the eating of the customary goose. Samhain, or Hallows, ends the tide of reaping and the witches' year. The winter presided over by the Lord of Misrule begins. The festival is celebrated with the customary sword dances, the sword here being associated with the chthonic spade and ploughshare, symbols of the God of Death.

The Dumb Supper may be performed in honor of the beloved dead, and wine and bread be ceremonially offered to them, the latter in the shape of a cake made in nine segments similar to the square of Earth. Candlelit turnip or pumpkin-heads and the last remnants of harvest-fare often provide decoration.

As always, it is a matter of personal preference as to exactly how a Sabbat is to be celebrated, always bearing in mind your few basic fundamentals, namely, the "drawing down" of the sun and moon, the ceremonial dances, the symbolic marriage of heaven and Earth, and the communal feast.

So there you are.

Finally, a few notes on practical Sabbat details.

Sabbat Music

Often this is of the recorded variety, usually utilizing old folksongs or traditional airs. However, the "folk" content, magically speaking, is not essential. What matters, of course, is the rhythm, which must be conducive to dancing, and the evocative content of the music. Religious music can work very well. But, here again, you will have to use your own judgment carefully. For instance, medieval plainsong and organ music in most instances are singularly inappropriate, but some of the recorded medieval pipe and tabor tunes of a semireligious nature work very well. Again—experiment.

The traditional Sabbat musical instruments are the harp and lute, worthily replaced by the guitar nowadays; the flute, often replaced by the recorder; and the drum or tabor, nowadays usually the tambourine. The traditional witches' drum, however, is of interest here. Usually composed of a box or broad hoop of wood, over which is stretched tightly laced animal hide or vellum. On this should be painted an eight-pointed star composed of two interlaced squares, again representing the solar year and the four elements. It should be divided in the center by a line linking the opposite corners of one square; on one side of it, half the star is stained red and the other blue, signifying summer and winter, death and rebirth, male and female.

Some witches perform a divination with the drum, throwing devil's-apple seeds upon its surface, and reading an augury from where and how they land in relation to the diagram.

Finally, there is the witch's bell, sometimes used in certain rites for striking knells, as well as in some exorcisms. This may be made out of magical electrum or simply be an antique handbell, the older the better.

Sabbat Incense

Summer Variety: (Beltane, Midsummer, Lammas, Michaelmas)
Fennel
Thyme
Rue
Chervil seed
Chamomile
Geranium
Pennyroyal
High-grade church incense

Winter Variety: (Hallows, Yule, Candlemas, Lady Day)
Bay laurel
Vervain
Wormwood

Ivy leaves
Fir branches
Solomon's-seal *(Polygonatum multiflorum)*
High-grade church incense

Sabbat Cakes

Basically any recipe containing honey, salt, wine, and oatmeal may be used. Here is a typical one.

Mix:
- 1 tablespoon honey
- ⅓ cup shortening
- ½ cup brown sugar
- 1 tablespoon white wine

Add:
- 1½ cups flour
- ¼ teaspoon baking soda
- ½ teaspoon salt
- 1¼ cups oatmeal

Optional: cinnamon, allspice, cloves, or ground cardamom

Combine well, adding water if necessary to make into rollable dough. Cut into small crescent-shaped cakes and bake until light brown in a preheated oven at 350 degrees about 15 minutes.

Sabbat Wine

Any red wine will do for this. During the winter Sabbats many covens drink this mulled with addition of aromatic herbs and spices. A mixture of sweet and hard ciders and brandy, simmered with cinnamon sticks and clove-stuck oranges may also be used.

However, some ambitious witches make use of the following cordial as an additive or accompanying drink. It is very complicated to make and requires distilling, but it is highly appropriate as a summer Sabbat beverage.

Take:
- 6 oz. hyacinth blooms
- ¼ lb. violet petals

- ¼ lb. wallflower petals
- ¼ lb. jonquil petals
- 1 oz. orris powder
- ½ oz. powdered mace
- 2 oz. orange or lemon essence
- ¼ lb. lily of the valley flowers

The process is this:

Bruise the hyacinth petals, orris root, and mace together with one gallon of alcohol in a glass container toward the end of March, in fact when the hyacinths are in season. Toward the end of April, add the jonquils, and then the wallflowers and lilies of the valley. The liquid must then be well-stirred every day for a week, at the end of which time, the liquor should be distilled off very slowly and carefully, preferably using a *bain-marie*.

The flowery essence is very potent and, in fact, is more in the nature of a perfume than a real liqueur. However, I am informed it makes an excellent additive for the wine, if not consumed by itself.

Thus concludes this witchcraft primer. Many things, of course, remain to be said and will have to wait for a later date.

The rudiments, however, are here presented. The old gods are not dead. They live still, ever ready to harken to man and his requests.

You need but ask; the way is open to you.

Let us celebrate the return of the old ones!

So mote it be!

APPENDIX 1

The Planetary Hours

WHEN your magical operation is not organized to coincide with a specific event, such as your victim's sleeping or waking hours, if you plan on being true to a fully traditional point of view, try to perform your witchcraft on the relevant "planetary day" at the right "planetary hour." Failing this, simply the right planetary hour will suffice, always and in every instance observing the correct phase of the moon, of course.

The days and hours of the sun should be used for operations concerned with honor, power, glory, and the Arts; those of the moon for dreams and female fertility; those of Mars for defense and attack; Mercury, for divination; Jupiter, for wealth, lust, and male fertility; Venus, for romantic love; and, finally, those of Saturn for works of necromancy, binding, and all works of darkness.

The Planetary Hours

A.M.

	☉ Sunday	☽ Monday	♂ Tuesday	☿ Wednesday	♃ Thursday	♀ Friday	♄ Saturday
1	Sun	Moon	Mars	Mercury	Jupiter	Venus	Saturn
2	Venus	Saturn	Sun	Moon	Mars	Mercury	Jupiter
3	Mercury	Jupiter	Venus	Saturn	Sun	Moon	Mars
4	Moon	Mars	Mercury	Jupiter	Venus	Saturn	Sun
5	Saturn	Sun	Moon	Mars	Mercury	Jupiter	Venus
6	Jupiter	Venus	Saturn	Sun	Moon	Mars	Mercury
7	Mars	Mercury	Jupiter	Venus	Saturn	Sun	Moon
8	Sun	Moon	Mars	Mercury	Jupiter	Venus	Saturn
9	Venus	Saturn	Sun	Moon	Mars	Mercury	Jupiter
10	Mercury	Jupiter	Venus	Saturn	Sun	Moon	Mars
11	Moon	Mars	Mercury	Jupiter	Venus	Saturn	Sun
12	Saturn	Sun	Moon	Mars	Mercury	Jupiter	Venus

P.M.

☉ Sunday	☾ Monday	♂ Tuesday	☿ Wednesday	♃ Thursday	♀ Friday	♄ Saturday
1 Jupiter	Venus	Saturn	Sun	Moon	Mars	Mercury
2 Mars	Mercury	Jupiter	Venus	Saturn	Sun	Moon
3 Sun	Moon	Mars	Mercury	Jupiter	Venus	Saturn
4 Venus	Saturn	Sun	Moon	Mars	Mercury	Jupiter
5 Mercury	Jupiter	Venus	Saturn	Sun	Moon	Mars
6 Moon	Mars	Mercury	Jupiter	Venus	Saturn	Sun
7 Saturn	Sun	Moon	Mars	Mercury	Jupiter	Venus
8 Jupiter	Venus	Saturn	Sun	Moon	Mars	Mercury
9 Mars	Mercury	Jupiter	Venus	Saturn	Sun	Moon
10 Sun	Moon	Mars	Mercury	Jupiter	Venus	Saturn
11 Venus	Saturn	Sun	Moon	Mars	Mercury	Jupiter
12 Mercury	Jupiter	Venus	Saturn	Sun	Moon	Mars

APPENDIX 2

Glossary of Witch Words and Terms

Adept	A master of the magic arts
Alraun	Talismanic image made from rowan wood
Altar	Magical table of practice, usually placed center circle
Amulet	Magical mascot or "lucky charm"
Arcana	Secret formulae or process. Also used to denote deck of Tarot cards, the Major Arcana being the "trumps" numbered from 0 to 21, the Minor being the 56 "pip" and "court" cards
Athamé	Witches' black-hilted knife
Averse	Black, or evil, usually applied to magical processes
Baculum	Witches' rod, staff, wand, or "broomstick" used in divination and certain fertility spells
Balefire	Ritual coven fire
Ban	To curse
Bane	Poisonous or destructive thing. Banishing exorcism (q.v.). Often applied to an herb, *e.g.*, hemlock
Barrow	An elven or Celtic burial mound often used by coven for Sabbat covenstead
Beltane	May Eve witch festival
Bind	To cast a spell on, also, to practice ligature (q.v.)
Bolline	An Athamé, often curved like a sickle
Brigid	February 2nd Eve witch festival—Candlemas

Cabala	(1) Body of lore stemming from early Chaldean and Mesopotamian traditions, later incorporated within certain rabbinical texts, (2) practical magical processes deriving therefrom
Candlemas	(*q.v.* Brigid)
Chalice	Magical cup used for philters and libations
Charm	Spoken or chanted words of magical intent
Cingulum	Witches' cord or girdle
Cone of power	"Cone" of collective witch power raised by assembled coven within circle to forward a certain aim previously decided upon
Conjuration	An act of summoning a demon or shade
Contact	Demon, deceased human or "god" coven instructor
Coven	Witches' group of not more than thirteen members
Covendom	Three-mile radius of coven's domain
Covenstead	Place where coven meets
Cowan	Uninitiated intruder
Cromlech	Welsh word for dolmen (q.v.)
Dagyde	Witches' image-needle or pin
Demon	Nonhuman spirit (*see* Foreword and Chapter 1)
Deosil	Turning clockwise and sunways
Devil	"Little god," title for the magister as representative of one of the Mighty Ones
Divination	Magical method of exploration or inquiry into a situation
Dolmen	Elven structure of stone. Megalithic monument. Often used as covenstead by witches
Eidolon	Wraith or fetch. Witch power formulated into semi-tangible human shape
Elemental	Witch's magically created familiar (q.v.)
Elements	Cognate "of the Wise": fire, air, earth, and water. The four basic modes of manifestation of matter and energy according to arcane lore
Elf fire	Need fire or Wildfire. Flame to light coven balefire produced without the use of metals

Glossary of Witch Words and Terms

Elvenfolk	Descendants of the witch gods, or Mighty Ones; Prytani or Faeryfolk
Esbat	Weekly or fortnightly witch meeting
Evil eye	Involuntary Eye biting (q.v.)
Evocation	Conjuration, often to visible appearance
Exorcism	Magical operation of purifying something from all alien influences
Eye biting	Cursing with a glance—overlooking
Familiar	(1) Coven totem animal, (2) witch's pet animal, (3) elemental servant
Fascination	Process of casting a spell upon someone using only the projection of witch power in close personal proximity
Fell	Baneful (q.v. Bane)
Fetch	Wraith (q.v.)
Glamour	Fascination
Goetia, goetic	Pertaining to medieval sorcery (q.v.)
Grimoire	Book of magic belonging to individual or coven, Book of Shadows
Hallows	Halloween, Samhain, or Shamain, November 1 Eve witch festival
Hexagram	Six-pointed talismanic star made of two interlaced triangles
Honorian script	Witch runes
Imbolc	Oimelc, Brigid (q.v.)
Incantation	Charm (q.v.)
Incubus	Male wraith form projected for purposes of sexual intercourse
Invocation	Calling down of power, beseeching the indwelling of a god
Jewel	Talismanic item of witch regalia
Lady	(1) Female leader of coven, (2) female ruler of an elf-rath

Lammas	August witch festival—Lugnassad
Ligature	Magical binding of person in order to prevent him accomplishing a specified thing or course of action
Linking	Commemoration. Process of mental identification with past adepts or appropriate symbols within a magical operation
Living Fire	Elf fire (q.v.)
Lugnassad	Lammas (q.v.)
Lycanthropy	(1) Chain-dance "assumption" of animal form, (2) projection of wraith in animal form
Magic	The ancient lore of the Watchers, comprising the knowledge of certain powers resident within the deep mind of man, by means of which natural law can be affected without using the generally recognized channels of communication. Parapsychic manipulation. The use of magic is witchcraft
Magistellus	Elemental servant (q.v. Familiar)
Magister	Master; male leader of coven
Magnetism	Term deriving from Anton Mesmer's eighteenth-century theory of witch power
Magus	Male practitioner of magic, wizard
Maiden	Coven title conferred upon the Lady, sometimes the Lady's daughter
Mandragore, Mandrake	Plant *Magistellus*
Mighty Ones	The ancient witch gods, Watchers, or Sons of Heaven
Mommet	Alternative to poppet or voodoo doll
Necromancy	Evocation of the dead
Need fire	Elf fire (q.v.)
Northways	Anticlockwise, widdershins, against the sun
Object link	Material sample impregnated with magnetism of proposed victim or subject of magic (as opposed to power object, q.v.)
Officer	Third coven leader. Magister's lieutenant, also known as the Man in Black, Verdelet, and the summoner

Oimelc	Imbolc (q.v.)
Old Ones	Mighty Ones, archetypal witch gods derived from legends of the Watchers
Overlook	To voluntarily cast the evil eye or eye bite (q.v.)
Pact	Initiates signature in coven register given as written pledge of silence
Pendulum	Witches' divination device
Pentacle	(1) Talisman, (2) five-pointed star—pentangle or pentagram
Power object	Material object charged with witch power and transferred into victim or subject's presence to effect a certain result; psychic battery
Puppet (poppet)	Mommet (q.v.)
Rath	Celtic word for elven dwelling
Repercussion	Phenomenon of reproduction of injuries received by projected wraith form on entranced parent body
Runes	(1) Ancient magical script or hieroglyphic alphabet, (2) spells
Sabbat	Witches' meeting at quarterly and cross-quarterly festival
Samhain	*See* Hallows
Scry	To divine by a show stone or mirror
Seal	A demon's signature or summoning diagram, sigil
Seeing stone	Show stone or crystal ball
Servitor	Familiar (q.v.)
Shade	Spirit of a dead person
Siderite	Witch amulet of lodestone
Sigil	Seal (q.v.)
Simple	Philter derived from a single herb
Sorcery	Magic, often of an adverse nature
Southways	Deosil (q.v.)
Speculum	Magical mirror or crystal for scrying in
Spell	Magical operation

St. John's (Eve)	The midsummer witch festival
Succubus	Female wraith form projected for purposes of sexual intercourse
Summoner	Officer (q.v.)
Talisman	Power object (q.v.)
Theban	Honorian script (q.v.)
Thurible	Chafing dish or incense burner
Transvection	(1) Levitation, (2) projection of the wraith form
Vampire	Predatory wraith form
Verendum	*Baculum* (q.v.)
Vibrations	Magical atmosphere around person, place, or thing
Vortex	Cone of power (q.v.)
Walpurgis Night	Beltane (q.v.)
Wand	*Baculum* (q.v.)
Warlock	Originally term of abuse meaning "traitor," now used generally within the United States to signify wizard (q.v.)
Watcher	(1) Elemental guardian, (2) Old One (q.v.)
Werewolf	Predatory wraith form
Widdershins, Withershins	Anticlockwise, northways
Wildfire	Elf Fire (q.v.)
Witch	One skilled in the ancient wisdom; originally used for both sexes, now generally only for female
Wizard	Male equivalent of witch, wise man
Wraith, wraith form	Projected astral body. Mobile form of witch power ensouled by witch's exteriorized consciousness
Yule	Midwinter witch festival

Bibliography

MANY of the following books which have been referred to or quoted from in the text, notably the older dates of publication, are unfortunately rare and out of print. As such, they are only available for study in major libraries and then, in many cases, only in their original languages. Though many of the points of view of the respective authors are conflicting, the works are important documents for research, presenting as they do the basis of many of the modern witch's beliefs and practices.

I have classified the type of book and its chief value under appropriate headings.

Historical Background

A good groundwork of fifteenth-, sixteenth-, and seventeenth-century witch beliefs current throughout Britain, the European continent, and America can be obtained from consulting the following source books:

Bodin, Jean, *De la demonomanie des sorciers*. Paris, 1580.
―――― *Le fleau des demons et sorciers*. Nyort, 1616.
Boguet, Henry, *Discours des Sorciers*. Lyons, 1608.
Delrio, M., *Disquisitionum magicarum libri sex*. Mainz, 1612.
Harrison, G. B. (introduction by), *The Trial of the Lancaster Witches*. London, Peter Davies, 1929. (Originally published, 1612.)
Hopkins, Matthew (the notorious witch finder general), *The Discovery of Witches*. London, 1647.
James I of England, *Daemonologie*. Edinburgh, 1597.
Levin, D. (editor of trial transcripts), *What Happened at Salem?* USA, Twayne Publishing Inc., 1952. (Reprinted from *A Handbook for English*. Harvard College, 1950.)
Scot, Reginald, *Discoverie of Witchcraft*. London, 1584. (Ed. by M. Summers and republished London, 1930; contains much of Wierus' *Pseudomonarchia Demonorum*.)
Sprenger, James, and Kramer, Heinrich, *Malleus Maleficarum*. Nuremberg, 1494. (Trans. by M. Summers and republished London, Pushkin Press, 1928; also republished London, Folio Society, 1968.)

Handy compendia dealing with and summarizing all these works are:

Lea, H. C., *Materials towards a History of Witchcraft*. Philadelphia, University of Philadelphia Press, 1939.
Robbins, Russell Hope, *Encyclopedia of Witchcraft and Demonology*. London, Spring Books, 1959.

The Witch Cult

Gardner, Gerald B., *Witchcraft Today*. London, Rider, 1954.
——— *The Meaning of Witchcraft*. London, Aquarian Press, 1959.
——— *High Magic's Aid*. London, Michael Houghton, 1949.
Hughes, Pennethorne, *Witchcraft*. London, Longmans, Green, 1952.
Leland, Charles G., *Aradia, or the Gospel of the Witches*. London, David Nutt, 1899.
Lethbridge, T. C., *Witches, Investigating an Ancient Religion*. New York, Citadel Press, 1968.
Murray, Margaret, *The Witchcult in Western Europe*. London, Oxford University Press, 1921.
——— *The God of the Witches*. London, Faber, 1934 (paperback, Anchor, 1960).
Valiente, Doreen, *Where Witchcraft Lives*. London, Aquarian Press, 1962.

Relevant Mythology

Evans, Sebastian, *The High History of the Holy Grail*, translated from French. London, Everyman, 1910.
Evans-Wentz, *The Fairy Faith in Celtic Countries*. New York, University Books.
Frazer, Sir James, *The Golden Bough*. London, Macmillan, 1922.
Graves, Robert, *The White Goddess*. London, Faber and Faber, 1948.
——— *The Greek Myths*. London, Penguin Books, 1955.
Guest, Lady Charlotte, *The Mabinogion*, translation. London, Everyman, 1906.
Kerenyi, *The Gods of the Greeks*. New York, Grove Press, 1960.
Kirk, *The Secret Commonwealth* (1691 ms.). Second ed., London, D. Nutt, 1893; Eneas Mackay, Stirling, 1933.
Leland, Godfrey, *Etruscan Magic and Occult Remedies*. New York, University Books, 1963.
Maltwood, K. E., *A Guide to Glastonbury's Temple of the Stars*. London, James Clarke, 1929.
Massingham, H. J., *Fee; Fi; Fo; Fum, or the Giants in England*. London, Keegan Paul, 1926.
Ovid, *The Metamorphoses*. London, Penguin Books.

Spence, Lewis, *The Minor Traditions of British Mythology*. London, Rider, 1948.
—— *The Fairy Tradition in Britain*. London, Rider, 1948.
—— *Magic Arts in Celtic Britain*. London, Rider, 1945.
—— *Mysteries of Britain*. London, Rider, 1928.

Cabalistic Magical Practice

Barratt, F., *The Magus*. London, 1801 (republished New York, University Books, 1967).
Crowley, A., *Magick in Theory and Practice*. New York, Castle Books (originally published 1929).
—— *777*. London, Neptune Press, 1955.
Fortune, D., *The Mystical Qabalah*. London, Williams and Norgate, 1935.
Levi, Eliphas (Alphonse Louis Constant), *Transcendental Magic*, trans. by A. E. Waite. London, Rider.
Regardie, I., *The Golden Dawn* (4 vols.). Aries Press, 1938, -39, -40.
Scheible, J., *Das Kloster* (12 volumes in German containing texts of practically every medieval grimoire). Stuart and Leipzig, 1846.
"Solomon," *Sepher Maphtheah Shelomo*, Hermann Gollancz, ed. London, Hermann Gollancz, 1914.
—— *The Testament of Solomon*, McCown, ed. Leipzig, 1922.
—— *The Greater Key of Solomon*. Chicago, De Laurence Scott, 1914.
—— *The Lemegeton, or Lesser Key of Solomon*. Chicago, De Laurence Scott, 1916.
Thorndike, L., *A History of Magic and Experimental Science* (8 vols.). New York, Macmillan and Columbia University Press, 1923–58.

Modern Developments of Witch Power

Jung, C. G., *The Interpretation of Nature and the Psyche*. London, Routledge and Kegan Paul, 1955.
Muldoon, S., and Carrington, H., *The Projection of the Astral Body*. London, Rider, 1951.
"Ophiel," *The Art and Practice of Astral Projection*.
Reich, Wilhelm, *The Function of the Orgasm*. England, Panther Books, 1968.
Reichenbach, Baron, *Letters on Od and Magnetism*. London, Hutchinson, 1926 (republished New York, University Books, 1968).
Rhine, J. B., *The Reach of the Mind*. London, Faber & Faber, 1948.
Sudre, R., *Treatise on Parapsychology*. London, George Allen & Unwin, 1960.

Herbal Lore

Culpepper's Herbal.
Gerard's Herbal.
Leyel, F., *The Magic of Herbs*. New York, Harcourt Brace, 1926.
Ransom, F., *British Herbs*. England, Penguin Books, 1949.

Arcane Traditions

Blavatsky, H. P., *Isis Unveiled* (2 vols.). New York, J. W. Bouton, 1877.
────── *The Secret Doctrine* (Third Point Loma ed., 2 vols.). Point Loma, Calif., The Aryan Theosophical Press, 1925.
The Book of Enoch, Charles, R. H., ed.: London, Society for Promoting Christian Knowledge, 1962.
Ginsburg, C. D., *The Kabbalah*. London, Routledge & Kegan Paul, 1863 (reprinted 1956).
Iamblichus, *De Mysteriis*. London, Stuart and Watkins, 1821 (reprinted 1968).
Mathers, S. M., *The Kabbalah Unveiled*, trans. of Knorr Von Rosenroth's *Kabbala Denudata*. London, Redway, 1887.
Simon, Maurice and Sperling, Harry, *The Zohar* (5 vols.). London, 1931, -34.
Spence, L., *Atlantis in America*. London, Ernest Benn, 1925.
────── *Encyclopedia of Occultism*. New York, University Books, 1960.
Waite, A. E., *The Kabbalah*. New York, University Books.
────── *The Brotherhood of the Rosy Cross*. New York, University Books.
────── *The Holy Grail*. New York, University Books.